D1736555

THE IMPORTANCE OF BEING FURNISHED

THE IMPORTANCE OF BEING FURNISHED

FOUR BACHELORS AT HOME

R. TRIPP EVANS

ROWMAN & LITTLEFIELD
LANHAM • BOULDER • NEW YORK • LONDON

Published by Rowman & Littlefield
An imprint of The Rowman & Littlefield Publishing Group, Inc.
4501 Forbes Boulevard, Suite 200, Lanham, Maryland 20706
www.rowman.com

86–90 Paul Street, London EC2A 4NE

COVER (clockwise from top left): *Portrait of Charles Leonard Pendleton* (ca. 1861). Ambrotype with hand tinting (1 7/8" x 1 3/8"). Gift of Fred Stewart Greene, 04.1466. Courtesy RISD Museum, Providence, RI / [Maker unknown], Jabot, France (1824) (detail). Silk (76" x 63 1/4"). One of a set of curtains and matching seating upholstery ordered by Charles Russell Codman from Paris in 1824. Museum Purchase with funds provided by a friend of Historic New England, 2005.14.1. Courtesy Historic New England / Charles Hammond Gibson, Jr. (1904). Photograph by J. E. Purdy. Gibson House Museum, Boston, MA / Henry Davis Sleeper (ca. 1906). Courtesy History New England / China, Qing Dynasty (1636–1911). *Vase*, 1700s. Porcelain (12 ½ inches, height). Bequest of Mr. Charles L. Pendleton (04.370). RISD Museum, Providence, RI / Ogden Codman Jr., Bar Harbor, Maine (1887). Photograph by Thomas Newbold Codman. Codman Family Papers, courtesy Historic New England.

COVER (background): Detail, side chair (American, 1830–1845). Collection of the author.

BACK COVER: Beauport, the Sleeper-McCann House, garden (eastern) façade. Photograph by Matthew Cunningham. Courtesy Historic New England.

OPPOSITE TITLE PAGE: Charles Hammond Gibson Jr. (Olympia Studio, 1915). Gibson House Museum, Boston, MA.

OPENING QUOTATIONS: (1) Emily Post, *Etiquette* (New York: Funk and Wagnalls, 1922), 296; (2) Elsie de Wolfe, *The House in Good Taste* (New York: The Century Co., 1913), 15.

British Library Cataloguing in Publication Information Available

Library of Congress Cataloging-in-Publication Data

Names: Evans, R. Tripp, 1968- author.
Title: The importance of being furnished : four bachelors at home / R. Tripp Evans.
Description: Lanham : Rowman & Littlefield, [2024] | Includes bibliographical references and index.
Identifiers: LCCN 2023048122 (print) | LCCN 2023048123 (ebook)
| ISBN 9781538173954 (cloth) | ISBN 9781538173961 (epub)
Subjects: LCSH: Interior decorators--United States--Biography.
Classification: LCC NK2004.2 .E93 2024 (print) | LCC NK2004.2 (ebook)
| DDC 747.092/66420973--dc23/eng/20240116
LC record available at https://lccn.loc.gov/2023048122
LC ebook record available at https://lccn.loc.gov/2023048123

For Mom, who taught me a great story is like a beautiful house:
It must be lovingly built, surprising, and disdainful of all economy.

And for Ed, who taught me a great marriage plays by the same rules.

ALSO BY R. TRIPP EVANS

Grant Wood: A Life

Romancing the Maya: Mexican Antiquity in the American Imagination, 1820–1915

CONTENTS

ACKNOWLEDGMENTS

It is wonderful to be able to trace a book's origin as clearly as I can this one. On November 19, 2011, my husband Ed and I met our friends Anne Barrett, Todd Dundon, Laurel Sparks, and Hannah Barrett at a bar in Boston's South End. Over Manhattans that night, Hannah—whose brilliant painting series *Tales from the House of Gibson* (2010) (see figure 3.14, p. 119) would debut at Childs Gallery the next day—insisted I should write a book about Charlie Gibson and his fellow bachelor, Ogden Codman Jr. Anne, once a curatorial intern at Beauport, suggested I add Henry Davis Sleeper to the mix. Twelve years later— and with Charles Pendleton now part of the gang—I can officially thank the Barrett sisters. The next Manhattans are on me, ladies.

Exactly a decade later, it was two friends from Historic New England (HNE) who pushed the book from the archives into print. When Lorna Condon and Ken Turino asked me in 2021 to guest curate an HNE exhibition drawn from my bachelor homes research, I was thrilled to accept—if terrified by the thought that I now had to *write* the book. Thank you, Lorna and Ken, not only for lighting a fire under this project but also for the myriad ways you have supported it: Ken, for connecting me with Rowman & Littlefield, and Lorna, for your tireless assistance during my happy months at HNE's archives (there are still times I want to shout out to you, "Wait'll you hear what Ogden's said *now!*"). My thanks go out, as well, to Lorna's wonderful team—especially Christina Pochilo, Stephanie Krauss, Donna Russo, and Leah Netsky—who made me feel like one of the Otis House gang.

As I embark on the last year of planning for the HNE exhibition, I'm grateful to be part of another creative and hardworking team—including Ken, Lorna, Julie Solz, Erica Lome, Keith Ragone, Adam Brooks, Karla Rosenstein, and Michaela Neiro. Without the material and moral support of friends like Candy Adriance, Wendy MacGaw, and J. P. Couture, there would have been no show to plan. You are my Dabsville 2.0.

Curatorial staff at the houses I researched for this book—and many others, at sites adjacent to this project—have been incredibly generous with their time and knowledge. It has been a joy to work with them all. I offer my profound thanks to Elizabeth Williams for helping me better understand Charles Pendleton and the context of his collection; Wendy Swanton, Meghan Gelardi Holmes, and Todd Gernes for ushering me into Charlie Gibson's colorful world; Wendy Hubbard, Camille Arbogast, and Prentice Crosier for their deep knowledge of the Codmans, one and all; and Beauport site managers Pilar Garro, Martha Van Koevering, and Kristen Weiss—and all their talented guides—for leading me through the house's wonderful complexity. (Stephen Bridges, I admit there were moments on your epic "Nooks and Crannies" tour that I nearly hid in a closet for an overnight stay.) Working with Shana McKenna at the Isabella Stewart Gardner Museum introduced me to a side of the famous collector I'd never known—and in my wide-ranging conversations with Corinna Fisk and Jennifer Newell, I felt ushered into the magical circle of "Doc" and Red Roof.

Three scholars' work, in particular, served as guiding lights for this study. Will Fellows first opened my eyes to the rich stories of gay men in historic preservation; his *A Passion to Preserve: Gay Men as Keepers of Culture* (2004) is a landmark guide that I return to frequently, with great admiration. For its masterful treatment of three understudied, utterly fascinating women, Lisa Cohen's *All We Know: Three Lives* (2012) continues to be a revelation to me. Her profound meditations on style, the nature of fame, and the importance of the ephemeral have deeply informed this work. (And though in the past decade I feared her subject Esther Murphy's fate—my book, like hers, seemed forever about a third completed—I can now thank both Lisa *and* Esther for their inspiration.) Last, every student of Beauport stands on the considerable shoulders of scholar Philip A. Hayden. I am grateful for his exhaustive documentation of the house and its creator, and eagerly look forward to his forthcoming study of Sleeper.

This book has benefitted from a wonderful editorial and production team. I owe a great debt to my agent, Rob McQuilkin, whose support for the project never flagged over its many years of development, and whose advice when it came time to pitch the manuscript was incredibly helpful. I'm grateful, in turn, to my editor at Rowman & Littlefield, Charles Harmon, who enthusiastically took a chance on the project when my passion for it outweighed my sense of direction. On the production side I offer sincere thanks to Lauren Moynihan at Rowman & Littlefield for her expertise and patience, and Alex Cummins at Io Labs for making the book's illustrations truly sing. Last, I wish to thank my dear friend and developmental editor, Susan Dearing, for her invaluable insights, sharp eye, and much needed encouragement. The book is much richer for her wisdom and talents.

Given my project's focus on fascinating houses, I must also thank the friends who've lent me *their* marvelous homes to write, edit, or escape this book. Ed and I are grateful to Kersti Yllö for the rugged beauty of Balanced Rock in Jonesport; David Potter for the majesty (and green chili burgers) of Galisteo; Peter Karczmar and Cathy Lund for their dreamy, Beauport-y Dach in Tiverton (home to our merry COVID-19 pod); and Jeff and Abby Jenkins Boal for the swellest casa in all NoLita. The inspiration of your magical homes and generous friendship runs throughout these pages.

Above all I owe this book to you, dear Ed. From that first conversation about a "bachelor book" in a South End bar, to the amazing dinner you're making us as I write these words—and all the meals, cocktails, trips, advice, laundry, editing, cheerleading, and bribing in between (I haven't forgotten about the wallpaper offer)—you have enthusiastically ridden shotgun for the entirety this project. I love you and wouldn't want to be furnished with anybody else.

A bachelor's house has a something about it that is very comfortable but entirely different from a lady's house, though it would be difficult to define wherein the difference lies.
—Emily Post, *Etiquette* (1922)

A house is a dead giveaway.
—Elsie de Wolfe, *The House in Good Taste* (1913)

INTRODUCTION

BEAUTY AND THE BACHELOR

Nowadays all the married men live like bachelors,
and all the bachelors like married men.[1]
—Oscar Wilde, *The Picture of Dorian Gray* (1891)

In 1983 my grandmother sold her Richmond, Virginia, home to two unmarried men. For the life of her, she couldn't understand what two bachelors wanted with a rambling Queen Anne–style house in a faded Historic District—a home originally built for a large family and virtually untouched since 1898. I wasn't confused in the least. Without ever meeting the new owners, my closeted, fifteen-year-old self understood precisely who these men were and what had attracted them to 1821 Park Avenue. I was in love with the house, myself. From its wainscoted stairs to its high ceilings and anachronistic rooms (a sleeping porch, a telephone room!), it held an almost embarrassing fascination for a teenage boy more properly interested in cars or lacrosse. This book is about that couple's, and my own, aesthetic ancestors—figures who brilliantly exemplified the first golden era of the "bachelor house" and paved the way for these two men to feel utterly at home at 1821 Park Avenue, despite the raised eyebrows of its seller. (The house, I should add, was never in better hands.)

The following chapters offer intimate portraits of four such pioneers, men whose homes now all serve as public museums. In order of their appearance here they include: Pendleton House (1906) at the Rhode Island School of Design (RISD) Museum in Providence, built to replicate the Federal-era home of gambler-collector Charles Leonard Pendleton (1846–1904); the Codman Estate (c. 1740) in Lincoln, Massachusetts, home to five generations of the Codman family and redecorated in its final stage by renowned designer Ogden Codman Jr. (1863–1951); Gibson House in Boston's Back Bay, an 1860 townhouse preserved by its last private owner, the prolific poet Charles Hammond Gibson Jr. (1874–1954); and Beauport (1907) in Gloucester, Massachusetts, the eclectic masterpiece of interior decorator Henry Davis Sleeper (1878–1934).

More or less historical contemporaries—the men's lives overlapped entirely from 1878 to 1904—they appear in the following pages from oldest to youngest (my apologies to the youth-obsessed Gibson, who is Sleeper's elder by four years). However coincidentally, this sequence follows a kind of "Goldilocks" scale of the owners' physical presence in the houses. We start with Pendleton, who moved only late in life to 72 Waterman Street—the grand home RISD recreated for its museum wing—and then only as a renter. Codman lived at his family estate just ten years in childhood and spent his final decades as an expatriate, whereas Gibson's residency at 137 Beacon Street reversed this model. Traveling abroad for many years as a young man, he returned permanently to his family home in 1933 and rarely left it until his death in 1954. As the builder and sole owner of his home, Sleeper occupied Beauport continuously from its completion in 1908 through its quarter-century of expansion.

This logic may explain the homes' sequence, but it doesn't answer the larger question: Why *these* four men? Over the course of my research, friends and colleagues have often pointed out rich examples of other historic house museums created by bachelors—including the George Eastman Museum in New York, Henry Chapman Mercer's Fonthill Castle in Pennsylvania, and Robert Neal and Edgar Hellum's Pendarvis in Wisconsin, to name just a few. Ultimately I selected the men in this study for their strikingly similar backgrounds. Because they all share the same period, region, class, social networks, and vocation (all were involved, to lesser or greater degrees, in professional interior decoration), I was able to cast their dazzling range of styles in higher relief. By doing so, I hope to demonstrate that the era's insistence on individual expression defied even the potentially leveling influence of their shared profiles. Second, despite the regional specificity of these case studies, in each we encounter a man whose story speaks to the period's bachelor house phenomenon more broadly.

And what is this "bachelor house phenomenon"? Here I refer to a particular convergence of factors—historical, literary, economic, and sexual—that, for the first time in the modern era, established the single man's household as an aspirational domestic model.

It begins with Oscar Wilde.

When Wilde conducted his popular, yearlong American lecture tour in 1882, two of my subjects were young men (Pendleton and Codman) and two preadolescent (Gibson and Sleeper). No surviving evidence confirms whether the first two attended the writer's lectures, but as adults all four men entered a world profoundly reshaped by his message. Wilde professed the Aesthetic Movement's "art-for-art's-sake" credo—a radical insistence that artistic creativity must be divorced from moral purpose. Beauty, this movement's adherents believed, constituted an end unto itself. Translated to the realm of domestic design (Wilde's most frequently delivered lecture in 1882 was "The House Beautiful"), this message sought to replace the home's traditional aims—the nurturing of family or inculcation of Christian virtue—with the presumably higher calling of individual artistic expression. Addressing "the youth of the land" (a constituency that included neither women nor married men), Wilde proclaimed: "the passion for beauty engendered by the decorative arts will be to them more satisfying than any political or religious enthusiasm, any enthusiasm for humanity, any ecstasy or sorrow for love."[2] Not only was marriage nonessential to domestic happiness, Wilde's argument ran, but it might even present an impediment. Homemaking was best suited to the single man of means—a figure who could collect, design, and entertain unencumbered by the demands of family life.

Pendleton, Codman, Gibson, and Sleeper were the very men Wilde had in mind: acolytes of beauty whose collections, homes, and even whose very persons exemplified his decree that "the secret of life is art" (and by "art," he meant *artifice* as much as creativity). In assembling his unparalleled collection of Chippendale furniture, the reclusive Pendleton lived for visual perfection—a goal he achieved not only at the cost of his "enthusiasm for humanity" but even sometimes at the expense of the works' authenticity. Codman was himself so enamored of eighteenth-century style that he codified the era's principles in an authoritative 1897 treatise. Though generally restrictive in his tone, he reassured readers that any false element in decoration (a faux finish, a dummy window) was acceptable as long as it provided visual pleasure. For Gibson, no beauty matched his own gilded youth and poetic voice—and so he arrested them forever in his home, oblivious to his own aging body and the vicissitudes of taste. At Beauport Sleeper orchestrated beauty in a surprising range of forms—through color, line, scale, pattern, and even visual humor—with little regard to his rooms' historical accuracy or collection's provenance.

Long before Wilde's arrival in the United States, American readers eagerly consumed fictional tales of bachelor domesticity. (The very popularity of such works explains, in part, audiences' receptivity to his message.) Donald Grant Mitchell's *Reveries of a Bachelor* (1850), narrated by a wise and well-housed bachelor, went into more than fifty editions and spawned a host of imitators. Notable among these was Oliver Bell Bunce's novel *A Bachelor's Story* (1860), which led in turn to his long-running *Bachelor Bluff* series, beginning in 1881. The decade that followed Wilde's tour produced such mainstream successes as Israel Zangwill's *The Bachelor's Club* (1891), Frank Chaffee's *Bachelor Buttons* (1892), Arthur Gray's *Bath Robes and Bachelors* (1897), and the 1900 hit play "A Bachelor's Home." In this same period a number of notorious works (often but not all imported titles) cast the bachelor home as a site of thrilling depravity. These include J. K. Huysmans's *Against Nature* (1884), the book Wilde once called his "bible"; Ralph Adams Cram's *The Decadent: Being the Gospel of Inaction* (1894); Wilde's own *The Picture of Dorian Gray* (1891); and the vividly pornographic *Teleny, or The Reverse of the Medal* (published anonymously in 1893, but often attributed to Wilde). Bachelor fiction of both types remained popular well into my subjects' young adulthood. Indeed, Guy Wetmore Carryl's paean to bachelor domesticity, *Far from the Maddening Girls* (1904), is dedicated to none other than Sleeper himself.

There were two primary drivers for the popularity of the bachelor novel. First, in the latter nineteenth century the United States witnessed an enormous rise in the number of unmarried men, particularly in cities. In Boston, for example—the nearest urban hub for my subjects—an astounding sixty-three thousand adult men remained unmarried in 1890 (representing nearly a third of *all* males in the city, of any age).[3] These highly concentrated populations of single men produced, in turn, their own subcultures: bachelor clubs, athletic associations, gambling dens, and even dedicated apartment buildings. Popular magazines glamorized bachelor living for its married and unmarried readers alike. In its 1899 feature "Luxurious Bachelordom," *Munsey's Magazine* proclaimed "the bachelor . . . has become master of the comforts and luxuries of a home of his own, with all the resources of capital and science to minister to his every need."[4] Modernity itself, it seems, had made wives redundant.

The second, related factor was an emergent misogyny regarding women and the home. By celebrating the domestic lives of unmarried men, writers in this period sought to "reclaim" the American home, long considered the exclusive sphere of women, and recast it as a masculine ideal. To do so they suggested that the goals of modern homemaking—the cultivation of beauty, individual style, and sensual comfort—were simply beyond a woman's ken. As Bunce's Bachelor Bluff pronounced: "when a woman is not slovenly, she is often so neat, trim, precise, methodical, and circumspect that she excludes all color, all freedom, all *tone* from her house."[5] Insisting that only men were capable of producing the subtle effects required to create a home, he continued:

It is not sufficient to say there is no dust, no untidiness. We must have active ideas at work. We must have colors and sights and sounds. . . . To render a home a heaven of the senses—women are usually too virtuous to do this. Daintiness in man takes an artistic form; in women, it assumes a formidable order, a fearful cleanliness.

To insist that female virtue and cleanliness were anathema to a home's cultivation was a shocking reversal of Victorian attitudes. Worse was to come. In Carryl's 1904 novel, the mere presence of a female *visitor* threatens the environment of his bachelor narrator, who insists women were no more welcome in his home than "a fly in the cream jug."[6]

The repeated claim that some men were more adept than women at creating sensual interiors—and that they were happy to do so without female companionship—raises the specter of the period's sexually suspect bachelor aesthete. Here, too, Wilde provides a foundational model. For all his popularity as a lecturer and writer, he was widely lampooned on both sides of the Atlantic as a limp-wristed effeminate. Indeed, when Wilde gave his first lecture in Boston the event nearly ended before it could begin; as he prepared to take the stage, sixty Harvard students in blonde wigs pranced arm-in-arm down the aisles of Boston Music Hall, striking fey attitudes before the roaring crowd. (Wilde defused the situation only by imploring the audience to "save me from my disciples.")[7] Even those who wrote admiringly about bachelors' homes couldn't resist an occasional wink about their subjects. Chaffee's *Bachelor Buttons*, for example, euphemistically presents its bachelor homeowners as "light hearted fellows, all more or less artistic" who entertain "blonde young lads" and prefer *marrons glacés* to molasses.[8] By the century's end the protective veil that once shielded these "artistic" bachelors had, to a large degree, disappeared. As Lord Caversham pronounced in Wilde's *An Ideal Husband* (1895)—produced the same year its author would be convicted of sodomy—"bachelors are not fashionable anymore. . . . Too much is known about them."[9]

And what is known of these four men? There is ample evidence that Codman and Gibson conducted a host of same-sex affairs—indeed, as I discovered in researching this book, a string of letters from the 1890s even reveals the former's pursuit of the latter. Most of Sleeper's personal correspondence is now lost, but his surviving letters confirm his lifelong romantic infatuation with his Gloucester neighbor, Piatt Andrew. As for Pendleton, his sexuality remains something of a mystery—as does most of his adult life. It is my own belief, however, that his obsessive privacy, all-male circle of intimates, passion for antiquing, and veneration of just one woman (his mother) point to the likelihood he was homosexual. Certainly, we read the same implicit assumption in contemporary accounts the collector.

Some may question whether the men's sexuality matters at all to our understanding of their homes, and to a certain extent I might agree. In the Venn Diagram of my subjects' sexuality and homemaking, the spheres do not entirely overlap; yet it would be as irresponsible to ignore the points where they coincide as it would be to suggest this alignment was experienced similarly by them all. However varied their experiences might have been, the choices they made as designers and collectors greatly depended upon their relationships with those who crossed their threshold—and not least with those who shared their hearts and beds. It is critical to understand, too, that desire, even in the absence of sexual activity (perhaps especially in its absence) was as powerful a force in these men's lives as sustained partnerships or consummated affairs.

From Jean Baudrillard's landmark study *The System of Objects* (1968) to our own time collecting has often been characterized as a form of sublimation, sexual or otherwise—or alternatively as an anticipatory response to loss (that is, hoarding). This book challenges both claims. In the homes of these four men we encounter not the repression of desire, but its creative and joyful expression; and though they lost much in their lives, we do their homes a disservice if we consider these spaces merely as consolation prizes for a missing partner. Far from substituting for human relationships, the men's environments often grew directly *from* the loving relationships their owners fostered. In the end, as Kevin Murphy has said of Beauport, "if it were only about the pathological desire to acquire objects" or safely channel a romantic urge, "it would be a lot less interesting space than it is."[10]

Why *was* it so important for these men to be furnished? This question may be answered in multiple ways for each man. For Pendleton it was initially more important to be furnished than to be *housed*, as only in his final years did his collection find a permanent home. When at last it did, his object was to transform his home into an elaborate stage set—and by the end of his life, to ensure its translation into the *facsimile* of a set piece. In Codman's case the lure of his family's material past was ever present, both as a matter of prestige and as a portal into the world of his eighteenth-century ancestors—men whose virtues, and vices, echoed uncannily in his own life. For his part, Gibson perceived in his home the nativity of his literary career and the milieu of his gilded youth; neither substantially adding to nor subtracting from his parents' furnishings, he nevertheless proclaimed their collection essential to his own identity. Alone among this group, Sleeper celebrated neither family nor personal ambition in his home. Rather, Beauport's mesmerizing interiors constituted a love offering to the community he formed on Eastern Point—and to Andrew, above all.

Before we cross these men's thresholds, it is important to consider what it meant for them to be "at home." The phrase suggests the comfort and gratification they derived from their environments, but it also conjures their period's formal practice of receiving visitors. For a bachelor to announce he was "at home" was an important way to wield social power. First, it suggested that his was a fully formed household, worthy of a social call. Second, the rules governing this ritual allowed him to manage who entered his private space and who did not, a privilege not always extended in the outside world. Third and perhaps most importantly, the custom provided an opportunity to present his most private self within a semipublic setting. Such a controlled performance required tremendous skill, but it often led to great rewards (even love). As Emily Post once observed: "A possible reason why bachelors seem to make good hosts is that only those who have a talent for it make the attempt."[11]

The men you are about to meet had this talent in spades. Our hosts for the following chapters, they will fascinate, charm, exasperate, and inspire—and like their fictional near-contemporary, F. Scott Fitzgerald's Jay Gatsby, they will also drift tantalizingly out of reach. This book is a love letter to them all—to their houses—and to *their* passion for their homes. In a society that measured men's worth by their progeny or profession, they demonstrated that a home, even one imagined or lost, held a power stronger than death.

ONE

PENDLETON'S GHOST

How would you like to live in Looking-glass House, Kitty? . . . Oh, what fun
it'll be, when they see me through the glass in here and ca'n't get at me![1]
—Lewis Carroll, *Through the Looking-Glass and What Alice Found There* (1871)

On the morning of June 27, 1904, the *Providence Journal* reported that Charles Leonard
Pendleton, city benefactor and "well-known collector of antique furniture," had died
peacefully at his grand Federal-era home.[2] Readers learned that the late collector was born
in 1849 to Henry Pendleton, attended Phillips Academy, and earned his law degree from
Yale. The integrity of this lawyer-connoisseur, the obituary noted, matched that of his
collection—one that held "no articles of doubtful value to the smallest piece of crockery"
and that would soon take its place in a magnificent wing he had endowed at the Rhode
Island School of Design (RISD). "Arranged and furnished as the home of a gentleman of
means and taste one hundred and fifty years ago," this wing's rooms would, in turn, reflect
the donor's own patrician roots and unimpeachable good taste. In closing, the *Journal*
offered that Pendleton had never married.

Of all these details, the newspaper reported just three correctly: Pendleton had
attended Phillips Academy, never married, and was now dead. Born three years earlier
than reported, to *John* Pendleton, the collector descended from a prosperous if not
precisely blueblood family in rural Westerly, Rhode Island. His father was a farmer. As for
his record at Yale, Pendleton lasted just one undergraduate semester there before being
ignominiously expelled; and though he later earned a degree from the Albany School of
Law, there is virtually no record of his professional practice as a lawyer. Indeed, for most
of Pendleton's adult life his sources of income varied considerably. Gaining—and far
more frequently losing—vast sums through high-stakes gambling and stock speculation,
he spent his last decades dealing in valuable, if not always genuine, antiques. Pendleton
would die in a rented home he could ill afford, leaving an estate so riddled with debt that
it threatened the very gift he promised RISD. He provided no funding for the wing that
bears his name.

If Pendleton's contemporaries found him a cipher—a man "rather solitary in
his tastes . . . [who] lived strangely apart from his fellowmen," by one contemporary's
account—then present-day visitors to the RISD Museum's Pendleton House find his
memorial equally mystifying.[3] In seeking to mimic the stately homes that neighbor the
wing on Benefit Street, architect Edmund Willson did his job only too well. Pendleton
House may belong to the museum, but its insistently domestic character denies any

1.1
Exterior view of
Charles Pendleton
House (1906) at the
RISD Museum. Author
photograph.

association with it. Indeed, like its reclusive namesake, this "house" appears to shrink even from those who walk past. Its elaborate wrought-iron gate and imposing front door never open, no smoke ever appears from any of its four chimneys, and the windows on its north face remain permanently shuttered. Standing like a caricature of the imposing homes that surround it, Pendleton House inspired, in turn, its own art installation in 2017. That year RISD students Cameron Kucera, Makoto Kumasaka, and Vuthy Lay created *White Wall*—a temporary work that engulfed the wing's cast-iron fence in a spiky web of whitewashed bamboo.[4] Recalling the thorny palisade of Sleeping Beauty's castle, the barrier dramatically reinforced the wing's inaccessibility while also suggesting that an enchanted figure lay within.

If the exterior of Pendleton House projects the impenetrability of a tomb, then its entry points within the museum appear almost *too* accessible. Visitors to its rooms feel as if they are trespassing in private spaces: an upper hallway lined with bedrooms, the china closet of a small dining room, or an alcove beneath a staircase. The experience can feel as disorienting and accidental as it does transgressive. (As artist Aaron Pexa has observed of Pendleton House, "You can never actually go there . . . you just happen upon it.")[5] Like the illusory environments Alice found through the looking-glass, everywhere in Pendleton House there are uncanny absences and false elements reminding museumgoers this is only the facsimile of a home. Here one finds no bath, kitchen, closet, or nursery; several of the house's windows, and all eight of its fireplaces, are sham; and if you give the walls a good rap, you will hear not the gentle thunk of horsehair and plaster but the unforgiving ping of poured concrete.

Even those who understand they are passing through a stage set may not fully appreciate the contradictions its collection presents. Taking the rooms' descriptive panels at face value, most visitors assume their furnishings derive entirely from Pendleton's gift and faithfully replicate the arrangements of his former home. Neither is the case. Others come away believing the collector single-mindedly promoted eighteenth-century American craft and insisted upon absolute authenticity in the works he acquired. Untrue, as well. From its design to its installation Pendleton House represents, in the words of one former museum administrator, "a lie built upon a lie built upon a lie."[6] Therein, of course, rests its fascination. And here, too, lies the genius of Pendleton himself—a man whose valuable collection was matched only by the grandeur of the eighteenth-century avatar it allowed him to create. Pendleton may never have lived in this house, but he does haunt it.

REPRODUCTION OF A GENTLEMAN

A scattering of graves at the River Bend Cemetery in Westerly, Rhode Island, is all that remains of Pendleton's family. Looming above the modest headstones of his grandparents and their descendants stands a massive granite block dedicated to Pendleton himself, its scale reflecting his position as the family's last male descendant. If his monument serves as an exclamation point to seven generations, then the oldest stone in this plot raises a question mark: the empty grave of Pendleton's paternal grandfather, Captain William Pendleton (1787–1819). This wealthy sea merchant died at thirty-two aboard the schooner *Victory*—a vessel depicted along the tombstone's crown, its sails drawn and crew vanished (below this ghost ship, the stone's epitaph notes the captain's internment on Bermuda).

His widow Anna Taylor Pendleton outlived him by half a century, supported by her sons William and John (Pendleton's father) and sharing a home with her unmarried daughter Loesa, a revered local schoolteacher.[7]

Given Westerly's small circle of local gentry, it is perhaps unsurprising that Pendleton's father and uncle both married their Pendleton cousins. John and his wife Rhoda were therefore each the great-grandchild of Colonel William Pendleton (1704–1786), once the wealthiest man in the town.[8] In subsequent generations, despite (or perhaps because of) a number of Pendleton intermarriages, the family's wealth and much-compounded name appear to have diminished. Comfortably well off if not affluent, Pendleton's father was one of the town's principal farmers and served as Westerly's tax assessor.[9]

Aside from his 1846 birthdate, we know little about Pendleton's childhood. He received his early education in Westerly, likely beginning in his Aunt Loesa's classroom, and though he was little involved in politics as an adult, the adolescent Pendleton appears to have been caught up in the excitement surrounding the start of the Civil War. In the earliest surviving photograph of the future collector, an 1861 tinted ambrotype, the fifteen-year-old Pendleton proudly celebrates the Union cause. Within a gold frame reading "The Union Now and Forever," he appears in a Union military jacket, stylish necktie, and felt hat. The blushing young man in this image is only playing at war: he is at once an awkward teenager, a soldier, and a dandy. Though Pendleton would never enter a battlefield, this blending of private and public personas, of real and imagined selves, became a lifelong habit.

Two years after sitting for his portrait, Pendleton enrolled at Phillips Academy in Andover, Massachusetts. It was an unusual choice, given his age, for at seventeen his peers would likely have been preparing for college rather than secondary school—and in 1863, of course, they might just as easily have been preparing to join the Union army (a possibility that undoubtedly occurred to Pendleton's father, who received an excuse from military service the year before).[10] However unorthodox, his parents' decision reflected the expectations of their class. As the oldest incorporated secondary school in the United States, Phillips Academy offered a pedigreed history as well as a clear pathway to an elite college and profession. When Pendleton graduated at nineteen, his parents must have been gratified by his acceptance to Yale—and doubtless, they were relieved that his time at Andover outlasted the war by a comfortable three months.

Pendleton's high school years appear to have been happy ones. His fondness for

I.2

Portrait of Charles Leonard Pendleton (ca. 1861). Ambrotype with hand tinting (1 7/8" x 1 3/8"). Gift of Fred Stewart Greene, 04.1466. Courtesy RISD Museum, Providence, RI.

this period is reflected by the large collection of scrapbooks and ephemera he saved from the time, an unusually detailed record of a life that in later years went almost wholly undocumented. The account book he kept at Phillips Academy reveals his first experience as a dealer—he sold a stamp collection in 1864 for $2.25—as well as his early taste for the good life.[11] After depositing $25 from his father in August 1864 for "sundries," he added insistently "not cigars!" (suggesting these were an item bought on other occasions); and in January 1865 he spent $55, the equivalent of twelve weeks' tuition, for an overcoat from a stylish tailor.[12]

Classmates' inscriptions in Pendleton's senior classbook suggest his early penchant for games of chance (one noted Pendleton's competitive checkers game) as well as his reputation for betting (another wrote that the only bet he dared take with Pendleton was that "we will have a 'gay' time at Yale").[13] If these entries hint at the activities of Pendleton's later life, then his classbook also illuminates a contrast between his youthful and adult selves: the reclusive collector, it appears, had once been a popular and sociable young man. Pendleton's peers address him with a variety of affectionate nicknames, including "Pen," "Penny," and even "Pengy," and all close their inscriptions with various versions of "your true friend." (In one exceptional example, a boy filled an entire page of his classbook with the looping inscription, "Everlastingly yours.")

An enthusiastic scholar at Phillips Academy, where he excelled in ancient Greek and joined the Philomathean Literary Society, Pendleton entered Yale in the fall of 1865 fully prepared for its academic rigor.[14] The social landscape at the college, however, was another matter. In his freshman semester, he encountered a baffling range of twenty-one different secret societies, eating clubs, and fraternities, each with its own competitive "rush" for entry and many requiring substantial initiation fees. In his only surviving letter to his father, Pendleton asked for funds to join a secret society; whether the request was granted or not is unknown, yet none of the society's published rosters from 1865–1866— indeed, none of Yale's social clubs from this time—lists him as a member.[15]

Faculty Records from 1865–1866 suggest the postwar students of Yale College could be a boisterous and even dangerous group. Infractions recorded by the Faculty Secretary ranged from mundane crimes (dishonoring the Sabbath) to ludicrous stunts (commandeering the college bells) to outright hooliganism (instigating brawls between the classes, dismantling Yale's entry gates, and in one instance, "stamping holes through the floor of the recitation room").[16] Repeated infractions included harboring loaded weapons, drunkenness, lying to police, throwing projectiles from dormitory windows, and hazing freshmen. Sanctions ranged from simple warnings for students who committed small transgressions to expulsion for those guilty of the most serious crimes.

Pendleton, as it would turn out, belonged to the latter group. In a frustratingly brief entry for March 21, 1866, the Faculty Secretary recorded: "Pendleton '69 on a/c of improper conduct in relation to a female shall be dismissed."[17] The nature of his infraction remains a mystery, yet some form of trial appears to have dragged on until the following June; that month Pendleton's classmate Edward Copp received a warning "for testifying in the case of Pendleton, to the faculty, to things which he had no reason to believe true except that the accused told him that they were so."[18] Both of these charges against Pendleton—improper conduct with a woman and the presumption that his word was, *a priori*, worthless—were among the most damning accusations that could be made against a young man of his time and class.

No record exists of Pendleton's reaction to his dismissal from Yale, but the trauma it inflicted is clear enough. From this year forward the formerly sociable, nostalgic young packrat became an increasingly secluded figure intent upon erasing all documentary evidence of his private life. His class at Yale, too, appears eager to have forgotten him. In the minutes for the sixth annual meeting of the Class of 1869, held in 1875, the editor tersely wrote: "Charles Leonard Pendleton left the class second term Freshman. . . . We advise future historians not to trouble themselves to learn further details concerning him."[19] When his class published its biographical record twenty years later, his name was followed by a single word: "unknown."[20]

His classmate's warning aside, the circumstances of Pendleton's expulsion deserve closer attention. "Improper conduct in relation to a female" might have meant a host of things in 1866. Given how freely the Faculty Record describes students' assaults upon one another and members of the town, it appears unlikely Pendleton physically harmed a woman. "Improper" suggests a social, and likely sexual, impropriety, but even here we are faced with a number of possibilities. Was Pendleton caught visiting a brothel? These certainly existed in postwar New Haven. Was the episode connected to an initiation ritual? Given the sexual dimension of some of Yale's secret society rites, this, too, is plausible (though if true, the initiation resulted in no club membership).

The sexual culture of Yale as a whole may provide some insight into the charge. In a speech he gave at an 1872 class dinner, Pendleton's classmate Copp—the same student disciplined for giving false testimony on his behalf—opined that "the maidens of New Haven mourn the departure of '69 and complain that subsequent classes have been unable to fill the gap left vacant."[21] Copp clearly intended this final phrase, uttered at a boozy stag event, as a double entendre—one that pointedly questioned the masculinity of Yale men who could not, or would not, "fill the gap." In an environment of such swaggering heterosexuality, had the nineteen-year-old Pendleton felt pressure to engage in improper sexual conduct? Or was he simply a natural Casanova, caught in a lawless act of passion?

RISD curator Christopher Monkhouse believed the latter. In his 1986 catalogue for Pendleton House, he wrote that the collector's expulsion from Yale "may explain why Pendleton kept his private life thereafter very much to himself. In fact, for the purpose of entertaining women . . . he would eventually maintain a *pied-à-terre* in New York City."[22] Pendleton did keep a New York apartment, yet one wonders—given his keen sense of privacy and the absence of any documentary evidence—how one might conclude he entertained women there. (Certainly, among the fast gambling set he later joined, an affair with a woman would hardly have required secrecy.) Setting aside the question of Pendleton's clandestine affairs with women, we are faced with his unusual choice to remain unmarried, a decision that set him distinctly apart from his peers (93 percent of his Yale classmates would eventually marry).[23] His youthful indiscretion posed no insurmountable obstacle to marriage, and indeed might even have made the prospect more attractive as a form of public rehabilitation. Rather, by choosing permanent bachelorhood he only added to the lingering memory of his Yale disgrace the suspicion of sexual deviance. For by the end of the nineteenth century, as historian John Potvin has suggested, "the twin figures of the bachelor and the homosexual were all too often conflated."[24]

The ancient Greek motto Pendleton inscribed in his high school account book, οδον ευρησω η ποιησω ("I will find the way or I will make it"), was a fitting credo for the period following his expulsion. Determined or perhaps merely resigned to becoming a lawyer, as nearly half of his Yale class would do, Pendleton embarked on a clerkship with the Providence law firm Thurston, Ripley and Company.[25] (To supplement his income he served as a Justice of the Peace, an appointment made, however ironically, on the one-year anniversary of his final Yale trial.)[26] Pendleton followed his clerkship at Thurston, Ripley with a single academic year at the Albany School of Law. He was admitted to the New York State Bar on May 5, 1869.[27]

Hoping to relocate to New York City, Pendleton sought the support of his former employers. Their lukewarm letters of introduction suggest he had not made much of an impression. "I suspect New York is more or less full," partner Isaac Edwards wrote, "and yet there is often an opening for a young man"; for his part, Edwards's colleague Benjamin Thurston offered only, "[Pendleton] studied . . . for a considerable period in this office . . . and will do no discredit to our profession."[28] No surviving records indicate where, or even if, Pendleton landed a position when he moved to New York in the fall of 1869. In any event, his residency there lasted less than a year.

On March 30, 1870, John Pendleton died suddenly—and, one can only assume, painfully—from a steak bone that punctured his stomach wall.[29] He was just fifty-two. Three weeks later Anna Pendleton, the family matriarch since 1819, died at seventy-seven. The paired deaths of his father and grandmother must have dealt a profound emotional blow to the young man, and yet they also provided him the first financial security he had ever known. Inheriting the significant sum of $5,000 in cash along with sole ownership of the Pendleton farm, he moved back into his childhood home as nominal head of the family.[30] After his admission to the Rhode Island Bar in 1873, he began to split his time between Westerly and bachelor quarters at a downtown Providence hotel.[31] Although Pendleton identified himself as a lawyer for the 1870 census, in the following decade no Business Directories in Westerly or Providence confirm his practice of the law. It would appear that income from his family's farm—likely augmented by illicit gambling gains— allowed him to live semi-independently at this stage.

It was during this first flush of financial independence that Pendleton began to collect, making his first purchase at the 1876 Centennial International Exhibition in Philadelphia.[32] Intended to showcase the United States' industrial prowess, the fair made a centerpiece of the Corliss Centennial Engine—a colossal, forty-five-foot-high steam engine produced just a few miles from Pendleton's rooms in Providence. However impressive such a display might have been, it proved no match for the dazzling range of "artistic" furnishings Britain sent to Philadelphia. Indeed, the triumph of British design at the Centennial represented the first major American conduit for the Aesthetic Movement's ideals, setting the stage for Oscar Wilde's successful American tour six years later. As the *New York Sun* reported from the Centennial:

> The richness, solidity, and exquisite taste of every one of the pieces of artistic [British] furniture are unparalleled. Compared with them, the exhibits of American furniture appear as a heterogenous collection of showy parlour and dining-room sets ordered by a . . . Western upstart about to marry and fit up his residence.[33]

Caught up in the Centennial's enthusiasm for "art-furnishings" himself, Pendleton bought an antique bronze vase at the fair. Little is known about the work, which he sold in 1897, but it was likely a Chinese piece (the *National Republican* had advised all "Chinamaniacs" at the fair to buy quickly, noting the Chinese pavilion's brisk sales in ceramics, lacquers, and bronzes).[34] The acquisition is notable given his later passion for Chinese ceramics, a fixation that stemmed from the Aesthetic Movement's promotion of "exotic" handmade works in artistic décor.

If Pendleton's vase suggests his early attraction to Aesthetic Movement ideals, it is worth noting that, for a collector later touted as a champion of American decorative arts, he appears to have been unmoved by the fair's promotion of colonial antiques. As a centennial celebration, the fair featured a number of colonial-themed exhibits, among them a popular venue called the New England Kitchen of 1776. This exhibition-cum-restaurant displayed a range of antiques and cooking utensils that, as an ensemble, became one of the most recognizable tableaux of American collecting for Pendleton's generation—and yet he neither created such a display in his own home nor did he propose one for the wing that would bear his name. (The RISD Museum later attempted to correct this omission, proposing in 1921 to shoehorn a colonial kitchen into the building's basement.)[35]

The advent of Pendleton's collection coincided with a time and place particularly conducive to his new passion. Given its long history of furnituremaking and connections to the sea merchant trade, Providence supplied New England antique hunters with an extraordinary range of both old and reproduction furniture. Capitalizing on this established market, Walter Durfee, the enterprising young son of a wealthy mill owner, opened his antiques business in Providence in 1877—and four years later took on the thirty-four-year-old Pendleton as his silent partner.[36] Accompanying Durfee on three buying trips to England over the next two years, Pendleton dealt in both antique and reproduction furniture (and combinations thereof) while amassing his own collection.

Considering his modest quarters down the street from Durfee's shop, a small house Pendleton shared with two other boarders from 1882 to 1896, his personal collection at this stage likely represented business stock rather than furnishings for his own use.[37] Even toward the end of his life, when the grandeur of his home at last matched the quality of his collection, he continued to regard his furnishings as liquid assets. Unsentimental about these works, Pendleton periodically unloaded large quantities of furniture in public sales and constantly weeded out individual works to improve the overall quality of his holdings. In the words of his friend Luke Vincent Lockwood, Pendleton's collection represented the "constant elimination of the good for something better."[38]

In 1884, crushing gambling debts forced Pendleton to dissolve his partnership with Durfee. Following the breakup he took on local clients as a dealer-decorator; when wealthy bachelor Henry J. Steere built his colossal Barrington, Rhode Island, home, for example, Pendleton served as his furniture advisor. Completion of the Steere commission in 1886 found Pendleton reduced to any work he could find, including a clerking stint at Fenner's Wire Works, a downtown Providence metal shop. It was a humbling position for someone of his education and age, but the following year he seems to have regained his footing as a dealer.[39] In a high-profile 1887 sale he managed to purchase a number of important works, including several from the heirs of his erstwhile employers, the Fenner family.[40]

In their more lucid passages, Pendleton's cryptic account books from the 1880s onward reflect a wide range of scouting trips from New England to the South and Midwest. A posthumous 1918 profile describes Pendleton "touring the attics, the dim, old fashioned parlors and secondhand stores of New England" for his pieces, yet by the

1890s he was more likely to be found in high-end auction houses or the showrooms of New York City dealers like Thomas Clarke or Hawkins, Drake, and Sypher.[41] His clients in this period included patrician New Englanders like Rowland Hazard and George Palmer, as well as wealthy self-made men like Marsden Perry and Richard Canfield. Not only did Pendleton help establish these men as serious collectors, but he also took satisfaction in surpassing them as a connoisseur.

Pendleton shared more than a taste for antiques with Palmer, Perry, and Canfield, all of whom belonged to the world of high-stakes gambling. Whereas Palmer and Perry fueled this habit from legitimate sources—Palmer was a textile manufacturer, Perry a banking and utilities magnate—Canfield amassed his fortune from a string of illegal gambling houses in New York City, Newport, and Saratoga Springs, many furnished by Pendleton. In his 1882 memoir *Turf, Cards, and Temperance, or Reminiscences of a Checkered Life*, Pendleton's fellow Rhode Islander and Phillips Academy alumnus J. Richmond Talbot wrote about this circle of reckless young men "around the green cloth" who lost entire fortunes at the racetrack or in card games like Faro or Euchre. "If you pursue a fast life," the author warns, "each word written here will stamp itself upon your brain in characters of fire, and it may be *too late*!"[42]

It was often too late for Pendleton. The principal difference between his position and that of the high rollers with whom he associated was his narrower access to capital. For Canfield, Perry, or Palmer, eighteenth-century furnishings represented the reward for their sizeable legal or illicit gains; in Pendleton's case, these same antiques constituted his principal cash reserve and sole entrée to their world. As a friend and purveyor to these men, moreover, he also inevitably became their competitor—whether in the auction house or the betting arena—and it appears he often found himself in over his head. Twice more nearly bankrupted after his 1884 debacle, and deeply in debt upon his death, he proved himself a far better furniture dealer than card player.[43]

Nowhere was Pendleton's prowess as a dealer more publicly demonstrated than at a sensational two-day auction in December 1897. Covered in breathless style by the *Providence Journal*, this sale of nearly three hundred "works of art . . . had not been equaled since the eighteenth century."[44] The *Journal* eagerly noted the presence of blueblood attendees—among the bidders were members of Providence's Goddard, Ives, and Aldrich families—as well as the auction's impressive sale prices (a single table sold for over $1,000, "occasion[ing] a great deal of comment").[45] Most gratifying of all for Pendleton was the newspaper's insistence that "every piece was warranted to be a genuine antique . . . the reputation of Mr. Pendleton being an assurance of this."

It was an extraordinary moment for the collector. Not only had the city's oldest families endorsed his taste but they had paid him handsomely for it, ensuring the greatest financial security he had known as a dealer. Almost more valuable than the items he sold (indeed, one of the very reasons for their value) was the *Journal*'s insistence upon Pendleton's irreproachable reputation. With a single sentence, it seems, the long shadow of his Yale expulsion had magically lifted. ("How astounding the change!" as Talbot described the euphoria of a big win, "like the possession of Aladdin's lamp, every wish was granted.")[46] With this sale he learned that collecting not only held the power to burnish his character but to transform it outright.

STAGING A LEGACY

Several months before this 1897 auction, Pendleton had exchanged his downtown boarding rooms for a stately, Federal-era home on College Hill—a costly move that likely necessitated the sale of so many works. How he planned to remain in these expensive new quarters is a mystery (sales like his landmark auction were a rarity), yet it is important to note that he came to 72 Waterman Street as a tenant, not an owner. In 1897, the house belonged to Sophia Brown Sherman, granddaughter of Brown University's namesake and a direct descendant of Rhode Island founder Roger Williams. A prominent socialite in Newport and New York, Sherman belonged to the "Astor 400" that constituted, according to the *New York Times*, "the *beau-monde* of New-York to-day."[47] However respectable Pendleton's Westerly ancestry might have been, his assumption of this Brown family home represented a quantum social leap.

Beyond its connections to such a storied family, Pendleton's new home was a model of Federal high style. Built for wealthy sea merchant Edward Dexter in 1795–1797 (and thereafter familiarly known as Dexter House), the home is a classically articulated, five-bay design. Two-story-tall "giant order" pilasters frame its central bay like paired exclamation points, while the house's upper balustrade is crowned by no less than a dozen classical urns. At either end of its façade the house's walls are wrapped in chamfered wooden quoins that, in the style of the period, imitate cut stonework. Every inch of this street-facing façade was engineered to impress, as was its location. Originally located several blocks away at the corner of George and Prospect Streets, the house was moved to its current location in 1860. That year Sherman's father, John Carter Brown, ordered the house sawn in half and rolled uphill—a feat accomplished using cannonballs—to the higher elevation of Waterman Street.[48]

Pendleton's move to College Hill was, in its own way, even more dramatic. With the 1897 auction he had effectively sawn his own property in half, only to rebuild his remaining collection in a grander setting. This process of distilling his collection cannot be separated from the corresponding refinement of his public persona, one increasingly detached from the man himself. Like Henry James's collector-protagonist Adela Gereth in *The Spoils of Poynton*, published the year Pendleton moved to Waterman Street, his "whole life and collection had been but an effort toward completeness and perfection."[49] Residency in Dexter House

1.3
Edward Dexter House (1795–1797) at 72 Waterman Street, Providence, RI. Author photograph.

allowed him to banish forever the image of the tradesman with a murky past, emerging instead as a gentleman of taste and social equal of the Brown family.

If both house and man presented a carefully calculated façade, then the interior of the Dexter House offered its own theatrical opportunities for display. The home's sprawling five thousand square feet were divided into eight principal rooms. Its two grandest, the parlor and library, faced the street; within these, dramatic arched recesses framed Pendleton's most cherished pieces. Directly behind the rooms were the dining room and large kitchen, with four elegant bedrooms upstairs. The home's entry hall and upper hallway, each nearly ten feet wide, offered their own possibilities for impressive compositions. (Indeed, the number of works Pendleton managed to squeeze into these two spaces, alone, suggested an auction house more so than private home.)

To furnish Dexter House Pendleton employed the style he loved above all others: English Chippendale. An elegant, labor-intensive, and costly mode, the Chippendale aesthetic had flourished in Britain and its colonies from the mid-eighteenth century until the 1790s, its subsequent revival beginning just a few decades into the nineteenth century. (Some of the British firms exhibiting at the Philadelphia Centennial were making

1.4
Entry hall at Dexter House during Pendleton's residency [illustrated in Luke Vincent Lockwood, *The Pendleton Collection* (1904)]. Courtesy Digital Commons @ RISD and the RISD Museum, Providence RI.

Chippendale reproductions as early as the 1830s.)[50] Characterized by deeply carved mahogany, dramatic cabriole curves, and signature ball-and-claw feet, Chippendale's catalogue of decorative elements constituted the first truly national English style, even while it borrowed elements from Chinese design and the French Rococo.

Collectors in Pendleton's time knew Chippendale's work almost exclusively through his publications. The first cabinetmaker to issue an illustrated trade catalogue, Thomas Chippendale (1718–1779) produced his enormously successful *Gentleman and Cabinet Maker's Director* in 1754. Its scores of measured patterns, particularly strong in chair designs, present an eclectic mix reflected by the work's subtitle, "Elegant and Useful Designs of Household Furniture in the Gothic, Chinese, and Modern Taste." Whereas previous furniture styles in England had borne the name of the period's monarch, Chippendale was the first cabinetmaker whose name became synonymous with the furniture he produced— and indeed, with the furniture *others* produced, as well, for he inspired hundreds of imitators on both sides of the Atlantic. Demonstrating that furniture could hold the same feverish, covetous appeal of fashion, this new generation of cabinetmakers adopted the novel practice of labeling their work, indicating the pieces' prestige and long-term value.[51]

For eighteenth-century consumers, everything about the Chippendale style felt modern and exciting. As Warren Clouston wrote in his pioneering 1897 study of the cabinetmaker's work, the style "seem[ed] to have sprung into life almost at once."[52] Unlike traditional English materials such as oak, mahogany—a Caribbean wood first introduced to England in the 1720s—was strong enough to withstand dramatic curves and crisp carving. Paired with its sculptural possibilities was its potential for surface brilliance. Capitalizing on mahogany's flamboyant "figure" (the complex patterning of its grain), cabinetmakers polished it to a reflective sheen that dazzled in candlelight.

Nineteenth-century collectors like Pendleton prized Chippendale-style furniture, whether made in London, Philadelphia, or Newport, for many of the same reasons: its craftsmanship, investment value, and what Emma Rutherford has called the style's "haptic sensuousness."[53] With the passage of more than a century, the style had accrued new associations. To nineteenth-century eyes the style's virtuoso, handcrafted aesthetic served as a rebuke to the "cheap, gimcrack age" (as Henry James dubbed it) that mechanized furniture production had introduced.[54] For self-made men like Perry, Canfield, and Pendleton, moreover—all of

1.5
Model Chippendale style in Pendleton's collection. Note cabriole legs, virtuoso carving, and ball-and-claw feet. Side chair, American (ca. 1755–1775). Mahogany and yellow poplar (42" x 24" x 17"). Bequest of Mr. Charles L. Pendleton, 04.116. Courtesy RISD Museum, Providence, RI.

whom vied against one another for Chippendale-style works—the pieces also provided a desirable veneer of gentlemanly respectability and pedigree.

So closely was Pendleton associated with this style that, when fellow collector Eben Howard Gay wrote his quasi-autobiographical novel *A Chippendale Romance* (1915), he based his character Mr. Remington entirely on the late Pendleton—even going so far as to reproduce an image of the entry to 72 Waterman Street as "Remington's Front Hall." A confirmed bachelor with a weakness for gambling, Remington is redeemed in the novel by his superb collection of Chippendale furniture. ("Whatever his private life may have been," narrator Harold Blake explains, "his love of the beautiful was as sincere as his taste was refined and discriminating.")[55] Yet even in his collecting Remington is presented as a cautionary example. Blake not only faults him for choosing his collection over true love but also for standing on the wrong side of period debates concerning furniture polish.

This question of finish was no small matter. Remington/Pendleton represented the so-called scrape school, which advocated stripping antique pieces and coating them with a glossy French polish meant to mimic the works' original appearance. "Anti-scrapers," on the other hand—including Blake and his love interest in the novel, Rose Lee—argued for retaining a work's historic patina. Lee feels that "scraping" created an unnatural look ("a hybrid *new-old* appearance that is neither one thing nor the other"), whereas Blake believes the process violated historical pedigree (a glossy finish, he declares, "in no wise equaled the satisfaction of viewing [a piece] as it had come down from our forefathers with all the earmarks of time").[56]

When Pendleton, Canfield, and Perry ("scrapers," all) refinished works to appear as if they had arrived directly from the maker's bench, the men collapsed the nineteenth century with the eighteenth—imbuing their collections with a dazzling newness and resurrecting the presence of the works' original aristocratic owners. (Comparing the "scrape" process to the revivification of a corpse, *The House Beautiful* declared in 1909 that "the rich beauty of mahogany is never greater than when under the operation of the scraper it is seen to emerge from its mummy-coat.")[57] No admirer of "the earmarks of time," Pendleton thus erased his pieces' past as thoroughly he had his own history.

However much his furniture evoked the immediacy of the eighteenth century, its arrangement at Dexter House would have baffled a gentleman of that era. Even a man of means from Chippendale's period would normally have possessed a single tall case clock and just one secretary bookcase—their function did not call for multiples—nor would he have possessed a large number of mirrors, which were among the most expensive items in a household. By contrast, Pendleton's home featured five tall case clocks, five secretary bookcases (three stood in the library alone), and no fewer than fourteen mirrors. And while an eighteenth-century household might have contained multiple dressing tables, it would have been unusual to encounter three in the same room (as in Pendleton's parlor), nor would a marble-topped side table—intended in the eighteenth century for serving alcohol—typically appear outside a dining room (Pendleton placed two such tables in his lower hall).[58]

Even more confusing to eighteenth-century eyes would have been the house's lack of society. Grand homes in the 1700s were designed for public display, yet by all accounts few visitors ever made it past the front door at 72 Waterman Street. However ironically, tea services—the most recognizable symbol of hospitality in an eighteenth-century household—were represented in staggering numbers in Pendleton's collection, crowding his shelves unused. (As Richard Marsh wrote in 1898, "ask a china maniac to let you have afternoon tea out of his Old Chelsea, and you will learn some truths as to the durability of human friendship.")[59] More troubling from a dynastic standpoint was the lack of any family life in the house, whether living or dead, as none of the portraits in his collection depicts a relative. If grand furnishings typically required an audience, then Pendleton appears to have committed himself to a life of inconspicuous consumption.

To understand the goals of 72 Waterman Street we must see it in the context of Aesthetic Movement ideals. The house was a shrine to beauty, not hospitality. "One glance at the superb furnishings of the hall," Eben Howard Gay wrote of Pendleton/ Remington's home, "revealed for the first time, to my delighted gaze, the possibilities of artistic furniture."[60] Pendleton's 1904 Deed of Gift to RISD reveals that visual interest was everything to him; in typical passages he describes a tall case clock as "one of the most interesting that the owner has ever known" or a table whose "lines are absolutely without flaw."[61]

The full "possibilities of artistic furniture," of course, cannot be understood without considering the supporting role that rugs, paintings, and colored glass played in the house's *mis-en-scène*. Jewel-toned, artfully distressed Persian and Turkish rugs glowed against Dexter House's dark, highly polished oak floors, prized as works of art in their own right. Pendleton's paintings functioned similarly, providing blocks of mellow color against walls painted in newly fashionable ivory or gray tones. Of the paintings he donated to RISD in 1904, nearly half are golden Dutch landscapes with bright blue skies; others feature European aristocrats painted in resplendent costumes. Cast in the rosy glow of Bohemian cut glass pendant lights, this constellation of objects created a unified artistic effect that was neither cozily domestic nor strictly museological.

Perhaps the most important visual partner to his furniture was Pendleton's collection of Chinese porcelain. Beyond their inherent value, he prized these pieces for the vivid range of colors they introduced—an effect intensified by their juxtaposition with dark, flamed-grained mahogany. In *A Chippendale Romance,* Blake goes into ecstasies over Remington/Pendleton's Chinese porcelains, cataloguing a display of

> peach blooms, sang-de-boeufs, mazarins, clair-de-lunes, lapis-lazulis, café-au-laits, turquoise-blues, powdered blues, black hawthorns, and a ginger jar in deepest ultramarine blue, with its transparent glaze that is a caress to the touch.[62]

Pendleton waxes nearly as poetic in his Deed of Gift, describing "liver colored," "seaweed green," and "clotted blood red" vases and carefully distinguishing between "powder," "slate," and "robin's egg" blues.[63] (Twice he appears to throw up his hands, resorting to the phrase "very unusual coloring.")

While the surfaces of Pendleton's furniture sparkled with Chinese porcelain, the interiors of his bookcases and cabinets held an even larger collection of eighteenth-century English salt-glaze earthenware, primarily Whieldon pottery. The work of ceramicist Thomas Whieldon (1719–1795) was popular with Aesthetic Movement collectors, who admired its acidic combinations of yellow and green or "tortoise-shell" effects. Yet the sheer quantity of Whieldon ware in Pendleton's collection suggests more than just an admiration for its palette. His fetishistic hoard of seventy-eight Whieldon teapots alone—none apparently put into service—exemplifies the "china mania" of his period while also exhibiting a troubling gender confusion. In the late nineteenth century china collecting was primarily perceived as a womanly activity, taken up only by men who fell outside societal norms. (Describing one such collector in 1892, china expert Alice Morse Earle writes: "it is needless to add he was a bachelor.")[64] As if to remove the problematic male china collector from Pendleton House altogether, *The House Beautiful* noted in a 1915 profile that the museum's salt-glazed pieces were "highly prized among New England housewives who attended carefully to their china closets."[65]

Nearly as troublesome for a bachelor like Pendleton was his fondness for the Chippendale style itself. Its luxurious character challenged self-effacing bourgeois respectability, conveying a glamour more associated with high-style bachelor's lodgings or clubs than a family home. (In its 1899 feature "Luxurious Bachelordom," *Munsey's Magazine* sighs over the "mahogany . . . and gorgeous embroidered eastern stuffs" found in New York's most fashionable bachelor apartments.)[66] And while furniture terms are generally anthropomorphic—words like *figure*, *arm*, *leg*, *knee*, *seat*, *spine*, and *carcase* all evoke the human body—Chippendale's hallmark features also suggest a stereotypically masculine form. These include the famed strength of its wood, often cut against the grain to create dramatic silhouettes; its muscular carving, naked surfaces, and widespread legs; the strained tenons of its ball-and-claw feet; and the phallic form of its sturdy cabriole supports. Appropriately enough, in Pendleton's day the descriptor used more than any other to praise Chippendale pieces was the masculine-sounding "handsome"—a term Pendleton himself used no less than seventeen times in his Deed of Gift (in one instance even committing the telling typographical error "mandsome").[67]

Given Pendleton's bachelor status, insistence upon privacy, and taste for handsome furniture, the question inevitably arises: Was he homosexual? Blake nearly asks this of himself in *A Chippendale Romance*, addressing the reader: "What do I know of pretty girls' kisses? A lone bachelor, self-banished, bent on a mad chase for—something he can't find! Am I not paying too dear a price in my worship of the beautiful?"[68] Whether or with whom Pendleton might have engaged in a same-sex affair is, in the end, immaterial. More important to consider is how external audiences perceived his profession and lifestyle, a factor that may explain his wish for a respectable, historically distant avatar. Although it belongs to a slightly later period, Cole Porter's song "Let's Do It" echoes the assumptions Pendleton's period inevitably made about his profession:

> The Belgians and the Greeks do it,
> Nice young men who sell antiques do it.
> Let's do it, let's fall in love.[69]

Beyond the question of his sexuality, there were other reasons Pendleton might have felt the need for public rehabilitation. For a man who sought the thrill of high-stakes gambling, the hunt for valuable antiques likely implied a similar range of vices: envy, greed, and the venality of deception. Whether or not he acted on such impulses is, again, less important than the popular belief that, as a bachelor collector, he surely must have. Indeed, several popular novels from this period feature unmarried men whose aesthetic sensitivity appears to *stem* from their immoral character (a reflection, itself, of the Aesthetic Movement's uncoupling of art and virtue). In Henry James's *The Golden Bowl*

(1904), for example, it is the suspect Prince Amerigo who perceives the flaw in the antique bowl of the novel's title, a defect the innocent Maggie Verver is unable to detect. Frankly admitting a connection between larceny and collecting, one of the unmarried men in Richard Marsh's novel *Curios: Some Strange Adventures of Two Bachelors* (1898) declares: "All collectors steal! The eighth commandment was not intended to apply to them" (to which his fellow bachelor responds, "think of the tastes we have in common").[70]

Whatever other vices we might detect in Pendleton's collecting habits, we know he often overrestored or "married" pieces he handled, combining portions of multiple antiques or embellishing older pieces with new elements. (Speaking of a wall cabinet in the Pendleton Collection, RISD curator Thomas Michie once declared it "not a fake, exactly"—a phrase that might have served as Pendleton's business slogan.)[71] Partnering with talented Providence furniture makers like Morlock and Bayer, Pendleton felt no qualms about sacrificing historical purity to achieve a more successful look. In an account book entry from the 1880s, for example, he notes buying an authentic eighteenth-century chest to which he added a new scroll top, replacement handles, and glossy finish, eventually selling the piece as an "original" for three times his purchase price.[72]

Pendleton's most audacious counterfeit was the richly carved, double chair-back settee he showcased in the recessed niche of his library. At the time of his gift to RISD he insisted this settee, the prize of his collection, represented the work of the Anglo-Dutch master carver Grinling Gibbons (1648–1721).[73] The actual story of this settee reflects, in microcosm, the problematic character of Pendleton's collection and even of the collector himself. Today RISD owns *two* settees matching the one photographed in his library; neither, however, belongs to the eighteenth century. Rather, the museum dates

1.6
Pendleton's "Grinling Gibbons" settee, likely a refurbished Victorian reproduction. Morlock and Bayer, American, 1877–1908 (cabinetmaker); Charles Dowler, American, fl. 1866–1924 (carver); R.H. Breitenstein, American, fl. 1869–1945 (upholsterer), *Double Chair-Back Settee* (1905). Mahogany (40 ½" height). Gift of the Estate of Mrs. Gustav Radeke, 31.146. Courtesy RISD Museum, Providence, RI.

them to 1903 and 1905 and attributes both to the Providence cabinetmakers Morlock and Bayer. Stories that Pendleton commissioned two copies of his beloved settee shortly before his death only compound the mystery—for not only does 1905 fall the year after Pendleton died, but it would also appear that the antique model for these two copies has gone missing.[74]

Closer inspection of the bill for the 1905 Morlock and Bayer settee dispels some of this confusion. Its principal fees include repairs ($74), recarving ($70), and reupholstery ($12), with the paltry sum of $7 for labor. In other words, the cabinetmakers made no new settee in 1905—instead, they appear simply to have overhauled an older piece, presumably the antique prototype for the settee made in 1903. In the 1980s, however, Christopher Monkhouse identified even this reworked "original" as a Victorian reproduction, patterned on an eighteenth-century *single*-backed armchair in London's Sir John Soane's Museum.[75] Did Pendleton realize his treasured settee was a contemporary work? A look at his Deed of Gift provides a clue. We know Pendleton commissioned six side chairs from Morlock and Bayer to match his cherished "Gibbons" settee, yet in the Deed he attributes them all—settee *and* side chairs—to Gibbons. Whether this entry represents seven lies or just six, it does not reflect well on him.

Ironically, the detail that betrays the settee's nineteenth-century origin is the head of a cherub carved into its back rail (a feature absent from the armchair at Soane's Museum). Like a metaphor for truth in dealing, this angelic feature seems to suggest that furniture never deceives, only unethical collectors do. Indeed, if Pendleton hoped to scrape and polish his legacy, then it was primarily through his furniture that he could do so—not only given the value of his gift to RISD but also because its works were themselves described in terms that suggest human virtue. With an irony now apparent to us in hindsight, critics in Pendleton's day praised his collection as "genuine," "authentic," and "worthy"; the ensemble displayed "integrity," "honesty," and "transparency" while never appearing "imperfect or doubtful."[76]

Pendleton profited, too, from the virtues ascribed to the works' original makers. As Ada Rainey wrote in her 1915 profile of Pendleton House:

> One leaves this fascinating house with a sigh of regret. . . . There is such a feeling of high-bred distinction, of consistently carried out ideas, which emanate from things that are genuine. Surely the people who made and lived with these chairs, tables and desks had much of the sterling qualities that the material objects possess, or they would not have made them or treasured them so dearly.[77]

Drawing the line between collection and collector even more clearly (if also insisting that taste provided a convenient cover for poor behavior), interior decorator Elsie de Wolfe wrote in 1913:

> What surer guarantee can there be of a person's character, natural and cultivated, inherent and inherited, than taste? It is a compass that never errs. When people have taste they may have faults, follies, fads, they may err, they may be as human and honest as they please, but they will never cause a scandal.[78]

As if to confirm her words, the 1986 catalogue of the Pendleton Collection declares: "whatever the deficiencies of Pendleton's . . . judgment, he compensated for them when it came to planning for the future disposition of his museum."[79]

By the time Pendleton commissioned the reproduction of his Victorian settee, he knew his time was running out. The considerable debt later discovered by his executor suggests his continued residence at Dexter House was likely in jeopardy; and as early as the summer of 1903 the fifty-eight-year-old had begun treatment for malignant melanoma (described in one period account—aptly enough, given his penchant for masking—as "cancer of the face").[80] As the eighteenth-century Massachusetts minister Joshua Bradley once famously sermonized, "all must leave their seats, their houses, and enter the mansions of everlasting happiness or misery and punishment."[81] Pendleton faced leaving his seat whether he lived or died, but the scheme he proposed in 1904 would transform his earthly home into a "mansion of everlasting happiness" inhabited by his own apotheosis.

THE FINAL GAMBIT

Through negotiations with RISD's museum director Eleazer Bartlett Homer, Pendleton pledged in May 1904 to leave the entirety of his collection to the school. (Homer, who knew him through Canfield and Perry, had "watched with amusement their competition in collecting.")[82] Praising Pendleton following the announcement of his gift, RISD President William Carey Poland conflated the virtuous labor of eighteenth-century craftsmen with that of the collector. Like these men, he declared, "you have spared yourself no toil, no persistent effort, no sacrifice, that you might make your collection one of unrivalled excellence."[83]

Founded in 1877, RISD—like Pendleton's collection itself—traced its origin to the Philadelphia Centennial. Inspired by design work at the fair's Woman's Pavilion, Providence philanthropist Helen Rowe Metcalf persuaded the Rhode Island Committee of Centennial Women to apply the group's remaining funds to found a coeducational school of design. Some form of a museum had existed at the school since its founding, but it was not until 1893 that it evolved into a public space at RISD's new 11 Waterman Street home. Two years after Metcalf's death in 1895, her husband Jesse built a museum addition in her memory—yet even these new galleries could not absorb the contents of Pendleton's sprawling home.

The day after Pendleton finalized his gift, the *Providence Journal* reported that his collection would be housed in a new, fireproof structure adjacent to the current museum and paid for by the Metcalf family (a detail the paper failed to include in Pendleton's subsequent obituary). The *Journal* noted, "it is intended that the collection shall be housed in a building which in its arrangement and disposition shall follow very closely those of the old house in which Mr. Pendleton now lives."[84] The interior of the new structure would faithfully mimic the layout and arrangements of 72 Waterman Street, while its exterior would only nod to Dexter House as a starting point. (Unsurprisingly, Pendleton insisted the façade of his memorial should embrace an even grander version of Georgian style.)

The other, more significant alteration to the mansion's identity involved a sleight of hand regarding its ownership. Early reports claiming that the wing paid tribute to the home where he *lived* soon gave way to the more durable impression that it replicated a historic house he *owned*.[85] Pendleton undoubtedly intended to sow this confusion, for only by claiming permanent (if posthumous) ownership of the home could he resolve the volatile nature of his reputation, finances, and address. One of the greatest gambles he ever made, it continues to pay dividends in our own day. In a typical version of the building's origin story written in 1975, *The Magazine Antiques* explained: "It was Pendleton's wish that . . . his own 1790s house be reproduced as exactly as possible."[86]

Some have suggested Pendleton's models for this wing included the aristocratic English house museums he visited in the 1880s, but a more likely prototype lies closer to home and nearer the end of the collector's life. In 1902 Stanford White designed a Georgian Revival "art house" in New York City for Pendleton's friend and fellow collector Thomas Clarke; completed the same year Pendleton leased his own New York apartment, Clarke's home and quasi-public gallery were an instant critical success. As the *New York Sun* gushed:

> Mr. Clarke has produced what may literally be called an art home . . . a home absolutely unique, and as beautiful as it is individualistic. There is nothing like it in New York . . . [and] it is bound to effect fortunate results in the tasteful influences which will go out from it through the owner's personal friends.[87]

Indeed, in its formation of a unified, artistic "picture" presented to the public, Clarke's gallery points directly to Pendleton House four years later. Here, too, period rooms would exert "tasteful influences" on visitors in the guise of a domestic setting, banishing as Clarke had himself any "suggestion either of a museum or a fad, so blended and adapted to their places and uses are these works."

When Clarke visited Providence in the weeks prior to Pendleton's death, his friend shared Willson's plans for Pendleton House—a design Clarke praised for its dignity and fitness "to enclose [Pendleton's] beautiful art possessions."[88] The architect's sumptuous presentation drawing formed part of the Indenture contract Pendleton signed with the Metcalf family, a legal agreement decreeing the finished building would be "a house of Georgian architecture . . . in accordance with the plan annexed to this instrument . . . [and] subject only to trifling changes."[89]

Stephen Olney Metcalf, who would bear the costs for the building, must have paused before signing this document. The Georgian mansion Willson proposed not only surpassed the grandeur of 72 Waterman Street, but it also eclipsed nearly every historic home in the city—including the nearby John Brown House (1788), then owned by Pendleton's friend and rival collector Marsden Perry. Willson's proposed design followed the basic outlines of Dexter House: five bays wide, it terminated in quoined edges and featured a second-story Palladian window crowned with a balustrade. Yet whereas Dexter House's façade features wooden clapboarding and elements that only mimic stone detailing, Willson's design called for brick walls and genuine stone detailing throughout, including an additional layer of quoining and a baroque scrolled pediment over the structure's central bay. As with the collection Pendleton assembled, Willson's design represented "the elimination of the good for something better."

The month before he died Pendleton wrote Metcalf's sister, Eliza Metcalf Radeke, "that you should find time to remember and be sorry for one so sick—so unfortunate as

myself, touches my heart deeply."[90] Pendleton surely realized his own misery would soon be visited upon her brother, who learned upon the collector's death that his estate lay in considerable debt. Leaving assets in the amount of $20,862.31, mostly tied to the value of his collection, Pendleton had stacked up liabilities to the tune of $38,892.01—over half of which was owed to Canfield in the form of gambling debts.[91] Before embarking on the new building, Metcalf settled this deficit in part by selling off some of the very works the wing was intended to contain.[92] More disappointingly, he was also forced to ask Willson to scale back his original design, resulting in the elegant if more modest structure the museum eventually built (see figure 1.1, p. 2).

If the collection and building ultimately survived Pendleton's final financial embarrassment, however altered in form, then the memory of the man himself was quickly fading from view. Five months after his death Pendleton's mother, the last of his immediate family, died at eighty-four. Donating Pendleton's ambrotype portrait to RISD that year, a young Westerly man named Fred Stewart Greene explained he was only able to acquire this rare image from Rhoda Pendleton's estate because "the remaining relatives do not care for Mr. Pendleton."[93] With the flawed, living man safely removed from the scene, the institutional project to introduce his gentleman-avatar could now begin. Central to this plan was the seemingly endless repetition of a particular phrase: "Pendleton aimed to create a home in which a gentleman of wealth and taste from the last quarter of the eighteenth century might have lived."[94] Variations of this declaration appear in sources too numerous to count—from museum copy to newspapers to catalogues and shelter magazines of our own day. Sometimes the home is characterized as English or colonial, and occasionally (if paradoxically) as "typical," yet the elements "gentleman" and "taste" have remained constant up to the present, when the validity of these terms is contested if not rejected outright.

This summoning of a generic, eighteenth-century figure might appear at odds with Pendleton's insistence that the new wing bear his name. The language of his gift is clear. The collector declared the building "shall be . . . a perpetual memorial of himself and of his family," his works "forever known as 'The Charles L. Pendleton Collection,'" and the building named "The Pendleton Museum."[95] Yet in these instances the famously private Pendleton seemed determined to memorialize his name as a symbolic emblem rather than a specific tribute to himself. In this he no doubt shared the attitude of his cousin Everett Hall Pendleton, who wrote in *Early New England Pendletons* (1956):

> Those Americans who possess old and honored names . . . may be rightfully proud of their heritage. . . . As it passed to his children, to his children's children, and their children, it became the symbol not of one man but of a family, and all that family stood for. Handed down from generation to generation, it grew inseparably associated with the achievement, tradition, and the prestige of the family . . . a badge of family honor . . . and the most treasured possession of those who bear it.[96]

Pendleton had never treated his name with the same care he showed his other possessions—witness its appearance in the Yale Faculty Records or on the unpaid notes left to his executor—but in death he ensured that it, too, would become an inviolable part of his collection. In turn, these objects would not only stand in for past generations of Pendletons but also the future ones he had failed to produce. (As the author of the first catalogue of his collection claimed, Pendleton's patrimony lay in furnishings rather than descendants: "he could truly be called the father of art as applied to furniture.")[97]

Pendleton House opened to the public on October 22, 1906, thanks to the heroic efforts of Willson and Metcalf. Struggling with poor health for much of the building's construction, the architect died prematurely from Bright's Disease just five weeks before the wing's opening. While he continued to pay off the debts from Pendleton's estate, Metcalf managed to save the collection—not only keeping it mostly intact but also ensuring its future in Providence (Pendleton's will stipulated that if RISD failed to construct this wing, ownership of the collection would revert to the Museum of Fine Arts, Boston).[98] Acknowledging the importance of Metcalf's patronage, Willson had labeled his blueprints for the wing not "The Pendleton Museum," as the collector had insisted upon, but rather "Mansion for Stephen O. Metcalf." For its part, RISD honored Metcalf by installing a prominent silver plaque in the wing that reads: "This House was built and presented by Stephen O. Metcalf, Esq." (Pendleton's name is conspicuously absent from the inscription.)

The recurrence of these domestic labels begs the question: Why would the museum designate this purpose-built wing as a "house" or "mansion" when it would never function as such? The institution could quite easily have met Pendleton's requirements—arranging his collection in substantially the same way the collector had—without implying that the space once served as a private home. Nor was this domestic designation restricted to the museum's communications. Periodicals from the time of the wing's opening frequently referred to it as an "old house" or "furnished mansion"—and even when just a year old, Pendleton House appeared in Rhode Island's Old Home Week, a festival devoted to the city's historic houses.[99]

The wing's identification as a home is linked to the novelty of its interior scheme. Its period rooms were the first in a long line of such installations in American museums, reaching their most extensive expression at the American Wing of the Metropolitan Museum, inaugurated in 1924. The period room depends upon visitors' suspension of disbelief, whereby historic works transform the museum space into a domestic one; as one journalist wrote of Pendleton House in its early years, "with an atmosphere of comfort and old-time cheer in every room, this old house was made to be inhabited."[100] But whereas later period rooms tended to feature genuine architectural fabric from the period represented, Pendleton House presents a more complicated model. Not only did this wing constitute a contemporary reproduction of spaces that were themselves a form of Victorian stagecraft, but it also mimicked the private realm of an individual known to its first curators. For this reason Pendleton House summons the very hybrid Rose Lee warns against in *A Chippendale Romance*: a "*new-old* appearance that is neither one thing nor the other."

As with any reproduction, there are telling differences between Pendleton House and its model, some subtle and others more striking. Willson's scaled-down exterior bears little resemblance to Dexter House, beyond his inclusion of an upper-story Palladian window, yet the museum wing's parlor and library recall their 72 Waterman Street counterparts fairly closely—with one notable exception. For reasons that remain a mystery, Willson not only exchanged the position of these two rooms, but he also moved the staircase from left to right, thereby rendering Pendleton House a mirror image of Dexter House. Other differences stem from the public nature of the wing. Its halls, stairs, and interior doorways are wider, its ceiling slightly higher, and its points of access (all but one located at the rear of the wing) more numerous.[101] And whereas an invitation to 72 Waterman Street would have been a rare occasion, Pendleton House in its early days offered daily "calling hours" by way of its Benefit Street entrance.[102]

If Pendleton House served as the collector's primary memorial, then the lavish catalogue of his collection, printed the year after his death, constituted its own kind of monument. Written by Luke Vincent Lockwood—Pendleton's friend, lawyer, and fellow furniture aficionado—*The Pendleton Collection* (1904) sold for the considerable sum of $150, its run limited to just 160 copies. Bound in tooled morocco leather and lined with green watered silk reverses, this massive illustrated tome was—like the collection's new home itself—precisely the sort of work a gentleman of wealth and taste from the last quarter of the eighteenth century might have owned.

Lockwood's dedication emphasized Pendleton's commitment to Aesthetic Movement principles, praising the collector's "delicate sensitiveness to the beautiful" and insistence on "pure styles," all of which had produced "a collection of gems each perfect in its way."[103] Frequently returning to this theme of artistic unity, Lockwood explained that Pendleton had aimed to build "a consistent collection which, when completed, combine[d] a beautiful home with a museum."[104] Offering a virtual tour of 72 Waterman Street with half a dozen full-page photogravures, the author provided readers a voyeuristic thrill— not only given the secrecy that once enshrouded these spaces but also because these

I.8
Installation view of
Charles Pendleton
House at the RISD
Museum, 2015.
Courtesy RISD
Museum, Providence,
RI.

environments now existed exclusively as museum facsimiles.[105] Particularly telling are the images of Pendleton's china closets, where densely packed English and Chinese ceramics fill every inch of the open shelves. For a catalogue dedicated to the collector's sense of "simplicity and quiet elegance," such images suggest a dazzling form of excess, at best, or at worst a shameful hoarding.[106]

The removal of Pendleton's household to the museum led to more than just the recontextualization of individual items. Beginning the year before the wing officially opened, and continuing into the 1930s, RISD identified Pendleton House by the new moniker, "Colonial House."[107] Similarly, the collection's Deed-stipulated name was eventually expanded to "The Pendleton Collection of Colonial Furniture."[108] This insistence upon the collection's colonial American character inspired an enthusiastic response from early visitors; according to a 1907 trustees' meeting, the wing was "besieged by groups of colonial enthusiasts hoping to hold elaborate costume parties in the newly installed rooms."[109] In 1915 the museum institutionalized this romantic association, honoring the collector with an engraved plaque that concludes: "by the Gift of his Collection

[Pendleton] has left a notable contribution to the Memory of Colonial Days."[110] (Donated by collector Henry Harkness Flagler, the plaque was surely intended as a corrective to the more centrally located one honoring Metcalf.)

A closer examination of Pendleton's gift challenges the notion of its essentially colonial composition. Chinese and English ceramics represent more than 80 percent of his gift, and of the furniture he donated, English and American pieces appear in nearly equal numbers (fifty-nine versus sixty-two works, respectively—and of these American pieces, ten belong to the late nineteenth or twentieth centuries). In fairness, the dizzying volume of Pendleton's ceramics can hardly be compared to the weightier presence of his furniture, nor does this accounting of his American pieces convey their great value. But the question remains: Did Pendleton assemble his collection as an homage "to the Memory of Colonial Days"? Not exactly. Given the scarcity of scholarship regarding colonial furniture in his day, Pendleton did not even realize how many American pieces he owned—and in the decades following his death, a number of works he believed to be English were reattributed as American. Most telling of all, Pendleton's highly descriptive Deed of Gift uses the term "colonial" just six times; and of the seventy-nine pieces of furniture Lockwood deemed worthy to include in his catalogue, he identified only nine as American.

Was Pendleton a champion of American design, as distinct from English tradition, or did he simply find in American pieces an admirable reflection of English style? The latter was more likely the case. Lockwood's own faint praise for American furniture undoubtedly reflected his own attitude:

> There was no such furniture made in America in the eighteenth century as the best of that made in England. . . . On the other hand, the best of the pieces in America, for beauty of line and quality of cabinetmaking, although lacking in the details of design in which their English mother excelled, are by no means to be despised.[111]

Not only did Pendleton show no marked preference for American over English design, but he may not have recognized any substantial distinction between the two. In the landmark catalogue for the 1909 Hudson-Fulton Celebration in New York City, the first major exhibition devoted to American decorative arts, its authors declare: "The history of American furniture is comprehended in the history of English furniture," adding that "almost all of the remaining furniture in the Colonies and States up to 1825 is English in character."[112]

Even the colonial home Pendleton wished to memorialize at Pendleton House would have been perceived through an English lens. In Edith Wharton and Ogden Codman Jr.'s authoritative *The Decoration of Houses*, published the year Pendleton moved into Dexter House, the authors deny the very existence of a distinct colonial style ("as a matter of fact," they claim, "'colonial' architecture is simply a modest copy of Georgian models").[113] Willson's original design for Pendleton House might have recalled Philadelphia's magnificent colonial mansion, Mount Pleasant (1761)—yet for Willson, Pendleton, and even Mount Pleasant's architect, this Georgian mode ultimately referenced high-style *English* design. (The *Providence Journal* itself made this transatlantic link, printing Willson's design alongside the headline, "A Royal Gift.")

In the decades immediately following Pendleton's death, his reputation as an advocate of colonial furniture may be explained, in part, by Americans' widespread enthusiasm for the Colonial Revival style—yet why does this reputation persist today? Scholar Linda Young offers that, in any house museum, the character of the nation always supersedes the character of the owner; visitors want to know how the owner's life or collection illuminates their own national story.[114] To consider the Pendleton Collection fundamentally American in character, then, reduces its messy complexity—and, in turn, papers over the collector's own problematic history. For most audiences, the image of a patriotic philanthropist is vastly preferable to that of a bachelor enamored of artistic furnishings, a New Englander drawn primarily to high-style English furniture, or a solitary man passionate about colorful Chinese urns and English tea sets.

If Pendleton's collection is today primarily associated with American decorative arts, this is also due to the ways curators have distilled and recontextualized his gift. The American masterworks from his collection stand out all the more emphatically today given that his English pieces are mostly removed from view (only nine of the original fifty-nine remain in the house). Reduced, too, is the number Chinese ceramics he once displayed—and entirely absent are his rugs, English silver, and paintings. Over the course of the past century Pendleton House has become more thoroughly Americanized, as well, with scores of works the collector never laid eyes on. To replace Pendleton's middling "Old Masters," the museum sought American paintings whose quality matched the best of his eighteenth-century American furniture. These include three important John Singleton Copley portraits the museum acquired in 1907 (see his 1764 *Portrait of Governor Moses Gill* in figure 1.8, p. 23), as well as Gilbert Stuart's iconic 1805 portrait of George Washington—a 1922 addition that, more than any other work, marked Pendleton House as a colonial shrine.

Even more significant than the museum's introduction of colonial American "inhabitants" was its addition of earlier American furniture and decorative arts. Primarily derived from Eliza Metcalf Radeke's large 1931 bequest, these acquisitions represent an aesthetic far removed from Pendleton's taste. Whereas he particularly admired high-style, heavily carved, English work from the mid- to late eighteenth century, scraped and polished to a glamorous finish, Radeke's gifts comprise older and generally plainer American pieces dating as far back as the seventeenth century and bearing all the romantic marks of their histories. If his works conjure the flash of an eighteenth-century bachelor hall, gentleman's club, or gambling den, then Radeke's pieces suggest family life, the romance of generational ownership, and the charm of self-taught craftsmanship.

Pendleton's strategy to disappear into his own memorial wing was perhaps more successful than he intended. Excepting the ubiquitous Pendleton ceramics, only thirty-nine other works from his nearly thousand-object gift remain on display. Indeed, even if one were to include his ceramics, the extent of his collection now shown constitutes less than 10 percent of his 1904 gift and about a quarter of wing's entire inventory. Such a protracted progress into semi-obscurity raises the question: Do Pendleton House's ersatz settings and collector still matter? In recent years, contemporary artists' surprising answer has been a resounding "Yes." Not only have these rooms inspired thoughtful new work, but the collector's long-dormant avatar has also been fully reanimated.

THE AFTERLIFE OF PENDLETON HOUSE

In 1969, the RISD Museum invited Andy Warhol to guest curate a series of installations in its galleries, drawn exclusively from material in the museum's storage vaults. In her foreword to the exhibition catalogue, collector Dominique de Menil cast Warhol as a kind of sorcerer:

> The world of art lies asleep. To break the spell unusual gifts or thorough preparation is needed. . . . It takes ardour, curiosity, patience to attune our ears to the "Voices of Silence." It takes also oracles and priests. . . . If critics and scholars can open many doors, only seers and prophets open the royal gates. . . . For what is beautiful to the artist, becomes beautiful.[115]

Matching de Menil's tone, RISD Museum director Daniel Robbins declared: "the art that [Warhol] chose from our reserves will reverberate with all the repressed meaning that the passage of time has left adhering to each piece. . . . Warhol's choice will have become part of their expanding meaning."[116]

Just as Pendleton House had introduced the idea of the period room, *Raid the Icebox I with Andy Warhol* represented the first contemporary artist's intervention within a museum setting—a similarly powerful model that has become a widespread practice. Yet in 1969, and in Warhol's hands, few knew what to expect.

De Menil's call for patience was well urged. When *Raid the Icebox I* opened in the spring of 1970, the artist's installations maddened RISD trustees and curators while leaving the public mostly baffled. To expose the very artificiality of the museum as an institution, Warhol installed random assemblages of works in the galleries—stacking pieces against walls, hanging them from industrial racks, or jumbling them together in storage lockers. Around these he littered the floor with the detritus of the storeroom itself, sandbags and cardboard boxes sharing space with sixteenth-century altarpieces. Robbins admits that "there were exasperating moments when we felt that Andy Warhol was exhibiting 'storage' rather than works of art," yet this was of course the artist's intention.[117]

The artificiality of Pendleton House would seem to embody the very attitude Warhol sought to dismantle, and yet the figures of Warhol and Pendleton themselves share more than one might first expect. Both yearned for an avatar—Warhol famously proclaimed in 1963 his wish to become a robot—and each maintained strictly private homes, curated with unimpeachably patrician furnishings that belied their personal reputations and backgrounds.[118] (As Warhol once quipped, "if you can't hide what you are where you *live*, where can you hide it?")[119] Ultimately the anarchic spaces of *Raid the Icebox I* only cemented Pendleton's legacy, for in its radical experimentation, this show would eventually "[re]open the royal gates" to the collection and its wayward father.

Artist Beth Lipman was the first to exhume the collector's avatar from storage. Her 2008 installation, *After You're Gone*, featured a ghostly suite of furnishings in the RISD Museum's Daphne Farago Wing, a modern structure built alongside Pendleton House in 1993. Lipman's installation included a large wooden table heaped with glass vessels and fruit; two empty portrait frames cast in opaque black glass; a collection of 500 glass snails and two squirrels; and a full-size, cast-glass replica of Pendleton's double chair-back settee titled *Settee (after Grinling Gibbons)*. Installing her settee in a niche that recreated the one in

Pendleton's library, Lipman also recalled the period room that lay just a hundred feet away.

Lipman explains that her title "alludes to what remains after death," the objects that stand in for their absent collector.[120] Drawn to the still life tradition throughout her career, she exploited the genre's synthesis of excess and decay in *After You're Gone*, presenting an opulent scene interrupted by legions of crawling snails and the chaotic appearance of rodents. Her medium itself suggests the *memento mori* tradition attached to the still life. "Glass represents mortality," Lipman has noted; "it is strong and fragile, elusive and concrete, fleeting and eternal. It frustrates your ability to visually own what you see."[121] Indeed, drained of all color, the glass carcase of *Settee (after Grinling Gibbons)* stood in this setting like a thing embalmed.

If the theme of absence hovered over this installation, then Lipman's scene also conjured a spectral presence. Acting like mirrors, her empty glass "portraits" invited the viewer to bear witness to the scene, gazing across the overladen table to the empty settee. The twinning effect of these portraits and the double chair-back suggest both the viewer's presence and Pendleton's, or perhaps the collector and his avatar.[122] By evoking the aftermath of a banquet, moreover, Lipman hoped to convey "an experience that's just taken place" and a seat only recently vacated.[123]

1.9
Installation view of *After You're Gone: An Installation by Beth Lipman* on view August 22, 2008, through January 18, 2009, at the RISD Museum. Lipman's *Settee (after Grinling Gibbons)* (2008) appears at right. © Beth Lipman. Courtesy RISD Museum, Providence, RI.

The trope of the spectral chair belongs to a long art historical tradition, stretching from Philippe Starck's lucite *Louis Ghost Chair* (2002) back to Gianlorenzo Bernini's seventeenth-century bronze, *The Chair of St. Peter*, whose depressed cushion suggests the saint's invisible manifestation. In her installation Lipman enlisted Pendleton's ghostly settee to question "what is beautiful, what is original, and whether that matters."[124] Commanding our attention as a one-of-a-kind virtuoso work of glass casting, the piece also represented a reproduction of a reproduction whose precise original never existed. In other words, it was the perfect proxy for Pendleton himself—a man who loved beauty more than truth.

Even the settee's unintended structural weakness, a flaw Lipman discovered only midway through its fabrication, suggested the fragility of Pendleton's public persona. The artist feared the piece might not be able to bear its own weight when displayed, but as someone who celebrates the possibilities of chance (not unlike the gambler Pendleton), she says she "made peace with the idea that [the settee] might disintegrate in public."[125] Remarkably, despite the extraordinary stress it endured, the work remained intact for the entirety of the installation. Only once it was removed from public view did it split in half.

In a subsequent intervention at Pendleton House, artist Aaron Pexa doubled down on the disorientation its spaces inspire. For *Backdoor @ the Pendleton* (2014), he covered the sidelights of the wing's back entryway with two brilliant neon-light signs; glowing in vibrant orange and hot pink light, they read "PEEP SHOW" and "ROOMS." Trained as an architect, Pexa wanted to call attention to this liminal space in the museum—a nondescript back door leading to a formal set of rooms—by forcing viewers to stop and ask, "Am I in the right place?" (Museum guards routinely fielded this very question throughout the installation's run.)[126] By suggesting the lurid signage of a pornographic arcade, Pexa

1.10
Installation view of Aaron Pexa's *Back Door @ the Pendleton*, on view February 21 through June 1, 2014, at the RISD Museum. © Aaron Pexa. Courtesy RISD Museum, Providence, RI.

created a humorous foil to the presumed respectability of Pendleton House—and yet he believes the arcade booth and period room are more alike than we might think. Suggesting the seediness of Times Square in the 1970s, Pexa's installation is as nostalgic, in its own way, as Pendleton House's Hepplewhite-inspired dining room.

The arcade booth and period room are linked, as well, by the complicated forms of looking—or peeping—they foster. At Pendleton House "you're standing behind a literal barrier," Pexa points out, "staring at velvet or chandeliers or whatever it is. It's kind of a bizarre experience."[127] By introducing the brash glow of neon, he attempted to expose the subconscious currents running between viewer and object—thereby short-circuiting the distance these rooms were designed to enforce and amplifying the sense of longing this separation was intended to create. As Pexa explains, he was "baiting us to look upon the home's contents with a more lustful eye."[128]

The anachronistic appeal of Pendleton House's period rooms proved irresistible to the artists who participated in the museum's fiftieth anniversary show, *Raid the Icebox Now* (2019–2020). Whereas Warhol's show represented a single artistic vision drawn solely from the museum's storage, this ambitious yearlong exhibition allowed eight artists free rein within the museum. Participants could create a unique curatorial project or an entirely new body of work, staging these in existing galleries, on digital platforms, or even in spaces beyond the museum. Of the scores of galleries available, three of the invitees chose to work with the Pendleton Collection and two of these three created installations within the wing itself.

Pablo Bronstein's installation for *Raid the Icebox Now* recalled Warhol's process if not his curatorial strategies. Collectively titled *Historical Rhode Island Décor* (2019), his work presented a range of furnishings from the museum's storage vaults, including six pieces from Pendleton's collection. Arranging these in a series of faux-period rooms, he wallpapered the spaces in saturated, acidic colors that illuminated the artificiality of the works' environments. By critiquing bourgeois obsessions with prestigious real estate and "good" furniture, the installation ultimately questioned the construct of the period room itself (a museum practice Bronstein pronounced, perhaps prematurely, to be in decline).[129]

When the artist mined the museum's storage for his installation, he "didn't want the best pieces," he simply wanted to create a certain look.[130] Exemplifying what he calls "plausible historical décor," his resulting period rooms conjured twentieth-century notions of WASPy good taste: starting in a living room, visitors proceeded to a space that evoked an auction sale room and arrived at last in a space that might have been a bedroom or a morgue. By insisting upon the rooms' "plausibility," Bronstein not only highlighted the period room's inherently theatrical dimension, but he also showcased its presumed authority as a representation of social class. And although Pendleton himself had always sought the best pieces he could find, Bronstein's installation of "good enough" works suggested one of Pendleton's own magic tricks: creating a seamless background against which individual personality might disappear.

Bronstein's final room, a windowless and tomblike space, featured dark wallpaper whose pattern suggested blocky masonry. At the center he placed the bed upon which Pendleton is likely to have died—a part-eighteenth-century, part-reproduction "marriage" whose hybrid nature has forever doomed it to storage (an astute collector himself, Bronstein claimed that at first glance he knew this was "a very, very bullshit piece").[131] The bed's most arresting feature is also its most deceptive: a deeply carved, Chippendale-style headboard

1.11

Pendleton's "married" bedstead. The rails and posts are English (mid-1700s), mahogany and oak (87" x 59 1/16"). Providence cabinet makers Morlock and Bayer (1877–1908) carved the central headboard, based upon Plate XLII in Thomas Chippendale's *The Gentleman and Cabinet Maker's Director* (1754). Bequest of Mr. Charles L. Pendleton, 04.099. Courtesy RISD Museum, Providence, RI.

added by Pendleton in 1900 to ensure, after his own fashion, a measure of plausibility.[132] Across from the bed Bronstein hung a seventeenth-century Dutch painting—not Pendleton's, but emblematic of his taste—featuring the Priests of Bel from the Book of Daniel (appropriately enough, men put to death for worshipping objects as idols). A marked contrast to the lighter satire of the previous two spaces, the funereal affect of this last room surprised even the artist in its final installation.[133] Like Lipman's *Settee (after Grinling Gibbons)*, this marriage-cum-deathbed appeared to have been only recently vacated.

Pendleton comes very much to life Bronstein's short film *In the Realm of the Realtor* (2019), created in tandem with his series of rooms. In this stylized performance (billed as a "Masked Ballet *en Pantomíme*"), a haggish realtor-witch shows a luxurious property to a new client. Identified only as "a strange dead man" and "true connoisseur," this character—played by Bronstein—wears a mask with Pendleton's handlebar moustache. The listing that the witch shows is in fact Bronstein's RISD Museum installation. Shot against a green screen, the actors appear to float through the three rooms, frequently dwarfed by the scale of the furniture. A satire of social ambition (the witch wears Chanel) and the banality of realtor-speak, the film's dialogue in several instances skewers the client's susceptibility to the erotics of furniture. "Slide your eyes across this wonderful seating statement," purrs the witch as she strokes a dark, Chippendale-style sofa, "[and] notice the elegant curvature of the humps." Responding, her client can only moan an ecstatic, "mahoooooogany . . ." In her final sales pitch the witch appears to summarize the Pendleton House project itself, telling her client, "you can finally cast the longest shadow. And if you do not possess it, someone else will."

Taking nearly full possession of Pendleton House during *Raid the Icebox Now*, the online arts magazine *Triple Canopy* and fashion house Concept Foreign Garments New York (CFGNY) partnered to create a multimedia installation under the collective title *Can I Leave You?* (2019). Their collaboration included a fashion show staged in Pendleton House; an installation of CFGNY garments throughout the wing; a three-screen video projected in the museum's media gallery; and an "augmented" version of Lockwood's 1904 Pendleton House catalogue posted online. Taken as a whole these interventions questioned the formation of American identity through the appropriation of Asian art, seen most pointedly in Pendleton's Chinese ceramics collection and Chippendale's own use of "orientalist" ornament.

CFGNY founders Daniel Chew and Tim Nguyen explain they wanted their Pendleton House fashion show, *Synthetic Blend V*, to "give the impression of the house being inhabited—or haunted—by those who don't belong in such a typical American

environment," adding "we told [the models] to be like ghosts."[134] Filmed without an audience, *Synthetic Bend V* features nine Asian men and women modeling a capsule collection. Walking through Pendleton House as if in a trance, they translate the wing's uncanny qualities into human form. The most notable "ghost" in this group is a gray-haired older man, the only such model in the show and the only to appear more than once (including one shot in which he appears with his double in the same frame). Whereas the show's others models sport streetwear, he wears a red silk smoking jacket with matching lounge pants—an outfit that suggests he is as much host as ghost. Stopping short of identifying this figure directly with Pendleton, *Triple Canopy*'s Alexander Provan concedes this model is "Pendleton-ish."[135]

As a companion installation to *Synthetic Blend V*, CFGNY and *Triple Canopy* exhibited the show's runway outfits throughout Pendleton House. Nodding to Warhol's arbitrary arrangements of 1970, the garments appeared to be randomly discarded in the room: draped over furniture, crumpled in piles on the floor, and even tacked to the walls. As Chew and Nguyen claim: "We wanted to be sort of really irreverent with the space. . . . [By] leaving the clothes around . . . it sort of brings this presence of a body."[136] If Pexa's neon signs summoned a locale of cheap sex, then CFGNY's installation seemed to illustrate the aftermath of romantic abandon, suggesting clothes discarded in passion or stripped away after a long night of clubbing (hanging in the dining room, in fact, were *Clubbing Pants with Yellow Pockets*).[137] The haunting, quasi-religious Sacred Harp music that accompanied these displays only further underscored their campy challenge to "good taste." (Chew has made this queer connection explicit in interviews, claiming CFGNY familiarly stands for "Cute Fucking Gay New York.")[138]

Footage of CFGNY's fashion show ran concurrently in the museum's media gallery with *Triple Canopy*'s three-channel color video, *If the Limbs Grow Too Large for the Body* (2019).

1.12
LEFT: Pendleton at the time of his gift to RISD (*Providence Journal*, June 9, 1904). RIGHT: The "strange dead man" from Pablo Bronstein's *In the Realm of the Realtor* (2019). © Pablo Bronstein. Courtesy of the artist; Herald St., London; and Galleria Franco Noero, Turin.

Projected on three walls, photographs of Pendleton House faded like a double exposure into historic images of 72 Waterman Street, vividly tinted versions of Lockwood's originals that alternated with ghostly photographic negatives. Surrounded by this hallucinatory montage, viewers literally saw through Pendleton House's artifice. An additional narrative element summoned CFGNY's theme of Asian exploitation; narrated by fictional Chinese characters who confront an eighteenth-century New England merchant, the video ended with their destruction of his home. Accompanied by sounds of shattered furniture and smashed ceramics, the projected images of Pendleton House/72 Waterman Street appear to go up in flames. When asked if *Triple Canopy* and CFGNY's interventions constituted their own attack upon Pendleton, Provan answered, "let's just say we were interested in representing a house attack and prompting visitors to imagine how and why such an attack might occur."[139]

If Bronstein, *Triple Canopy*, and CFGNY sought to dismantle Pendleton House in one form or another, then one contributor to *Raid the Icebox Now* aimed to exaggerate the excesses of its donor. Taking over a nondescript hallway within Pendleton House, artist Beth Katleman created a fully immersive environment—a room writhing with Rococo ornament, elaborate overdoor sculptures, cabinets bursting with figurines, and two large

1.13
Installation view of
Raid the Icebox Now with Beth Katleman: Games of Chance on view November 8, 2019, through July 11, 2021, at the RISD Museum. Photograph by Erik Gould.
© Beth Katleman. Courtesy RISD Museum, Providence, RI.

mirrors surrounded by cascading figural decoration. Composed of nearly ten thousand pieces of biscuit-fired porcelain, Katleman's *Games of Chance* suggested both the grandeur of an eighteenth-century pleasure pavilion and the impressive scale of Pendleton's china collection.[140] Yet as the artist warned visitors in her introductory wall text, "The world is still deceived with ornament."[141]

The "still" in this Shakespearian quote suggested a link between Pendleton's deceptions—whether as a dealer or donor—and Katleman's own, for nothing in *Games of Chance* was it seemed. Elements that initially appeared to represent traditional Rococo decoration turned out to be, upon closer inspection, casts from contemporary flea market finds: throwaway trinkets, toys, dolls, and kitschy figurines. Honoring Warhol's own elision of high and low in her work, Katleman's practice transforms these mass-produced items into luxurious handmade objects, fusing them into compositions that evoke fantasy, eroticism, or dark humor (an approach that one critic has labeled "pop surrealism").[142]

If Pendleton projected onto Pendleton House the false impression of patrician integrity, then Katleman challenged his project with a myth of her own. Presenting visitors with an invented origin story for the *Games of Chance* installation, her poker-faced wall text read:

> Rumors have circulated since the time of Charles Pendleton's death about an unusual private room that he had commissioned. Well over a century later, during the recent renovations of the RISD Museum, a miraculous discovery came to light.

The text went on to explain the accidental discovery of the room's contents, directing visitors to a video tour of the *Games of Chance* room hosted by members of a bogus group called the Antiquarian Research Society, or ARS. (Along with this video Katleman produced a creaky, early Internet–style website for ARS. The site was so convincing she received donation offers to the group.)[143] Suggesting discoveries of another sort, the wall text concluded: "The *Games of Chance* room may hold the key to the inner life of one of the most misunderstood geniuses of the antiquarian world."

Games of Chance marked Pendleton's ascendance and demise as a collector. Not only did Katleman's medium capture his mania for Chinese and English porcelain, in a general sense, but the room's two densely crowded china cabinets also specifically recalled their teeming counterparts at 72 Waterman Street. Referring to this room as Pendleton's private "closet of ostentation," Katleman suggested the collector had commissioned the room's eccentric curves and velvety whiteness as a decadent foil to the glossy dark mahogany and sturdy cabriole legs of his public rooms. This "closet," moreover, came fully stocked with its own skeletons. Using cast human bones as decorative elements, Katleman nodded to the elaborate ossuaries of Rome's Capuchin Crypt while also conjuring the vision of a looted tomb.[144] As if to illustrate Jean Baudrillard's declaration that the collection resolves the "irreversibility . . . of the relentless passage from birth to death," Katleman presented in harmony the sensuality of accumulation and austerity of the grave.[145]

Beyond its suggestions of Pendleton's collection, *Games of Chance* also pointedly summoned the collector himself. Above the entry to her installation Katleman placed the blindfolded figurine of Marilyn Monroe, cast in the role of the Roman goddess Fortuna. Representing the "blind luck" of the gambler, Fortuna's traditional blindfold also

1.14
(Detail) Beth
Katleman, *Paradise
Mirror* (2019).
Photograph by Erik
Gould. © Beth
Katleman. Courtesy
Jane and Paul Athanas.

suggested the figure of Justice—and certainly, Katleman meted out a kind of sentence in the room beyond. Along the space's western wall she chose "Paradise" as her theme, characterized by roulette wheels, harem girls, and cornucopias overflowing with coins. By contrast, the theme of the facing wall was "Shipwreck." Here Fortuna ushered in broken ship's wheels, nets, skeletal remains, and a tiny foundering ship whose sail featured Yale's coat of arms. Because the two walls' central mirrors faced one another, *Paradise Mirror* reflected infinitely in *Shipwreck Mirror*, with the viewer lodged between.

Katleman's Yale reference pointed to an important secondary theme in the room: Pendleton's presumed sexual indiscretions, beginning with his college disgrace. To decode this theme, one needed first to identify Pendleton's avatar in *Games of Chance*. Throughout the installation he appeared as the kindly and eternally grinning figure of Colonel Sanders, founder of Kentucky Fried Chicken, in guises one might not have expected from this popular character. In one instance, Katleman presented him as the drunken god Bacchus, complete with a grape leaf crown, while in others she portrayed him leering at figures of young girls (suggesting a link between fried chicken and "chicks"). In the most unnerving of these exchanges, featured in the room's *Paradise Mirror*, the artist fused Colonel Sanders's head with the body of a snake; coiled menacingly around a tree trunk, Pendleton's avatar lurks behind an unwitting female forest sprite. Whether or not Katleman was correct in imagining Pendleton's collegiate disgrace involved an underage girl, this theme of sexual transgression underscores the room's larger suggestion of illicit pleasure—whether derived from sexual misconduct, gambling, or compulsive consumption.

As if to defuse the darker elements of this theme, Katleman's faux-documentary "The Pleasures of Ownership" takes the viewer on a chirrupy tour of Pendleton House and its rediscovered room. (Katleman has described the film as "a fake tour of a fake room in a fake house.")[146] Hosts "Timmy" Blythe Piggot and "Maddie" Ball Woodcock—introduced as the founders of the fictional ARS—relate the story of the room's rediscovery in a bemused tone, attempting to reconcile its splendor with the sobriety of the wing's public rooms. While Maddie deflects inquiry into Pendleton's private life ("What are we to make of this lavish but confounding room?" she asks, adding, "not that it is our place to speculate"), Timmy lapses into reveries that suggest the collector's kinks. Standing before a Philadelphia highboy, Timmy sighs: "One could picture Mr. Pendleton alone with his trophy, proudly running his hand over the delicate grain of the woodwork and the smooth curve of the legs."

At the film's close Timmy wonders aloud, "Is it our place to pass judgment on a Titan of Tongue and Groove for enjoying specialized experiences beyond our comprehension?" Katleman seemed to think so. Although speaking strictly tongue-in-cheek by claiming this room "would hold the key to the inner life of one of the most misunderstood geniuses of the antiquarian world," she was not far off. By inserting this tomb within a tomb—a theater of pure id, staged within the very spaces built to hold it in check—she managed to pull off a minor miracle. Over the course of five brief months, she reunited Pendleton with his own damning ghost.[147]

"NOTHING TO SEE HERE, FOLKS."

Riddled as it was with errors and misstatements, Pendleton's *Providence Journal* obituary would doubtless have gratified its subject. The man who spent his last years safely tucked behind the figure of an eighteenth-century gentleman would now remain there forever—just as his rooms at 72 Waterman Street have today slipped behind the façade of Pendleton House. We are no more likely to meet the man, or enter his home, than we would have been in his lifetime. Indeed, it is a testament to the power of Pendleton's many attractive lies—found in his collection, his finances, and above all his personal history—that he has captured the enduring fascination of contemporary artists. Like them, Pendleton understood the power fantasy holds to transform life's messy banality into a thing of beauty.

One of the most enduring of recent interventions at Pendleton House was also its smallest. Unsanctioned by RISD and anonymously authored, the work was so inconspicuous that for many years it escaped the attention of museum officials. Yet in its own way—indeed, perhaps *because* its disguise was so intentional—the work was as fitting a coda to Pendleton's life as the museum wing it neighbored. Sometime between 2011 and 2013, an unknown hand replaced a brick in the museum's sidewalk with an embossed substitute.[148] Identical to its neighbors but for its message, it read simply: "MYTH." Sometime before the summer of 2023, it vanished as mysteriously as it had appeared.

1.15
[Artist unknown], *Myth* (ca.2011–2013). Embossed brick (8" x 3 ¾"). Author photograph.

TWO

DOUBLE VISION AT THE CODMAN ESTATE

> What do you call one's self? Where does it begin? where does it end? It overflows into everything that belongs to us—and then it flows back again. . . . I have a great respect for things! We're each of us made up of some cluster of appurtenances.[1]
> —Henry James, *The Portrait of a Lady* (1881)

> There's a portrait painted on the things we love.[2]
> —Sasami Ashworth, "Portrait" (2018)

In 1981 *Old-Time New England* magazine asked Thomas Boylston Adams to record his boyhood memories of the Codman family. A distant cousin of the Codmans, who had occupied the same Lincoln, Massachusetts, home for five generations, Adams equated them not with his own storied clan—descendants of President John Adams—but rather, seemed to conjure the *New Yorker*'s ghoulish Addams Family:

> Who lived in the Codman House we vaguely knew. . . . Sometimes we would see the Codman limousine come swaying out of the driveway, an immense contraption, long as a locomotive and high as it was long. . . . Sometimes figures were barely glimpsed within the huge glass cage. They were heavily swathed in black and wore large black hats . . . in mourning for their husband and father, who had always been dead.[3]

Communicating "only with shadows," Adams recalled, the Codman home stood in its isolated park like "a silent exclamation point"—an eighteenth-century pile shuttered and sunken beneath encroaching trees. Behind its forbidding façade the family's matriarch, Sarah Bradlee Codman, had "disappeared completely." When Adams's mother first entered the house in the 1930s—her car had broken down on a hot summer day—the family's youngest daughter, Dorothy, led her to a darkened parlor for a cool drink. "Within [the room] was a settled calm," Adams recounted; "everything that could happen, had happened. Nothing now would change."

Dorothy remained in these darkened rooms until her death in 1968. When the Society for the Preservation of New England Antiquities (SPNEA) acquired the estate the following year, the organization received along with it one of the largest documentary troves any American family has ever assembled. Covering a period of more than 350 years, the Codman Family Manuscript Collection occupies a staggering two hundred linear feet of shelf space. Comprising more than 100,000 letters, diaries, receipts, invitations, wills, and inventories, in addition to nearly 10,000 photographs and 1,500 items of clothing, it represents a record so dense as to be nearly paralyzing for researchers—who may find in these collections both the family's housekeeping accounts and the underwear they paid their staff to clean.

How might we reconcile such extraordinary documentation with the hermetic figures of Adams's account, a family "of no interest" even to their neighbors? The answer lies with the family's eldest son, celebrated architect and interior designer Ogden Codman Jr. An offstage figure in Adams's boyhood memories, Codman "somehow . . . had escaped" Lincoln to lead a glamorous expatriate life, rumored to be "wildly extravagant, [and] building a palace on the Riviera." Even among the bizarre coterie of this family, Codman is the "eccentric" one in Adams's account—code, perhaps, for the designer's acknowledged homosexuality—and yet he was far from an outlier within the family. Rather, he formed the very distillation of seven generations of family eccentricity, acquisitiveness, and ambition. Despite (or perhaps even because of) his self-imposed exile from Lincoln, moreover, Codman also constituted the house's most dedicated chatelaine. Writing to a local historian in 1904, he offered the uncharacteristic understatement: "I am probably the person who has taken the most interest in the property."[4] In truth, the house commanded his unblinking attention for nearly all his life.

Across five generations of Codmans, two seemingly inescapable patterns appear. First, family members tended to live beyond their ever-dwindling means, often spending money not strictly their own. Second, and with few exceptions, the Codman men made no lasting mark on their period's political, military, literary, or civic spheres—choosing instead to focus their energies on building and decorating. Given such a long line of gentleman-designers, it seems almost inevitable that Codman became one of the great tastemakers of his era and coauthor of its first definitive guide to interior decoration, *The Decoration of Houses* (1897).

When the Codmans weren't outfitting their Lincoln home they busied themselves with recording its contents: archiving plans and receipts, compiling endless inventories, and eventually documenting its rooms with a collection of "kodaks." This fixation reached its height with Ogden Codman Jr., who in addition to his inventories spent decades compiling the genealogies of his extended family—ancestors who built, renovated, or enlarged their home in reaction to, or sympathy with, the projects of their forebears. When Codman and his siblings donated their home and its contents to SPNEA, they turned this centuries-long, intergenerational conversation into a purely documentary exchange.

As a house museum the Codman Estate effectively presents the various generations' building projects and collecting habits, but it can never fully convey the inner lives of its former inhabitants—men and women who at times surely felt the house was cursed. Codman often spoke of a "terrible sadness" attached to the estate, beginning with the family's nearly ten-year exile from Lincoln when he was a child. Yet even from its earliest days, infidelity, insolvency, isolation, mental illness, and death have haunted the house—leading both to dramatic physical changes there and long periods of seemingly enchanted stagnation. The profound insularity of these cycles was never more apparent than in the family's last, long generation, which spanned from the Battle of Gettysburg to the Beatles' White Album.[5] Despite the cultural upheavals of this century, the siblings' singular focus on their home left little room for engagement with the outside world. As

Adams put it, theirs was "a family that had withdrawn from the life of the nation."

Did Codman escape the family curse? His residency at the house amounted to just a decade of his childhood and short stays as a young man; in the last decades of his life he became a virtual stranger there, visiting only twice between 1920 and 1951. Yet he fell more powerfully under the home's spell than any of his siblings, largely *because* Lincoln existed for him as an abstraction. The house represented the vanished world of his childhood, a monument to opportunities lost, and an emotional touchstone whose power intensified even as its reality faded. Lincoln served, too, as an important (if not always successful) counterweight to his penchant for excess. In a 1935 letter to architectural historian Fiske Kimball, Codman wrote that the "restraint and simplicity" of Lincoln had "prevented me from being carried away by eccentricities that otherwise might have proved too seductive."[6] Though spoken about his design practice, Codman's words also suggest the oppositions that defined his character. Throughout his life he felt torn between New England propriety and Continental decadence, respectability and promiscuity, intellectual substance and superficial flash. He had a profound respect for pedigree but hungered for the power new money could bring.

This Puritan-versus-Epicurean strain was something of a genetic inheritance.[7] Beginning with brothers John Codman III (1755–1806) and Richard Codman (1762–1806)—Codman's great-grandfather and twice-great-uncle, respectively—each generation of the family produced at least one stalwart Yankee and (usually more than one) extravagant rake. In Ogden Codman Jr., the last of his family line, these opposing natures combined. He revered his ancestors but loved himself, above all; he could be loyal and sentimental, but also manipulative and bitchy; and though he was an erudite designer of beautiful environments, he was also an unreconstructed snob with ruinously expensive tastes. As his cousin Florence Codman described him, he was "gifted, intelligent, obstinate, ambitious, obdurate, caustic, but never boring."[8]

"THE HANDSOMEST PLACE IN AMERICA"

In 1708 Charles Chambers (1660–1743), the wealthy sea merchant who founded the Chambers-Russell-Codman clan, made two important acquisitions: 275 acres of land near the future town of Lincoln, Massachusetts, and a ten-year-old ward named John Codman. Thus began the geographic and genealogical links to the Codman Estate of today, yet more than three decades would pass before a house appeared on the land and a half-century before a Codman lived there. Town records first indicate a house on Chambers's property in 1741, when his grandson, Judge Chambers Russell (1713–1767), completed an elegant summer home there. Built on land Russell would not inherit from his grandfather for another two years, the project established an important family credo: If you build it, the legacy will come.

Russell's home combined patrician style with a liberal, luxury-loving household—a formula that itself echoed across future generations of the family. Though modestly scaled at just six rooms, the home's two floors were built fashionably high and its first-floor rooms featured paneling in the latest English fashion. Within these spaces Russell and his wife, Mary Wheelwright Russell, created a home rather livelier than those of their conservative neighbors (the couple even celebrated Christmas, a practice still frowned upon in local circles).[9] Providing a glimpse of this environment where "the arts and ornaments of a courtier" were reportedly cultivated, Mary described in 1751 "much Gay company and Dancing" at the house as well as her own weakness for gambling ("I have already ingaged [*sic*] in as many . . . Lottery Tickets as I have Dollars to spare").[10]

The judge and his wife shared their home with Russell's protégé, a young law clerk named Jonathan Sewall. Sixteen years Russell's junior, Sewall was charismatic and strikingly handsome; in the words of his lifelong friend John Adams, he possessed a "soft, smooth, insinuating eloquence" along with a generous "fund of wit, humour, and satire."[11] However dazzling Lincoln's sole courtier might have been, his residency did not always make for an easy marriage. Indeed, in a satirical 1754 pamphlet attacking Russell for his support of the Excise Bill, its anonymous author implied the judge was married to *Sewall* rather than Mary. (Describing Russell in the feminine as "Madam Rutila, commonly appearing in a dark Russel [*sic*] gown," the author explained that "she" is "the Wife of a very fine, handsome Gentleman.")[12] It is perhaps unsurprising that when Mary acknowledged her brother Dudley's engagement in 1752, she wrote him: "There is no state of Life but something is wanting. . . . I wish you all the happiness that you can expect."[13]

Mary's death in 1762 and Russell's subsequent financial troubles put an end to this Lincoln ménage, ushering in a period of uncertainty concerning the home's ownership. In 1766 Russell sailed for England, having mortgaged the Lincoln house—then worth about £4,200—for the sum of £1,000, an amount that allowed him briefly to live in style once more.[14] Upon his death the following year the house transferred to his nephew, Dr. Charles Russell (1738–1780), along with a staggering £3,681 of debt and a £1,000 legacy to be paid his niece.[15] The economic landscape in the late 1760s was grim—real estate values plummeted with the arrival of British warships in Boston harbor—but within a year of the will's reading, Dr. Russell had the good fortune to marry a wealthy bride. Elizabeth Vassall Russell hailed from two of the colony's wealthiest Tory families, the Royalls and the Vassalls, whose fortunes allowed Dr. Russell to settle nearly all the debts on the estate. As if taking the baton from his uncle, he and his wife reportedly led a life at Lincoln "free from the more rigorous constraints of puritanism."[16]

In 1767, Dr. Russell invited celebrated Boston painter John Singleton Copley to Lincoln to create his portrait. Self-fashioning for posterity was nothing new to the family—painter Joseph Blackburn had painted Chambers Russell's portrait in 1755—but in this case the artist created a spontaneous pairing of the owner and his home. According to family legend, upon the completion of his portrait Dr. Russell attempted to open an expensive bottle of wine only to find his corkscrew missing. The next morning he awoke to discover Copley had painted a marvelous *trompe l'oeil* corkscrew on the cross-panels of his parlor door (the painter is said to have pronounced, "allow me, sir, to see to it that your house is never again without a corkscrew").[17]

However fanciful the anecdote surrounding this painting may be, the work indicates how the fabric of the house itself had become implicated in the family's image-making—and serves, too, as a talisman for Codman's later decorating philosophy, which allowed any degree of illusion as long as it pleased the eye. The coda to Dr. Russell's portrait is equally illuminating. As if to forecast the Oedipal conflicts, inheritance struggles, and impulsivity of the generations to come, Dr. Russell's daughter Catherine destroyed the painting in 1819 after learning it was bequeathed to her sister Penelope. Slicing her father's face from the portrait, Catherine hid the fragment from family members for the

remainder of her life. (In 1943, one of her descendants donated the abject relic to the Massachusetts Historical Society.)[18]

During the American Revolution and its aftermath the Lincoln house switched hands several times, its legal ownership often unclear. By 1775, the Russells and their Loyalist relations understood they could no longer remain in the colonies; that year the doctor and his family fled to Royall family property in Antigua, where he died five years later. Yet at the time of his death he no longer held legal title to the Lincoln property. With the Banishment Act of 1778, which nullified the property rights of Loyalist émigrés, ownership of the house had transferred to his father, James Russell, along with Chambers Russell's still unpaid mortgage from 1766.[19] James Russell rented the property to pay its taxes, but it was his younger son, the unmarried Chambers Russell II (1755–1790), who would finally discharge the mortgage on the house and assume its ownership.

In 1781, Chambers Russell II's sister Margaret "Peggy" Russell married John Codman III in the home's southeast parlor (the groom was the grandson of Charles Chambers's ward). When in 1784 the couple welcomed their second son, Charles Russell Codman, Chambers Russell II arranged to leave him the family home. Charles was just six when his uncle died in 1790—the boy had lost his mother, as well, the year before—and so the home's ownership temporarily reverted back to Peggy's father. Inviting his widowed son-in-law and grandsons to live at the house, James Russell retained its legal custodianship until his own death in 1798. Yet by this date John Codman III had assumed full control of the property, transforming it as to be nearly unrecognizable to the Russells. The Codman era had begun.

The Codmans had emigrated to the American colonies nearly half a century before the Russells, with the 1637 arrival of John Codnam in Salem, Massachusetts (his surname, only later spelled "Codman," may have derived from his native Codenham, a parish in Suffolk).[20] Eventually settling in Charlestown, the family made their living as merchant

2.1
LEFT: Surviving passage from John Singleton Copley's portrait of Dr. Charles Russell (ca. 1767). Oil on canvas (15" x 14 ½" as framed). Courtesy Massachusetts Historical Society, Boston, MA.
RIGHT: John Singleton Copley, *Corkscrew Hanging with Nail* (ca. 1767). Oil on original door panel (5 3/8" x 5 5/8" x 7/8"). Bequest of Ogden Codman, 1970.223. Courtesy Museum of Fine Arts, Boston, MA.

sea captains. In 1708, John Codman III's great-grandfather Stephen left a considerable estate of £631; therefore, by the time Stephen's orphaned son John (later known as John Codman I) became Charles Chambers's ward, the ten-year-old had a considerable a head start on what would become an even greater fortune.[21] By his fifties John Codman I was widely engaged in sea trade and other enterprises, including real estate and a local iron forge, but his life was cut short in 1755 when three of his enslaved workers fatally poisoned him. The body of one of the convicted murderers, a man known only as Mark, was placed on permanent display beside the Charlestown Common—a grisly monument Paul Revere reported seeing as late as 1775, and one that John Codman III, born just six months before the murder, would have known for the entirety of his young life.[22]

If the Codmans of earlier generations turned maritime trade into small fortunes, then John Codman III's successes in this arena eclipsed them all—and provided a model unmatched by any of his descendants. A year before his marriage the twenty-five-year-old Codman formed a sea-trading partnership with William Smith, son of Boston banker Isaac Smith. Codman and Smith traded a vast range of commodities, from shipping supplies to liquor, furs, cotton, iron, precious metals, and foodstuffs, in an international circuit that stretched from the West Indies to France, Portugal, Spain, and Holland. (Unceasing war on the Continent in the 1780s and 1790s considerably strengthened the prices of these American commodities.)[23] On land, Codman's investment in real estate, rope chandleries, and government bonds significantly increased his capital—and never more so than when Alexander Hamilton's Funding Act of 1790 caused his considerable bond holdings to triple in value.[24]

In the brief span of 1789 to 1791, Codman's family life changed even more dramatically than his financial prospects. With Peggy's death in 1789 and her father's the following year, Codman found himself a widower with two small sons and sole guardianship of the Lincoln property. A year after moving into the home, he married Catherine Amory and formed a new business partnership with his younger brother Richard—two decisions that had profound repercussions for the generations that followed. Newly married and now mostly unencumbered by Russell relations, Codman at last hoped to bring the Lincoln house into scale with his fortune. To rewrite the story of the Lincoln house—recreating it in magnified form, as if it had ever been thus—became his primary goal in the 1790s, and indeed, the family's central fixation henceforth.

Codman initially charged minor improvements at the house to Chambers Russell II's estate, but by 1794 he was paying for the work from his own accounts. The change was likely necessitated by the still unexecuted Russell estate, though it also reflected Codman's growing independence from his late wife's family. Indeed, in 1797—the year Codman initiated his most ambitious building program—the family's lawyer urged him to sell the property and therefore settle the estate. He refused, citing (however disingenuously) the "anxiety and distress" such a sale would cause "the female part of the Russell family," and added, "I have . . . determined to settle the estate myself according to my own ideas."[25] His ideas encompassed more than just the estate's fiscal management.

In his wide-ranging travels, Codman had developed a discerning eye for interior design. In a 1796 letter to Catherine he remarked: "I passed an evening at Mr. Hammond's . . . his [New York City] house and furniture in the best style. In short I recollect no one in New England who lives equal to him in such finished elegance."[26] In another note, written from London, he told his wife about the apartments of "Mr. Smith, a bachelor. . . .

By far the most elegant I ever saw, adorned with gilt carved work, and looking glasses all around."[27] Determined to match if not surpass the elegance of his merchant peers, Codman embarked on one of the grandest building schemes ever carried out at Lincoln.

Beginning in March 1797 Codman enlisted a small army of carpenters, bricklayers, plasterers, painters, and carvers to raise the house a full third story, double the footprint of its 1740 plan, and join the enlarged interiors with an elegant new staircase. From the Russells' former kitchen he created a formal dining room, and by extending an original ell at the rear of the house he added a long hall to the first floor. (The grandest public space in the new house, this room featured a floor specially braced for dancing.) On its exterior the house's provincial Georgian style received a Federal makeover, including porticoes with slender columns and sidelights, a crowning parapet, new shutters, and the replacement of the home's twelve-over-twelve pane windows with more fashionable six-over-sixes. In all, the renovations spanned eighteen months.

Despite these radical changes, the home's original profile and paneled interiors blended so harmoniously with the new construction that the structure appeared all of a piece—a sleight of hand that suggested the house had always rivaled earlier, grander homes like Boston's Thomas Hancock House (1737) or Cambridge's Vassall-Longfellow House (1759), two models Codman appears to have consulted. Catherine's cousin Rebecca Gore, soon to build her own Federal showplace in Waltham, declared the Codmans' home "the handsomest place in America."[28] Codman could only agree, telling his wife: "I do not know anyplace in America so much like Gentleman's seats in this country as Lincoln (dear Lincoln)."[29]

2.2
The Codman Estate (ca. 1740) in Lincoln, MA. The home's third-story addition, crowning parapet, and central (southern) portico reflect its 1797–1799 reconstruction. In 1862–1866, architect John Hubbard Sturgis added its quoining, window pediments, and eastern porch. Photograph by David Bohl. Courtesy Historic New England.

Lincoln had also become dear in another sense. By 1799 Codman had spent a staggering $15,000 of his own money on improvements to the house, $9,000 of which represented the 1797–1799 renovation alone.[30] Such a colossal investment begs the question: If Codman were not the estate's legal owner, why had he lavished so much money on its expansion? The question had also occurred to the Russell family. In a remarkable attempt to rewrite the legal record, Codman explained to Mary Russell in 1802:

> I never would suffer myself to become the means of giving you pain. . . . It is, however, now become proper that [my son] Charles and his connections know that the Estate at Lincoln was never given to him and that by the last codicil a great part of his residuary legacy was taken away. . . . According to the strict rules of propriety . . . the estate ought now to be sold . . . provided I was to become the purchaser.[31]

Codman closed with the rather unconvincing apology, "as I have prevented the will's being executed [by delaying the payment of its annuities], it is no doubt taking all the responsibility on myself." No codicil removing Charles's legacy survives, yet his father's insistence upon the "additional value I have given" to the home suggests he believed the improvements themselves—along with his eventual settlement of his brother-in-law's estate—justified this transfer of ownership.

However thorny the Lincoln question had become, it would pale in comparison to the financial entanglements of Codman's brother Richard, whose extravagance in the 1790s threatened to unravel the family firm itself. Two years after forming a business partnership with his brother, Richard sailed to Europe with six cargo ships destined for French markets. Landing in England in June 1793, he commissioned two portraits from John Singleton Copley while he prepared to establish himself in France. (Like his former sitter, Dr. Russell, the Loyalist Copley had fled the colonies at the start of the American Revolution.) The first was a charge from his brother, who asked Richard to bring the painter a John Johnston portrait of their late father for reproduction—a dynastic gesture that, like the expanded Lincoln house, would seem to suggest his father's portrait had *always* been a Copley (indeed, today only the copy survives).[32] Copley painted Richard's second commission from life. Portraying Richard on the eve of his French adventure, the artist captured the very moment of his transformation from New England patrician to Parisian rake.

Although the painter typically flattered his subjects by way of their material surroundings, rather than through their physical appearance, his portrait of Richard presents an image of arresting masculine beauty. Richard's sculptural profile and heavy brows are tempered by a soft, lingering gaze and full red lips; his black suit, crowned by a virtuoso passage of lace cravat, frames his features while cascading folds of red damask draw out the rosy tones of his flesh. The sitter's seemingly intimate engagement with the viewer suggests the document he holds so gently cannot possibly be related to business (Copley often alluded to his American subjects' professions in his work) but rather some form of romantic correspondence. Contemporary accounts of this handsome bachelor confirm the charisma captured in his portrait. Rebecca Gore, who had admired the Codmans' "handsome" New England home, later summarized Richard's Parisian life with more breathless appreciation:

He was living in as great a style as any, his establishment . . . as handsome and expensive and his mistress as beautiful as anyone's in Europe. . . . He himself is quite the accomplished man, the very man to enjoy himself in this fashion.[33]

Arriving in revolutionary Paris at the height of the Terror, "Citoyen" Richard Codman appears to have been little affected by the events of the day—with the exception of the buyer's market he discovered in French noblemen's property. Richard's Parisian spending orgy began with the 1794 acquisition of "eighty odd" Old Master paintings, negotiated on John's behalf from the dealer Jean-Baptiste-Pierre LeBrun.[34] Charmed by the prospect of adding these works to his Lincoln home, John did not yet appear to be alarmed by his brother's spending habits. In the year that followed the LeBrun purchase, Richard turned his eye to French real estate. Between 1795 and 1797 he purchased the Château des Ternes, located north of today's Arc du Triomphe; the Hôtel de Créqui, in Paris's fashionable Saint-Germain neighborhood; and the Château de la Thuilerie at Dammartin, set within a seventy-two-acre park northwest of the city.[35] Beyond this impressive portfolio, all purchased for his own use, Richard bought three farms outside the city and an apartment building near Créqui.

Because he paid for these properties with the firm's capital, either by gambling in speculative public funds or selling commodities from its ships outright (Créqui alone sold for 8,333 pounds of Pernambuco cotton), Richard later justified their purchase as corporate investments.[36] His scant communication with John, however, indicates otherwise. In 1795 he wrote his brother about "a house in town," "a beautiful country house," and "delightful château" he now owned, with no other particulars—nor does he mention the colossal amounts he was then paying architect Louis Emmanuel Aimé Damesme to renovate the properties.[37] No doubt to deflect his brother's concerns, Richard closed one letter home with a charm offensive: "How I long for the time when I can have a few weeks of ease at your Country House at Lincoln," to which he was sending "an elegant Muslin Gown with headdress compleat" for Catherine.[38] In the end it was a public scandal—both financial and sexual—that tipped off John to Richard's activities. With the help of his mistress Céleste-Rosalie Vans, who held power of attorney for her Salem sea merchant husband, Richard liquidated the Vans' Hôtel de la Ferté-Senneterre in 1798 for cash.[39] Both cuckolded and swindled, William Vans brought a lawsuit against the Codman family that would drag on until 1838.

It is difficult to imagine two brothers less alike. If Richard had become the quintessential expatriate rake, then contemporaries remembered John as the very model

2.3
John Singleton Copley, *Richard Codman* (1794). Oil on canvas (44 3/8" x 36 ¼" x 3 3/8"). Bequest of Dorothy S.F.M. Codman, 1969.779. Courtesy Historic New England.

of Yankee respectability. Later eulogized as "a truly respectable citizen, of manners gentle . . . of habits industrious and enterprising, with an understanding clear and masculine," John was "a warm, sincere, pious believer in the Christian religion" and a man "formed for every domestic endearment."[40] The reverse mirror image they present would define the family from this stage forward. The Codmans' vacillations between propriety and excess, family and self, responsibility and heedlessness are indeed no better illustrated than in the brothers' simultaneous building projects. On one side of the Atlantic workmen feverishly clambered over the Lincoln house, its every brick and clapboard part of an expansive dynastic project; on the other, Damesme commanded an army of upholsterers, gardeners, and furniture dealers for his American client, creating environments that existed solely for beauty and pleasure—and at any cost.

As early as 1797, John wrote one of his French creditors: "We are perfectly tired of [Richard's] continuance in that Country and wish he was as much so."[41] At the conclusion of the Lincoln renovation project he decided to confront his brother directly in Paris, preceded by a summer in England. In July 1800, John wrote Catherine, "I can gather but little about Brother Richard, he must have spent a great deal of money"—adding, without a hint of irony, how much he enjoyed London shopping ("as to the shops it is almost impossible to get out of them without making a purchase").[42] The most important acquisition John made that summer was his own portrait from Copley. Here he projects none of the sensuality of Richard's image but rather the stolid form of a successful New England merchant (if one who privately felt the ground shifting beneath his feet). Writing Catherine before he departed for Paris that fall, he admitted that the situation with Richard was "too serious to me who am paying the fiddler to enjoy the sport . . . but I do not despair."[43]

The showdown between the brothers took place in October 1800. "The exact state of my Brother's concerns . . . were too confused and mortifying for him to explain," John wrote.[44] Unable to cover Richard's colossal debts "without doing injustice to my own family"—Richard owed a staggering £33,000 to his creditors—John insisted his brother liquidate his properties to buy French products, thereby turning his châteaux into cargo once more.[45] Humiliated and bankrupt, Richard left Paris for South America in 1802 before returning the following year to Boston. There, according to one family historian, his "charm and wit made him a great favorite" despite his reduced circumstances.[46]

Having saved the family firm and paid the outstanding the debts on Lincoln, John

2.4

John Singleton Copley, *John Codman III* (ca. 1800). Oil on canvas (45 ½" x 37 ½" x 3"). Museum Purchase, 2016.62.1. Courtesy Historic New England.

looked forward to the life of a country squire. "I am quite tired of business," he wrote his wife, "and determined to withdraw entirely from it."[47] In 1803, just three years after his return from France, he died at forty-eight. Three years later, his penniless brother was also dead. However brief their lives, the afterglow of the combined "fireworks of [their] grandeur"—as one contemporary described Richard's Parisian life—would extend well into the twentieth century.[48] John's colossal estate continued to fund the family's building projects from the grave, just as the legend of Richard's extravagance inspired them to live beyond their means.

INTERREGNUM, RESTORATION, AND EXILE

Orphaned on the eve of his majority, nineteen-year-old Charles Russell Codman did not have to wrestle with the problem of Lincoln's legal ownership. The question was whether he intended to keep the home. As a teenager he had favored Uncle Richard more so than his father—a situation that clearly worried John Codman. Writing Charles en route to his confrontation with Richard, he responded to his son's financial requests by explaining: "I am very willing you should have what is requisite . . . [but] a plenty of money is a bad companion in the pocket or at the command of any Young Man."[49] Not more than a year after taking ownership of the property in 1807, twenty-two-year-old Charles sold the Lincoln estate. Sharing this development in a remarkably brief aside to his brother, John Codman IV, he wrote: "As for news . . . I know of none myself. You have no doubt heard that I have sold the Lincoln farm . . . much under its real value," explaining "the increases in my expenses made it absolutely necessary."[50]

With this new influx of capital Charles announced his plan to travel abroad for an undetermined period, a scheme that raised alarms within the family. Writing their uncle William Amory, John Codman IV implored him to

> lead [Charles] by the hand into business, for at his age he must need a tactful friend and director. . . . He has an idea of going to Europe . . . I beg you to discourage it as much as possible, [for] a young man going to Europe without an object is in the greatest temptation . . . and he can be led into almost any thing.[51]

In the event, Charles did not leave for Europe entirely without an object. Between 1808 and 1812, he traveled the Continent collecting works of art, eventually forming one of the most extensive private art collections in Boston.

In 1817, Charles established himself at 29 Chestnut Street, a stately home on Beacon Hill designed in 1799 by the celebrated architect Charles Bulfinch. Here he demonstrated a passion for curating and decorating that would have impressed both his father and Uncle Richard. Enamored of French style above all, he contracted Parisian firms to furnish his Beacon Hill rooms. In a typical letter from 1824 he provided dealer Samuel Welles with minute instructions regarding furniture dimensions, fabric finishes, curtain linings, and cornices, all "made in the best style—rich but not gaudy" (asking for satin-lined curtains, he explained that silk always appeared *"mesquin"* [trifling] to him).[52] The interiors of 29 Chestnut Street would become the stuff of legend within the family, who for decades after the dispersal of Charles's estate spoke of its contents with a reverence second only to their love for Lincoln.

In creating this showplace, Charles demonstrated two important ways the Codmans' *modus operandi* departed from that of their Boston peers. First, while many of Boston's so-called Brahmin class would continue to build merchant fortunes for the first three-quarters of the nineteenth century, the Codmans' merchant past ended with John Codman's death in 1803. From this date forward the family's building projects relied entirely upon dividends and strategic marriages. Second, it is worth noting that by the date of his letter to Mr. Welles, Charles was a forty-year-old bachelor. In subsequent generations the Codmans' interior decorating would likewise fall to single and married men rather than to their female relations or wives. Indeed, it appears Charles was not even feathering his nest for a future bride—for when he married Anne McMaster in 1825, the couple left for France and remained abroad for the entirety of their brief marriage. (Anne would die in 1831, after delivering their second son.)

In the story of the Codman Estate, Charles is often presented as an anomaly: the figure who renounced the family seat and preferred France to New England. Yet to understand the arc of this house's, and family's, history we must consider the extraordinary pull France exercised on Codmans of every generation. When John Codman set out to retrieve his brother from Paris he told his wife: "the general opinion is that Richard has in habits and manners become so much of a Frenchman that it will be in vain for me to try to get him home."[53] Though he succeeded in bringing him back to Boston, his brother's Francophilia only appeared to increase in the generations that followed. Atypically for a Boston family of their class—which tended to take its cultural cues from England and regard anything French with suspicion—the Codmans felt a powerful attraction to France and exhibited a wanderlust unusual for Boston's insular elite (as a Beacon Hill matron once famously remarked, "Why should I travel when I'm already here?").[54] This restlessness stemmed not only from their love for French style but also from France's apparent endorsement of a pleasure-seeking life lived "without object"—a way of life the Codmans embraced more readily than most of their peers.

Returning to Chestnut Street with his two young sons following Anne's death, Charles married Sarah Ogden in 1836 and fathered three more children. With Sarah's death in 1844 and his own in 1852, their eldest child Ogden Codman [later Sr.] was left a twelve-year-old orphan. Sent to live with a tutor in New Bedford, Ogden became by his teenage years a spendthrift with little interest in schoolwork and perhaps too great an interest in clothing, stimulants, and the opposite sex. In 1854, Charles Russell Codman Jr. wrote his fifteen-year-old half-brother that his grades were "in the highest degree disgraceful to you" and the mark of a young man destined to be an "ignorant idler."[55] That year Ogden's other half-brother, James McMaster Codman, similarly castigated him for his "extravagant and foolish ideas in regard to your dress[,] . . . clothes which are so tight that they impede [your] movements" and made of flamboyantly "superfine material."[56] If the young man did not wish to become "something halfway between a coxcomb and an exquisite," his brother continued, "you had better give away . . . the bunch of charms dangling at your watch chain, [which are] very pretty for girls."

Ogden's account book from the following year shows a raft of charges for tailors, theater tickets, jewelry, photographers, cravats, and copious amounts of tobacco—while surviving letters to the sixteen-year-old include both love notes from girls and expressions of disappointment from his tutor's wife, who called his habits those of "an indolent sloth."[57] Young Ogden was also entangled with creditors; "I do hope the experience you have gone through will be a lesson to you," his brother Charles wrote him in 1855, "and I now give you fair warning that I shall not again interfere to extricate you from your difficulties."[58] Ogden reluctantly entered Harvard in the fall of 1857 ("you did not go, I am aware," his tutor's wife wrote him, "with any high anticipations") only to drop out in the second semester of his freshman year.[59]

The following summer, eighteen-year-old Ogden wrote James Bowdoin Bradlee to request his daughter Sarah's hand in marriage. Sarah was herself a month shy of sixteen. Describing himself as "one to whom there are no doubt objections and especially that of youth," he continued:

> I shall not come of age for two years but then peculiar circumstances have made me feel older and depend more upon myself than persons generally or at any age. I am an orphan. . . . With regard to my prospects I merely say that on becoming of age I shall come into possession of one-fifth of the income of my father's estate.[60]

Bradlee's response does not survive, but his reaction must have been mixed. A successful merchant prince along the lines of Ogden's grandfather, he had high expectations for his daughter's marriage. Given the close family and economic networks of Beacon Hill he would have known the esteemed Codman family, yet Ogden's prospects did not appear promising. Not only must the prospective groom—and certainly, Sarah—have seemed far too young to take such a step, but Ogden had shown no signs of commitment either to business or his education.

The marriage would have to wait. In June 1858, just weeks after he wrote Sarah's father, Ogden sailed for a four-month voyage to Calcutta. If his family hoped his time abroad might provide him with a sense of perspective about his future (Charles wished Ogden would "lead a more productive life when you return"), they were sorely disappointed. After reviewing his brother's travel expenses, Charles wrote him in a rage:

> I am really astonished and shocked at the state of things that your account discloses. During the six weeks that you were in Calcutta you spent about $2199 exclusive of the exorbitant $1167 for your passage to England and furniture for your cabin. What you have got for this is, I am informed, knickknacks . . . and extravagances in clothes and jewelry. If you do not change your habits and practice economy then [it] will be a very few years between you and the poorhouse. When all your property has been thrown away, you may judge for yourself how likely a person so indolent as you are and whose education is so imperfect, is likely to get on . . . the spendthrift propensities that you manifest are *vulgar*.[61]

Sarah appears to have harbored her own reservations about her fiancé, who entered Harvard's Law School that fall only to drop out in his first term and head abroad once more.[62] Although her parents provisionally granted permission for the engagement, Sarah insisted that it remain a secret and later destroyed her diary entries from December 1860 to August 1861, along with all letters to Ogden from the same period (an extraordinary step for a woman who later saved so much).[63] On October 26, 1861, the two were at last married. Under "occupation" on their marriage license, the groom recorded simply: "Gentleman."[64]

Armed now with his inheritance, Ogden planned to recapture the one legacy his father had denied him: the house in Lincoln. In the fifty-five years since Charles Russell Codman had sold the property it had passed through four different families, none of whom treated the home with the same reverence his ancestors had. (Upon his first visit to the southeast parlor at Lincoln, Ogden found it filled with racks for drying fruit.)[65] When he purchased the property from the Minns family in November 1862, its price reflected just how far the home had fallen. Now significantly reduced in acreage, it sold for just $12,000—a full $7,000 less than Charles Russell Codman had received for it in 1807.[66]

However foolhardy the Lincoln scheme might have seemed in 1862, Ogden had made a powerful dynastic gesture. The orphan whose "circumstances . . . have made me feel older" had reached back for the reassurance of his grandfather's generation. He would pass on this nostalgic quest to his son, Ogden Codman Jr., whose birth in January 1863 coincided almost exactly with the reclamation of the Lincoln house. Indeed, as if to abet his father's project from the distance of several decades, Ogden Jr. would one day include in his "family" genealogies all of Lincoln's owners from 1807 to 1862, a period he imperiously called the house's "inter-regnum."[67]

2.5
(Detail) Sturgis staircase at the Codman Estate. Spindles reproduced from Boston's Thomas Hancock House (1737). Author photo.

As if to mark the home's new chapter, Ogden Sr. rechristened the property "The Grange." By suggesting his was the home of a gentleman farmer—in the nineteenth century a grange indicated a country estate surrounded by farm buildings—Ogden honored John Codman's unfulfilled dream for his own life at Lincoln. By more specifically summoning the name of the Marquis de Lafayette's summer home, the Château de la Grange-Bléneau, Ogden also paid homage to his father. In 1830, Charles Russell Codman and his wife Anne had spent a month as Lafayette's guests at La Grange; after Anne's death the following year Lafayette sent Charles an eloquent condolence note, a letter Ogden Sr. cherished as a documentary link between the house and its new name.[68] To those of a more superstitious mindset, this connection to a French estate might have appeared ill fated. Until this moment France and the Lincoln house had always occupied separate spheres—and more often than not, the Codmans' French associations spelled bad news for the family.

Between 1862 and 1866, the Codmans' home underwent its second major transformation. Enlisting architect John Hubbard Sturgis, husband of his sister Fanny, Ogden amplified the house's Georgian elements by introducing "period" features absent from the Russell design. These included heavy chamfered quoins along the home's corners, pediments above the first floor windows, a terraced balustrade, and a new columned porch along the house's eastern façade (see figure 2.2, p. 43). The home's grand double staircase received a similar upgrade. Reducing the height of its risers to create a more stately ascent, Sturgis replaced the stairs' delicate Federal-era spindles with reproductions of more muscular examples from Boston's recently demolished Hancock House (1737).[69] When completed, The Grange's neo-Georgian scheme once more projected the glory of a past it could not quite claim.

If the exterior of The Grange addressed the property's past, however wishfully, then its interiors reflected the latest in contemporary fashion. To supply furniture, wallpaper, upholstery, and interior finishes Sturgis and Codman hired the New York firm of Léon Marcotte, whose work exemplified Gilded Age magnificence. (In his bestselling *The House Beautiful* of 1877, Clarence Cook later sniffed, "If you only want to be in fashion, have things that come from Marcotte.")[70] Dramatic additions included a new, brightly colored encaustic tile floor for the entry hall; dark paneling for the southwest parlor, now a billiard room; and an Elizabethan makeover for the dining room, complete with an elaborate strapwork ceiling. (Notable subtractions included the eighteenth-century paneling of the southwest parlor and upstairs bedrooms.) Joining the Marcotte furnishings at The Grange were a range of works from 29 Chestnut Street, long held in storage, along with pieces from Sarah's family at 34 Beacon Street. From this period forward, the home's interiors became a kind of historical index for the homes of the extended Codman and Bradlee families.

For nearly a decade the family lived the idyll Ogden had envisioned as a twenty-two-year-old. Not only did he avoid the poorhouse, but his tax returns for the late 1860s indicate an impressive income of nearly $12,000 a year.[71] An 1864 photograph of Ogden and Sarah, taken in Paris, presents the young couple's confidence on full display. Hand on hip in a swaggering pose, the darkly handsome Ogden remains every inch the dandy of his teenage years. For her part, Sarah wears a striking French gown and the self-assured gaze of a new mother. Within the following years the family would grow to include Alice ("Ahla") Newbold Codman, born in 1866, and Thomas Newbold Codman in 1868. By the time of Tom's birth, the family were living year-round at Lincoln and using the Bradlees'

2.6
Ogden Codman, Sr. and Sarah Bradlee Codman in Paris (1864). Photograph by L. Pierson, firm of Mayer and Pierson, Paris. Codman Family Papers, courtesy Historic New England.

Beacon Hill home as their in-town residence. Looking back on this period in 1902, Ogden Sr. described himself as a would-be farmer who led an uneventful if satisfying life. ("I saw no prospect of become a Rothschild," he wrote, but admitted his life "hasn't been an unhappy one.")[72]

The events of 1872 would alter the Codmans' financial prospects—and happiness—for years to come. In January Sarah lost her fifty-nine-year-old father, with whom she had always been close and who had done a great deal to support the young couple (the extensive renovations of The Grange were largely supported by the influx of Bradlee money). Though her father left an estate valued at more than half a million dollars, Sarah's mother, Mary Perrin May Bradlee, now controlled its disbursement.[73] Time would prove that Sarah did not have much to expect from her. On November 9, it was at her widowed mother's house that the heavily pregnant Sarah first heard news of a fire in downtown Boston. Raging through the night, what came to be known as the Great Boston Fire of 1872 eventually consumed sixty-five acres of land, including most of the financial district. By the time the smoke cleared, nearly eight hundred buildings lay in ruin—their combined loss only a fraction of the deeper financial implications of the fire, which wiped out valuable rental markets and sent Boston's insurance industry into collapse. Heavily invested in downtown real estate and fire insurance companies, the extended Codman family had in the space of twelve hours lost a considerable portion of its income.[74] On Christmas Day, Sarah gave birth to her fourth child and third son, Bowdoin Bradlee Codman, in an atmosphere of painful uncertainty. She refused to visit the burned district for a full year.[75]

In 1873, the Codmans were offered little relief. Global financial panics that year battered the US economy, already weakened by property losses in the Great Boston Fire and the Chicago Fire the year before. The family had little choice but to retrench, renting their Lincoln property and seeking a new life abroad. Sailing for France on October 4, 1874—appropriately enough, aboard a ship called the *Siberia*—they would not see The Grange again for ten years.[76] The choice to relocate to France had not been an easy one, but it had its own logic. Not only did the Francophile Codmans feel an affinity for the country, but they also realized the cost of living in France—still recovering from its brutal loss in the Franco-Prussian War—promised the possibility of exile without a drastic reduction in their lifestyle. For eleven-year-old Ogden Jr., however, the removal constituted a hardship from which he never fully recovered. Their time abroad was "a horrid nightmare," he later recalled, intensified by his fear that the family would never return to New England.[77]

By 1875 the Codmans had settled in Dinard, France, a sleepy resort town in Brittany popular with British expatriates. Here they moved into the modest Maison Crolard—located, ironically enough for this eternally backward-looking family, in the Rue de l'Avenir ("Road of the Future").[78] Their first years in Dinard were difficult ones, not only given France's postwar depression—Ogden Jr. remembered the town as a "wretched hole of a place"—but also due to personal losses.[79] Three days after Bowdoin's third birthday in 1875, the family lost their youngest son; Sarah's mother died in Boston two years later, splitting her estate between Sarah's sisters Fanny and Alice. Sarah did not record her reaction to this shutout from the family settlement, but it is telling that in her copious cartes de visite albums her mother's image is conspicuously absent.[80]

The family grew by two more in Dinard: Hugh Codman, born in 1875, and Dorothy Sarah Frances May Codman in 1883. Undoubtedly a surprise to her middle-aged parents, Dorothy began life as she would end it, her rambling name—like the house she would die in—a kind of clearinghouse for the family's history. Twenty years younger than Ogden Jr., Dorothy and he developed vastly different relationships with their mother. While Sarah ultimately granted her eldest son the authority of a coparent, she restricted her youngest daughter's freedoms, even in her adult years, as if she remained perpetually a child.

The decoration of the children's schoolroom at Maison Crolard speaks to their experience of exile. Here a large-format photograph of The Grange took center stage, placed at a child's height and hung across the room's corner like a religious icon. Taken just a few months before the Great Boston Fire, the image presents the house from a three-quarter perspective, revealing its full volume along the estate's sweeping drive. Drawing the viewer into this space are nine-year-old Ogden Jr., standing in a smart suit and holding his pony's lead; six-year-old Ahla, confidently astride her own pony in a flounced skirt; and four-year-old Tom, himself still in a skirt, regarding the viewer beneath one of his great-grandfather's chestnut trees. It is full summertime at The Grange, and the home's future appears assured by this new generation.

For the Codman children who remembered The Grange, the image stood as a daily reminder of all the family had lost. If Ogden Sr. had dreamed of reclaiming Lincoln to restore himself to his grandfather's generation, then his three eldest children—and Ogden Jr. above all—must have yearned to reunite with their own former selves, the home's most recent scions. When the teenage Ogden Jr. left his family for the first time in 1880, it is telling that he asked his mother to send him a copy of this photograph.[81] However painful the image surely was for him—a reminder "of all the things I might have done had I been [at Lincoln] instead of Dinard," he told his mother—it also held a mirror to his future potential.[82] His exile from Lincoln would one day end.

Dinard took much from Ogden Jr., but it also bestowed upon him, for better or worse, two lifelong legacies: a fetishization of wealth and its trappings, along with a melancholic yearning for Lincoln that even its proximity could not assuage.

2.7
LEFT: Exterior view of The Grange, Lincoln, Massachusetts (1872). Photograph by Barton Sprague.
RIGHT: (Detail) Nine-year-old Ogden Codman Jr. Codman Family Papers, courtesy Historic New England.

Codmans of every generation understood the power of money—and the sting of its lack—but Ogden Jr. developed from his youth a near obsession with making, acquiring, inheriting, and associating himself with great fortunes. Writing Sarah in his twenties he confided, "I always did like an atmosphere of wealth," adding, "I like having money and have always wanted money wherever I was."[83] Indeed, his lifelong insecurity surrounding money seemed only to increase in periods when he was flush with capital. (In 1896 he assured his mother, "if I ever can get enough money I shall be quite a person and possibly of use in the world"; he never could get enough, and when he did, he was of little use to anyone—least of all to himself.)[84] Wealth represented for Codman both a way back to the life he felt had been robbed from him, and the path forward to the one he believed he deserved—a sense of entitlement that extended to his family at large, for among his siblings none was more focused than he on the question of inheritances. "It is sad to lose relations," he wrote a friend after the death of his uncle Benjamin Crowninshield, "who don't leave you anything."[85]

Related to Codman's cupidity, if casting him in a more sympathetic light, is the powerful nostalgia he felt for Lincoln, the eternal symbol of his family's lost prestige. Separated from his childhood home from the age of eleven to nineteen, Codman developed a reverence for The Grange that an uninterrupted life there might never have inspired. What he forever called his "homesickness" even outlasted his return to New England. ("I can't bear the idea of never living [at The Grange] again," Codman wrote Sarah *after* his return to Boston, when residence at the family home was once again an option.)[86] The same feelings continued throughout his adult life. Halfway into his seventies and more than eighteen years after his permanent move to France, he wrote Tom: "I am just as homesick as possible" for The Grange.[87] The reason Codman could never cure this longing was that The Grange he missed so desperately had never existed. He pined only for the house, and the life, in his schoolroom photograph.

A PRODIGAL SON RETURNS

Codman's parents decided in 1880 that if he were ever to leave Dinard he needed professional training. Sent to learn banking in Bonn, Germany, the seventeen-year-old enjoyed his employers (two bankers who were "both very nice and enormously *fat*") but loathed clerking, and so he returned to the family that fall.[88] Increasingly concerned about his nephew's future, Uncle Sturgis wrote Ogden Sr. in November 1880:

> I hear that Ogden has left his school at Bonn [and] is now back again with you. If he is ever to live in America he ought to be educated there or he will be more or less unfitted for his life there. . . . Let me again make the offer . . . that he shall come live with us and finish his education. . . . It is for the boy's good. Make up your mind to the sacrifice.[89]

In the event, the Codmans sent their son back to Germany in 1882—this time to Hamburg, where he studied bookkeeping. However disconnected Ogden continued to feel from his studies, he wrote Sarah with some pride that

You would find me rather changed in some ways, I hope you would say for the better. I almost think I am a little less selfish than I was. . . . *And I am actually spending less than several of my friend who earn their own living . . .* a fact of which I am just a *little* proud.[90]

Sarah must have been unconvinced about her son's newfound maturity. Anxious to return to New England, Codman wrote her several months later:

I expect that at 19 all chances of turning over a new leaf are not lost. Give me the chance, let me go home *alone*, and let me stay there long enough *alone* to make the best of the chance. I happen to be very "*rangé*" [steadfast], but how would you tell when I left home whether I was going to be "*rangé*" or not?[91]

When the Codmans at last sent Ogden back to Boston in November 1882, the nineteen-year-old found it more difficult to adapt than he hoped. Dinard had sent home a changeling. Whether due to his own idiosyncrasies, the foreign habits of an expatriate, or both, Ogden found it difficult to break into the fully formed networks of young men raised in Boston. "I'm sure I would give anything to have been here the last four years [and] to have been . . . with others my own age," he wrote Sarah, adding, "I don't know as many fellows as I would like to."[92] Charles Russell Codman Jr. tried to reassure Ogden Sr. about his son's prospects, writing about Ogden Jr.: "If he has some peculiarities they are not of a kind that need cause anxiety."[93]

In the spring of 1883 Charles proposed a scheme to his brother. Telling him "frankly . . . I don't think you can expect [Ogden Jr.] to be able to earn his living as a clerk in the business sense," he advised instead that his nephew enroll at the Massachusetts Institute of Technology (MIT) "to give him a professional education."[94] A knowledge of architecture, he suggested, might allow him to "take up a business like Dick's." (Following the family's 1872 losses, Ogden Sr.'s brother Richard had turned to professional interior decorating.) Before Codman entered MIT in the fall of 1883, he wrote Sarah that he "would be able to make some friends as nice people send their sons there."[95] He was soon disappointed. Although he enjoyed his architecture courses ("it is the first time I have ever liked school"), he confessed to an abiding loneliness. Writing his mother in the loosely punctuated run-on style that became his signature, he explained:

The Institute fellows are awful *cads* I would not have any thing to do with them for any thing and all the nice fellows are in college Fortunately I am busy and evenings I can see anybody I choose still I don't see many young people. I am sorry on Ahla's account that I shall not be of any use to her [in securing a beau].[96]

Leaving MIT after just a year, Codman eventually asked for his name to be permanently expunged from their rosters.[97]

Codman's aimlessness in this period begs the question: Exactly where *were* his interests headed? He declared to Sarah around this time that "houses, genealogy, and furniture" were his three passions.[98] Among these, furniture was likely his first love. Throughout his life Codman's letters to his siblings contained vivid childhood memories of the placement, quality, and style of furniture in his extended family's homes. Even as a boy, he had roamed these rooms with an appraising eye. His related interest in genealogy—which served an important role in determining the provenance of these objects—had first blossomed in Hamburg. Writing Sarah from there in November 1881, he offered two important discoveries:

> The Codmans were much better people than I had any idea of. I also heard (from relatives) a good deal about papas great-uncle Richard and a nice? respectable! person he seems to have been!!! He had a most scandalous Lawsuit which has been published in a book which I must find when I get home.[99]

Codman's newly awakened interest in his family history—ancestors who were both better than he had reason to believe and thrillingly worse than he could have imagined—would occupy more of his adult life than his design career.

As for the houses Codman cites in this trifecta of interests, The Grange represented his primary focus. On December 5, 1882, just a few weeks after his return to New England, he made his first visit there since childhood. Reporting to Sarah that the house was "larger and grander" than he remembered, he noted, "the old parts are still very handsome."[100] Then living with the Sturgises, Codman began making multiple trips to The Grange in early 1883—to the likely exasperation of the Codmans' renters, the Hubbell family, who were asked to take him throughout the house to inspect its rooms. "Every time I go there I am fonder of the place," he wrote his mother, even if its neglect in renters' hands pained him.[101] Identifying himself directly with the house, he added, "I am so fond of it and when it looks shabby I feel as if I were in rags walking up Beacon Street."[102] Exhorting his parents to return to Lincoln, he claimed the house sorely needed "an owner's eye."

There were two impediments to this scheme. First, as late as 1883 it did not yet appear the family's finances had rebounded fully enough to leave Dinard. "If there was any chance of your being better off next year," Codman reasoned with Sarah, "then that would be a reason for a delay. But is there?"[103] Second, it appears that if Dinard inspired Codman with the prospect of returning to The Grange, then the family's time in France had produced the opposite effect in his father. In the same letter, Codman cajoled Sarah: "I am sure you will all soon like it better here with one exception, *Papa*, he will not find it so pleasant no doubt."

Enjoying greater freedoms abroad than did the rest of his family, Ogden Sr. decided that Continental life suited him better than the quiet existence of a gentleman farmer. As Adams recalled from his Lincoln boyhood, the Codman patriarch "liked good company and champagne and found occupation elsewhere."[104] In photographs from the 1880s, the middle-aged Ogden Sr. is, if anything, more stylish and commandingly handsome than in the first years of his marriage—a marked contrast to the long-suffering Sarah, who had gone gray and, at forty-one, was once again nursing a newborn. With The Grange's power over Ogden Sr. more or less permanently broken, his son stepped in to fill the vacuum.

Following the departure of the Hubbells, Codman attempted to hasten his family's return by sprucing up The Grange. When he bought a new straw rug for the drawing room in the summer of 1884, he wrote his mother that Lincoln now looked "ever so nice . . . to say that the place is looking lovely is not to do it half justice."[105] Turning his attention to his bedroom—a first laboratory for the future designer—he added an armchair upholstered in William Morris fabric, a Morris rug, and artfully draped fringed textiles. The completed room presented a far more contemporary look than the now dated interiors of the Sturgis renovation. Sending sketches of the final result to Sarah, he added: "I suppose Papa will scorn my furniture."[106] (In fact, it was Codman who scorned his father's choices. The days of the Sturgis interiors were numbered.) By the time his family at last sailed for home in fall 1884, The Grange had a new designer-in-chief.

Considering how closely associated Codman later become with French style, it is worth noting his love for English design in this period, particularly the work of William Morris. Writing Sarah in 1883 from his new bachelor quarters at 96 Charles Street, Codman praised the William Morris & Company furnishings he encountered at Boston's Foreign Exhibition that fall: "saw some very pretty rugs from Morris in London he has such pretty chintzes and wallpapers."[107] (To this he added, "English is the fashion The *Rage* so mind and let everything be as English as possible [at Lincoln] and get as much in England as you can *except Dresses*.") Not long thereafter he redecorated the grandest room at Lincoln, the southeast parlor, entirely in Morris fabric—a scheme likely carried out with help from Uncle Dick, an importer of Morris textiles and admirer of the English designer.[108] Mindful of the strains these redecorations might place on the family's straitened circumstances, Codman suggested to Sarah: "could you not sell the pictures [the Codmans' painting collection] if they are so valuable . . . and get furniture with the money!"[109] "Poor Lincoln," he added, "would need but little to make it the height of fashion."

Despite his claim that he planned to "make money first" when he returned, with only "a little curiosity to see Boston," the future designer had a slow start to his career.[110] First apprenticing with his Uncle Sturgis's firm, Codman later spent two "dreary years" working for an architect's office in Lowell, Massachusetts.[111] In the mid-1880s he worked briefly for the decorating firm A. H. Davenport in Cambridge, and in 1886 joined the Boston design office of Andrews and Jacques. (His cousin John Codman Ropes, who secured the job for him, wrote Codman: "I answered for your assidity and faithfulness: so be careful, my boy!")[112] It was not a good match. Three years later Robert Andrews fired Codman, writing in his letter of termination: "I express a regret common to your friends that your indifference to success in the profession you have chosen should be so marked."[113] Despite his poor showing at the firm, Codman made two important connections there: Herbert W. C. Browne and Arthur Little, who, along with Codman, would one day be known as the "Holy Trinity" of the Colonial Revival style.

Supporting himself with small decorating projects, often undertaken for his extended family,

2.8
Ogden Codman Jr. in Bar Harbor, ME (1887), a year after he joined the Boston firm of Andrews and Jacques. Photograph by Thomas Newbold Codman. Codman Family Papers, courtesy Historic New England.

Codman borrowed $1,000 from his Aunt Alice in 1891 to establish his own design office in Boston. (That year he appeared for the first time as "architect and decorator" in the Boston Directory.) It was not Boston, however, but the resort town of Newport, Rhode Island, where Codman's career hit its stride. A regular vacationer in Newport since the mid-1880s, Codman met future novelist Edith Wharton there in 1891. A distant cousin of the Codmans through the Newbold family, she formed an immediate, intense friendship with this "clever young Boston architect" and did much to launch his career. In 1893 she hired Codman to de-Victorianize her Newport home, Land's End—an 1864 structure designed by Codman's Uncle Sturgis. Despite the limited scope of the project, it sowed the seeds of Codman's later literary partnership with Wharton and led to his similar "correction" of Sturgis's designs at Lincoln. In a more important and immediate sense, the Wharton connection led to his first major design commission.

Sharing the news with Arthur Little in November 1893, a breathless Codman wrote, "I must just write a line tho' it is midnight and I am dead tired to tell you that I am to decorate the whole upper part of the Cornelius Vanderbilt [II] Newport villa. . . . The house is enormous!"[114] Dazzled by Vanderbilt himself as much as by the size of the commission, Codman told Sarah, "Just think what a client!!! The richest and nicest of them all. I can scarcely believe it is true. . . . I am going to thank Mrs. Wharton who brought this about."[115] Codman's purview at the Vanderbilts' oceanside villa, The Breakers, comprised thirteen bedrooms above the house's principal rooms; the first floor was to be decorated by the French firm Allard et Fils, and the house's overall design directed by architect Richard Morris Hunt.

Work on the house took nearly two years, not without considerable friction between Codman and Hunt. Surviving letters indicate that Codman's work was often too schematically rendered, measured inaccurately, and late (sometimes by months). When he accused Hunt of questioning the correctness of his designs, Hunt responded sarcastically that "your following in the footsteps of [Ange-Jacques] Gabriel"—famed architect to King Louis XV—was "no less certain" an outcome given Hunt's frequently required interventions.[116] To Codman, the unintended compliment doubtless removed the sting of Hunt's reprimand.

However difficult the young architect might have been, his eighteenth-century French interiors were a model of restraint in an otherwise overblown Gilded Age affair. In a letter to his mother toward the end of the project, Codman explained:

> The lower part of the house is intensely vulgar. . . . My rooms are a great contrast. They are just right and look as if intended for ladies and gentlemen. Mr. Hunt is to blame for most of the vulgarity I think. Of course the Vanderbilts wanted *magnificence* but they would not have minded good taste.[117]

For her part, Wharton was "much pleased" with Codman's designs but declared his clients were "entrenched in a sort of *thermopylae* of bad taste, from which apparently no force on earth can dislodge them."[118] Codman's career would increasingly rely upon such *nouveaux riches* clients, whose tastes he questioned and budgets he roundly ignored. Years later he declared to Sarah, "One cannot expect most of these people to be like ladies and gentlemen . . . when you think of what they were. I really think it wonderful they are not worse. However they *pay*."[119]

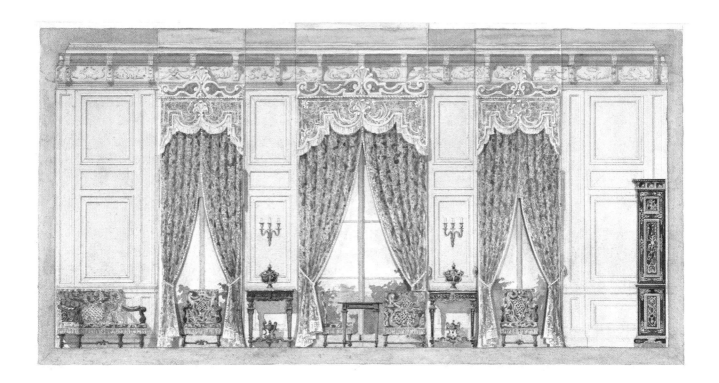

In the 1890s Wharton and Codman's relationship deepened into a complicated friendship/business/quasi-romantic affair. Calling Wharton "the cleverest and best friend I have ever made," Codman hung on her advice and continued to rely upon her social connections for work.[120] The pair referred to one another by the affectionate nicknames "Puss" and "Coddy" (Newporters labeling them with the portmanteau "Mr. and Mrs. Pusscod"), a practice that undoubtedly sat uneasily with Wharton's husband Teddy. Indeed, as Codman told Sarah in 1896, Wharton once declared to Codman in front of Teddy, "I really think I shall have to end by marrying you Coddy, I feel as if it will be my fate"—to which Codman responded, "you'll have to marry someone very rich first."[121] ("I thought it rather funny," he added to his mother, but "she did not quite seem to like it.")

Neither Wharton nor Sarah—nor, it must be said, Teddy—considered Codman a serious threat to the Whartons' marriage, for all likely knew Codman's sexual interest lay with men. Wharton, whose 1917 novel *Summer* included an effeminate architect based on Codman, once wrote a female friend that he was "a queer stick."[122] As for Sarah, Codman was often surprisingly frank with his mother about his attraction to men. In one letter he confided that he would skip the beach at Marblehead "as the Boys are not very attractive," and in another he characterized some of the men in his circle as "rather of the Oscar Wilde type."[123] What neither Wharton nor his mother realized, however, was the extraordinary extent of Codman's sexual activity in the 1890s—an underworld that blossomed for him at precisely the moment he was becoming a more public figure. First examined by David Doyle in 2004, the full dimensions of Codman's queer world were in his own day known to only a small inner circle, at the center of which stood Arthur Little.[124]

Codman's correspondence with Little between 1891 and 1903 provides a remarkable record—not only of their particular desire for, and liaisons with, other men but also of the homosexual mores of their time, place, and class. Notable, too, is the very fact that

2.9
Ogden Codman Jr., *The Breakers: Bedroom of Cornelius Vanderbilt II, Design for Window Wall* (ca. 1893–1895). Watercolor and pencil on paper (13 1/8" x 9 ¾", sheet). 51.644.73(15). Image © The Metropolitan Museum of Art. Image source: Art Resource, NY.

Codman saved these letters. While he possibly believed the sheer volume of his family's manuscript collection would ultimately conceal them—as it effectively did until the twenty-first century—Codman confessed to his brother Tom in 1935 how much he enjoyed rereading his 1890s correspondence with Little and doubtless realized others might, as well.[125] Doyle rightly suggests that these men, while understanding the need for discretion, perceived in their activities neither guilt nor danger—an attitude that appears to have survived even Oscar Wilde's 1895 conviction for "gross indecency," a case they followed with interest. Engaging in sex with other men, visiting underground same-sex bars and bathhouses, and collecting homosexual pornography did not in their eyes disqualify them as gentlemen. Quite the contrary, in fact, for they believed it was their class itself that exonerated them.

In the spring of 1892, Little asked Codman, "How is your smash on Walter Abbott getting on? You don't mention him so I *suppose* all sorts of things[, if] silence is golden what is screwing for [for] God's sake then?"[126] Frequent talk of their "smashes," both consummated and not, fills their letters in this period; between 1892 and 1894 alone, Doyle reckons, Codman romantically pursued at least fifteen different named men. Acknowledging the salacious nature of their correspondence, Codman wrote Little in 1894: "I found a very nice letter from you which had been opened in Paris . . . fortunately it was written *to be read aloud* so no harm was done to anyone's morals."[127] In an earlier letter clearly not meant for public consumption, Little honored his friend's sexual enthusiasm with a sketch for a new Codman coat of arms composed entirely of erect phalluses and bearing the enigmatic motto, "A Po Cocko!"[128]

The spaces where Codman conducted his affairs ranged from his bachelor quarters—he was now living in an apartment at 100 Chestnut Street—to semipublic venues in Boston, New York, Paris, and Rome. Speaking of a neighbor, Codman sighed to Little, "let us hope that Ben Allen will not be the only one in 100 Chestnut Street to have luck tho' I really have had my share" (Little asked in response, "have you been screwing Winnie Clarke lately?").[129] The men share stories, as well, of trysts and voyeurism at the Boston Athletic Club's Turkish Baths. Comparing them to the Turkish Baths in Paris and the West 28th Street Baths in New York, Little added: "it is all the difference, having a cock or not in cases of need."[130] In New York, the pair were enthusiastic patrons of The Slide, an infamous gay bar that briefly operated from 1890 to 1892. At the time of the bar's final raid, the *New York Herald* condemned "the unspeakable nature of the orgies practiced there" (Codman confessed to Little that nights at The Slide often left him entirely "used up").[131] Speaking of another, unnamed venue, Little wrote Codman: "Take care you don't bring [name illegible] boils again by too often visits there—what a thrilling thing you say that it is less tiring than the 'Slide!'"[132]

Both men acknowledged that Italy offered greater sexual opportunities than New York. ("You will have fun . . . if you care to look about," Codman told his friend, "I always heard the 'Slide' was mild compared to Italy.")[133] Here, too, the men encountered a bustling market in pornography. "I should think you might get some awfully queer engravings and photos in Italy," Codman suggested to Little when the latter traveled to Rome in 1891; "you might send me some photos anonymously to 100 Chestnut Street."[134] The following year Codman requested more photographs, instructing Little to send them "unmounted in an envelope without any letter [so] if they get lost it would not matter," reminding him that, in addressing the package to him, "for heaven's sake remember to put 'junior.'"[135]

We may assume Little fulfilled his request, for—remarkably—not only has the men's correspondence survived but so too has Codman's collection of same-sex pornography. Discovered nearly a decade after SPNEA took ownership of the Codman Estate, the collection was at first solely associated with Tom, the family's photographer. The brothers appear to have shared the collection, however, for though it includes images clearly taken by Tom, it also contains an 1899–1900 inventory in Ogden's hand and an envelope addressed to "O. Codman" from a New York printing lab, bearing the message: "The Law does not permit us to print some of these negatives."[136] Primarily dating to the late nineteenth century, this cache of images includes a number of works created by professional Italian studios, ranging from classicized male nudes to hardcore images of men engaged in sodomy and fellatio.[137]

Codman and Little's shared passions for design and same-sex adventure raises the question: Did these worlds overlap? It appears the line between the two sometimes blurred. Little wrote Codman in 1892, "I have bought [you] some more 'Neopolitan boys'—some are daisys!—such c_ks!! Also some architectural photos which are interesting and nice."[138] Little's apparent non sequitur points to Codman's collection of architectural images— an archive that eventually contained thousands of architectural photographs, particularly of historic interiors. In their own way, these images spoke as much about desire as his collection of Neopolitan nudes (indeed, mixed in with the Codman pornography collection are a number of images of French châteaux).

Clearly, sumptuous interiors held an erotic power for Little. Speaking of a palace on the Arno he exclaimed to Codman, "the silk walls!! And the muslin and embroidered curtains!! Oh my! My balls ache with delight."[139] In at least one case, arousal inspired design, in turn. Responding to Codman's request for more nudes, Little suggested the setting they might inspire:

> I begin to think it would be delightful to decorate and fit up a petit appartement particularly devoted to screwing. Only pink silk with "chaise longues" to wallow on and endless cushions . . . and lewd prints . . . and all the materials such as would bring out skin and hair etc. etc. etc.!!![140]

Codman's response is not recorded, but the friends were rarely of two opinions when it came to decorating or men.

At the height of this intense period of carousing, Codman coauthored with Wharton their landmark study, *The Decoration of Houses* (1897)—an erudite and often frosty treatise on architectural decorum. It is unclear which of the two initiated the project, but by December 1896 they were hard at work. Codman explained to Sarah, "Mrs. Wharton and I have been writing a book about decoration and architecture and that takes up time," adding, "she takes my notes and adds a good deal out of her own head. . . . It is very amusing to see my ideas in literary shape."[141] Most of the completed writing is likely Wharton's, yet the work's photographs, bibliography, and pronounced preference for French design all point to Codman. So, too, do the moments when the project was in greatest peril. Writing Codman a blistering letter in spring 1897, Wharton declared that his foot-dragging had driven her to regret taking on the project: "I hate to put my name to anything so badly turned out as the book is bound to be."[142] Dropped by their publisher, Macmillan, in May—due to Codman's highhandedness with their editor—the book was picked up by Scribner's that summer and published at Christmastime 1897. A resounding success from the moment it appeared, it has never gone out of print.

Although *The Decoration of Houses* was not the first American guide to home decoration—scores had appeared from midcentury onward—its outsized influence may be attributed to its systematic presentation of rules, authoritative tone, and lavish illustrations of homes "of some importance" (mostly European palaces, drawn from Codman's ever-growing photograph collection). Defending their use of such aristocratic models, designs that only a robber baron could have afforded, the pair offered a trickle-down theory of reform: "When the rich man demands good architecture his neighbors will get it too."[143] By declaring "proportion is the good breeding of architecture," dispensing advice about the proper outfitting of a ballroom, and frequently lapsing into untranslated French (good ormolu andirons are "almost *introuvable* [unfindable] today," the authors sigh), Wharton and Codman struck a tone of patrician discernment that clearly appealed to aspirational readers.

Their treatise—at one point provisionally titled *The Philosophy of Home Decoration*—championed with near-religious fervor the principles of order, hierarchy, and, above all, symmetry (which they dubbed "the sanity of decoration").[144] Banning any originality of expression ("to conform . . . is no more servile than to pay one's taxes"), the pair also railed against openness in interiors, demanding that stairs be tucked out of sight and doors firmly closed ("privacy is the first requisite of civilized life").[145] For good measure, they also condemned wallpaper, electric light, and Christmas trees.[146]

However much they derided originality, Wharton and Codman introduced at least one novel concept in this work. Challenging earlier design reformers like Clarence Cook and Charles Eastlake, writers who promoted "honesty" in decoration as a central principle, Wharton and Codman—as *The Nation* quipped—"snap their fingers at sincerity [and] have no horror of shams."[147] False doors and windows, concealed entrances, imitation materials, and illusionistic spaces were all allowable as long as these elements contributed to the visual pleasure of an overall design. Explaining it was the decorator's mission "not to explain illusions, but to produce them," the authors revealed more about their own work and lives than they might have realized.[148] Much of Codman's world, of course, was built upon a series of successfully managed illusions—while Wharton founded her literary career upon characters who often wield the power of a beautifully told lie.

Even before the pair completed *The Decoration of Houses*, Codman began to outline his next literary project: "a monograph about Lincoln called 'A New England Country Seat' . . . with illustrations from the plans and photos I have—a combination of genealogy and architecture."[149] Hints of the project appear in a draft version of *The Decoration of Houses*, which in one passage declares "[with stucco and carving] it is possible to obtain effects ranging from the grandeur of the Villa Madama to the simplicity of any wood-paneled parlour in an old New England country-house" (Codman drew a line through the passage, perhaps given his belief that The Grange's paneled parlor, at any rate, was the equal of any room at the Villa Madama).[150] Although the Lincoln book never materialized, Codman would undertake a significant "restoration" of the house in the late 1890s—a project that, much like the proposed book, was at its core a celebration of his eighteenth-century ancestry.

THE ASYLUM OF THE PAST

If *The Decoration of Houses* had inspired Codman to turn back to Lincoln's interiors, there were also personal reasons urging on the project. First, the house was nearing the centenary of John Codman's Federal-era makeover—an event Codman wished to mark by returning the home, as nearly as possible, to its pre-Sturgis appearance. In a second and related sense, his plan to erase his father's interventions reflected Ogden Sr.'s ongoing absence from Lincoln.

Around the time Codman won the Breakers commission, the Codmans—minus their eldest son—had returned to Dinard. This second period of retrenchment, likely brought on by the Panic of 1893, lasted four years. In 1895 Sarah's recently widowed sister, Alice, joined the family in France; remarking on the length of her stay, Codman wrote his mother, "I suppose Aunt Alice means to cling to you forever."[151] It soon became apparent that Alice planned to cling to his father alone. By 1897 Ogden Sr.'s romantic relationship with his sister-in-law was more or less an open secret, evidenced by the two-year trip they embarked upon that year. It is unclear how Sarah or the children initially reacted to this change, but they eventually appeared to regard the affair as unremarkable. In a 1903 letter to her father and aunt, Ahla asked: "next time you or Aunt Alice write Mère Cot will you please enclose the Russells' address in Geneva? To you both—your affectionate daughter Ahla."[152] (The fact that the children took this relationship in stride is, itself, a sign of their French worldview—as was their affectation, from about 1890 onward, to style their parents "Père Cot" and "Mère Cot.")

By 1897 the family's finances had sufficiently recovered to allow Sarah and the children to move back to Lincoln—without Père Cot. On the advent of their return Codman suggested a few changes to the house:

> I dare say I can try a few experiments in the garden now I have a little money to spend. . . . I am sure it will be fun to arrange the furniture and perhaps we can make the Drawing Room look better now it is no longer the fashion to crowd things so. I think we can abolish that awful Billiard table and make a nicer room of that.[153]

As it turned out, Codman's work at Lincoln from 1897 to 1900 involved far more than rearranging the furniture. Altering the architectural fabric of at least three rooms, he sought to erase his father's interventions at Lincoln while aligning the house—and himself—more closely with John Codman, the first in the family to reinvent a house not strictly his own.

Writing Dorothy and Hugh decades later, Codman claimed their Uncle Sturgis—and by extension, their father—had "tried to spoil Lincoln."[154] "I suppose that in 1862 no one thought anything old fashioned was nice at all," he continued, "[but] perhaps if he had left everything as it was I should never have been inspired with passion for putting things back as they were. But that has been a great pleasure to me." To return the house's upper bedrooms to their "original" state, Codman reinstalled their northern paneled walls and mantels in 1899. Using a historic drawing of the southwest bedroom as his guide, he created the impression that these interiors had never been touched—but as he had advocated in *The Decoration of Houses*, there was no harm in artistically rearranging the panels for greater visual power.[155]

By establishing 1800 as the historical end date for The Grange's "authentic" period of design, Codman marked more than just the centenary of John Codman's Lincoln makeover. For him and Wharton, 1800 represented the moment when aristocratic European design as a whole fell off an imaginary cliff (not one of their book's fifty-six plates illustrates an interior or object later than the 1790s). For Codman, too, this date had genealogical implications. His vast New England obituary collection screeches to a halt at 1800, after which date he believed families' bloodlines were as compromised as their decoration schemes. Given his fondness for "Bad" Uncle Richard, moreover, it is also no coincidence that 1800 marked the final year his ancestor enjoyed his ill-gotten string of French châteaux. After Richard's fall from grace, it must have seemed to Codman, the family lost a good measure of its brilliance.

For interior furnishings at The Grange Codman turned to the eighteenth century, as well. Chippendale chairs, French *bombé* chests, and a reproduction of Reverend John Codman IV's cane-back sofa, circa 1800, were all the order of the day. His father's billiard table was out. He even banished his once-beloved William Morris furnishings, replacing

2.10
Paneled southeast parlor at the Codman Estate, as redecorated in the late 1890s. Photograph by David Bohl. Courtesy Historic New England.

his bedroom wallpaper with an eighteenth-century French moiré design and removing the Morris curtains in the southeast parlor. In this room, the only one in the house to have retained its original colonial paneling, he introduced Louis XVI–style furniture upholstered in eighteenth-century patterns of *toile de jouy* fabric. By freely mixing colonial, English, and eighteenth-century French modes at The Grange—all circa 1800—Codman successfully integrated the tastes of John and Richard Codman.

The designer evoked his family's past in The Grange's landscape, as well. In 1900 he and his mother created a formal Italian Garden to the west of the house, whose pergola terminated in a "ruin" that evoked the Great Boston Fire—and by extension the family's expulsion from Lincoln. This so-called Exchange End of the garden featured salvaged columns from the Merchant's Exchange (1841), a building once part of the Codman portfolio and lost in the 1872 fire.[156] Constituting their own romantic nod to the past were the chestnut and mulberry trees John Codman had planted, specimens of which his great-grandson carefully documented in these years. Pasting a photograph of one ancestral tree in his family album, Codman labeled the image "stump and last branch of grandfather's mulberry"—an entry that erased a full generation.[157]

Codman capped this intense period of "restoration" in 1900 with a full suite of measured drawings, each showing the house as he believed it had appeared in John Codman's day. Erasing Sturgis's additions while retaining the name "The Grange, Seat of Ogden Codman" (notably without any suffix), he collapsed the house's two most significant earlier periods beneath his own drafting pen.

What should have represented springtime for The Grange felt for some of the Codmans like the sealing of a tomb. During the family's first stay in Dinard, Codman suggested to Sarah that she was "afraid to go to Lincoln . . . for fear of being stuck there."[158] In 1895 he returned to the theme, confessing "tho' I like Lincoln very much it is very sad there and I should hate to have to stay there always."[159] The house had brushed up against the funereal before (indeed, its very name traced back to a condolence letter), yet Lincoln's late-nineteenth-century melancholy suggests the stoppage of time itself. By turning back the clock to his great-grandfather's era Codman had halted the house's—and his family's—forward progress. Indeed, as if to symbolize this state of arrest, Tom's 1897 portrait of fourteen-year-old Dorothy, newly returned from Dinard, presents her in a hairstyle and gown from the mid-nineteenth century (her garment likely borrowed from Sarah's closet).[160] By collapsing his mother and sister's generations in this image—it was the last portrait he ever made of Dorothy—Tom consigned her to the past as surely as his brother relegated The Grange to the limbo of "circa 1800." The Codmans were a family both running out of time and standing outside of it.

2.11
Fourteen-year-old Dorothy Codman in a vintage gown (ca. 1897). Photograph by Thomas Newbold Codman. Codman Family Papers, courtesy Historic New England.

However frozen Codman's family and home might have become, his career in this period was moving dynamically forward. Now working from a New York City office, he was in high demand as an interior decorator—and, increasingly, the sole architect—for wealthy clients up and down the eastern seaboard, earning an average of $10,000 a year in the early 1900s (and in 1907 earning a peak salary of nearly $25,000).[161] Conservative and carefully studied, his work combined colonial American and eighteenth-century French sources, reconciling his passions for Yankee simplicity and the grandeur of the ancien régime. Though they are often praised for their "timeless" appeal, his designs represent quite a specific time, place, and point of view. The last gasp of the Gilded Age, these interiors flattered clients with a borrowed pedigree; designed to appear out of date from the moment they were built, these fanciful stage sets artfully disguised any use of modern materials or technologies.

Not all of Codman's contemporaries respected his work. Despite the success of *The Decoration of Houses* and the numerous high-profile commissions Codman had executed, architect Charles McKim warned Codman in 1897 that, while he would gladly sponsor the designer for membership in the American Institute of Architects, "interior decoration alone" would likely sink his nomination.[162] Some critics perceived in Codman's work a dangerous reflection of his own presumed effeminacy. In 1905, *Architectural Record* claimed the designer "gained variety at the expense of virility"—whereas Henry James declared, upon seeing the New York City apartment Codman designed for Wharton, that its rooms were "a bonbonnière of the last daintiness, naturally."[163] It is unlikely these barbs would have bothered the cocksure Codman. "I should never dream of caring what *the world* thought of anything I said or did," he once wrote Sarah, "unless it affected my pocket or prevented me from getting something I wanted."[164]

Codman's visual bravado in this period now extended to his own person. A paragon of dandified Edwardian fashion, he wrote the following runaway monologue to Little from London:

> You would scarcely recognize me now I am so smart. Single eye glass Boutonnière, grey or brown linen waistcoat varnished boots, top hat and cutaway coat or frock [coat] grey or black very smartest gloves everything from the swellest London people. I constantly see myself in the glass and wonder who it is, pink blue or mauve shirts butterfly ties etc. do make a difference—my moustach [*sic*] is curled like this [inserted sketch] the ends get nearly in my eyes.[165]

In 1903 Codman proposed another kind of makeover—an ambitious plan that would have dramatically altered The Grange's scale and rendered its authentic Georgian elements virtually unrecognizable. Referencing eighteenth-century houses even grander than John Codman's version of the family home—Boston's Shirley-Eustis House (1751) provided one of the models for this 1903 scheme—Codman repeated his great-grandfather's strategy of covering the home in retroactive glory. Proposing to raise the home's rear ell to a full third story, Codman imagined a monumental new eastern façade that would face a reoriented drive (thereby reducing the home's southern façade, its principal entrance since Chambers Russell's day, to the status of a side porch). Punctuated by two-story pilasters and a sweeping second-floor balcony, this commanding new façade would have sacrificed the home's historic integrity for a fanciful exaggeration of colonial style. (As Codman once confessed, he found most colonial houses "not architectural enough . . . to give me pleasure.")[166] Such a dramatic expansion of the house, of course, bore no relationship to the family's needs—or pocketbook. Rather, the scheme suggests a monument to the *idea* of the Codman family.

Had Codman carried out this plan, his mark upon the home would have eclipsed that of his great-grandfather—and certainly it would have removed all traces of his father. Ogden Sr. was in 1903 still alive, if now institutionalized at the McLean Hospital for the Mentally Ill in nearby Belmont, Massachusetts.[167] The circumstances of his health at this date are unclear, yet by 1902 it appears Alice had returned Sarah's ailing husband to her; Sarah, in turn, had committed him to McLean. It is perhaps no coincidence that Codman's grandest plan yet for The Grange should have materialized as his father entered his final decline. (Indeed, throughout Codman's life his relatives' imminent deaths often placed him in an anticipatory mood.) Yet by the time Ogden Sr. died in October 1904—a special Pullman car brought him home to Lincoln, where he lingered for days in a morphine-induced coma—his son's scheme for Lincoln's transformation, too, had been put to rest.[168] It was not his father's death that ended the plan, however, but an event that had taken place several weeks before: Codman's marriage to Leila Griswold Webb.

In 1897, the thirty-four-year-old Codman confessed to his mother, "I really think it would take a gigantic fortune to tempt me to marry now."[169] It was for this principal reason—if not, perhaps, due to her fortune alone—that he found Leila Webb irresistible. The forty-eight-year-old widow of railroad magnate Henry Walter Webb, Leila was seven years Codman's senior when they married and the mother of two teenage sons. Earlier that year Codman had built and decorated her home at 15 East 51st Street, yet no surviving letters from 1904 indicate their relationship had progressed beyond that of architect and client. When the pair announced their engagement just two days before their

2.12
Codman's proposed enlargement of The Grange (1903). Watercolor by W. F. Protz (16 1/2" x 24" sheet). Codman Family Papers, courtesy Historic New England.

October 8 wedding, press coverage was more sensational than congratulatory. Beneath the headline "Mrs. H. W. Webb Will Wed Again Saturday," the *New York Press* offered, "Her Social Friends Will Be Astonished to Hear of the Betrothal" (an observation the *New York Herald* echoed more tersely: "Society Genuinely Surprised").[170] Nor was interest limited to the couple's seemingly mismatched social rank. Describing Codman's New York City apartment as "a gathering place for persons well known in the artistic world," the *Press* added that Codman "was looked upon as a confirmed bachelor, and the sudden announcement will come as a surprise."[171]

From its start the marriage appears to have been a success, and not simply given the millions Leila inherited from her late husband. Writing Tom soon after the wedding, Codman offered that Leila cured "the feeling of loneliness that used to haunt me. . . . We have done everything together all day and every day—and I have enjoyed each moment."[172] Even in his first letter to Sarah after his father's death—the news had come two weeks into his honeymoon—Codman framed his tone-deaf condolences by speaking of his new life with Leila. "I cannot think I shall never see Père Cot at Lincoln again," he began, adding, "I was looking forward so much to showing him our new house."[173] (In another aside that must have stung, he mused, "Poor Aunt Alice what will become of her, you have us all to care for you but now she has no one.") He ended by telling her that Leila "seems to enjoy all our shopping as much as I do, we do too much however and both are rather tired." For Codman, the couple's shared interests in beautiful objects, travel, and sightseeing—all of which kept his chronic loneliness at bay—were enough to build a happy life together.

Over the course of their marriage the couple divided their time between New York City and France. In 1908, they took a Paris apartment at 60 rue de Varennes—Codman kept it for the next twenty-five years—and the following summer they rented the Château de Corbeil-Cerf outside the city. Codman's professional interest in the history of French châteaux, along with his fascination for Richard Codman's eighteenth-century holdings, led him in 1907 to begin *A Catalogue Raisonné of French Châteaux*—a sprawling project that eventually filled four hundred notebooks. Leila partnered enthusiastically in the catalogue, just as she shared in Codman's professional work by entertaining clients and providing a second pair of eyes with purveyors. The two remained inseparable on both sides of the

2.13
[Artist unknown], *Ogden Codman, Jr.* and *Leila Griswold Webb Codman* (both ca. 1904–1910). Oil on canvas (9" x 9 1/8" x 1 ½" each). Bequest of Dorothy S.F.M. Codman, 1969.874 and 1969.875. Courtesy Historic New England.

Atlantic (Codman once told Sarah in 1908, "I hate New York without her") until Leila's unexpected death, in January 1910, from surgical complications.[174]

Codman was devastated by her loss. ("What shall I do without my Darling," he wrote Tom, "It has all been like some dreadful nightmare.")[175] Predictably, Codman refracted his grief through the lens of his own pursuits. "I have been thinking over all sorts of plans for the future," he wrote Tom:

> I want so much to continue my work on the French châteaux she cared so much about it and [it] gave me such splendid opportunities. No one of course will ever care for it as she did and I shall long for her tender enthusiasm and sympathy very often.[176]

In the period following Leila's death, Codman's intense periods of loneliness returned ("Oh God that she could be here with us once more . . . I am terrified at being so alone"), but that summer at Corbeil-Cerf he cheered himself up with a new Rolls Royce and a proposed menagerie. "I am getting a *dog*!! (to me) [a] wild undertaking," he wrote Tom; "I am also thinking of a cat, a parrot, or a cockatoo! And some white rabbits! This will tend to gay up the place."[177] In response to Tom's invitation to Lincoln, he wrote, "I should love to be at Lincoln . . . and should no doubt be happy there, but I have been so happy motoring and working and playing in France in summer at Corbeil-Cerf and elsewhere that I could not give it all up and go back to my life as it was before I married Leila."[178]

There would be no returning to Lincoln, despite Sarah's insistence that Codman rejoin her brood—a strike for independence that would "doubtless appear to Mère Cot . . . revolutionary," he confided to Tom. Because Leila had left Codman the entirety of her estate, with the remainder to go to her sons upon his death (he would survive them both), her fortune provided him a measure of unprecedented control. The 1910s found him taking on fewer clients, spending longer periods in France, and diving ever more deeply into his beloved genealogies and châteaux research. Nor was he entirely alone. Starting the year before Leila's death, Codman hired a succession of young male secretaries—the last of whom, Francis White, remained with him from 1931 until Codman's death twenty years later. These men managed Codman's correspondence and social affairs, ran his various properties, and served as companions, often remaining close to Codman long after they left his employment. (One of his secretaries from this period, Robert Tritton, married even more advantageously than his former boss—and gave Codman one of his last major commissions in the 1930s.) Writing Sarah the summer after Leila's death, Codman told her about the arrival of "Chuffy" Sampson, a "great comfort, and a pleasant companion. He does not antagonize me as a cleverer person might."[179] Assuring his mother, "I think you will all like him," he added, "and if you don't you can blame yourselves for leaving me alone."

In truth, it was Codman who had left his family alone. In his absence his siblings had fallen ever more powerfully under Sarah's control. Not only did she continue to hold the purse strings at Lincoln, providing her adult children with allowances, but she was determined to restrict their avocations to Lincoln. Tom, once a promising portrait photographer, now primarily turned his camera on the young men who bathed in Lincoln's local swimming holes; a talented artist in her own right, and once the most well-traveled of the family, Ahla turned to painting scenes no further afield than the family property. When Sarah banned Hugh from accepting a violinist seat with the Boston Symphony Orchestra he became a ham radio enthusiast, communicating with the outside world almost exclusively from his boyhood bedroom. As for Dorothy—the youngest and least worldly of all the siblings—Sarah gave her a garden plot to tend near the carriage house. As late as end of the 1930s the Codmans' seemingly immortal nanny from Dinard, Bino, continued to attend the siblings.

The 1920s ushered in a particularly dark period for the inmates of Lincoln. After Dorothy suffered a nervous breakdown in 1920, Sarah committed her to a private mental treatment facility in Marblehead. Writing her mother in January 1921, the thirty-seven-year-old Dorothy demonstrated the power Sarah held over her behavior—and liberty:

> I could stand it a year if necessary, but I *would* like to have some idea of how long it is likely to be. And it certainly has done me good, for I see what a devil I am, and I wonder how you could have put up with me so long. . . . When I came here I thought *all* my nerves were on edge, but now I know it was only *some* of them! . . . I confess I'm crazy to go home! I've learned to appreciate home and the family, to see quite a number of my own faults, to think I'd rather live with my own people than away from them.[180]

Dorothy remained institutionalized in Marblehead, and subsequently in a Vermont clinic, for more than a year. When at last she returned to Lincoln, in the spring of 1922, her mother's health was in marked decline. Sarah died on June 25. Returning for her funeral, Codman found Ahla confined to her upstairs bedroom with an unnamed illness—a condition that had dragged on for years, treated with increasingly stronger doses of the barbiturate Veronal.[181] The family eventually committed Ahla to McLean, where she died at fifty-seven in November 1923. Looking back on this period Codman observed to Tom, "what bad luck poor Lincoln seems to have for you all."[182]

UNCLE RICHARD, REDUX

By the time of Sarah and Ahla's deaths, Codman had settled more or less permanently in France. Though he pined for Lincoln's historical context ("as poor Mère Cot used to feel the links with the past," he confided to Tom, "so am I beginning to feel"), he also felt relieved to be separated from "the sad and dreary memories" he associated with the house.[183] Years into his expatriate life, Codman admitted that the family home had *never* brought him joy. "[The Grange] is a lovely place," he wrote Tom in 1934, "[and] one should be able to be very happy there, but somehow I never was."[184] By this time, of course, the house was not much more than a figment for Codman. It was only Hugh, Tom, and Dorothy who experienced the day-to-day melancholy of the place.

When he closed his New York City office in 1920, Codman effectively ended his career as a professional designer—yet continued to decorate The Grange from across an ocean. His letters to Lincoln in the 1920s are filled with detailed instructions to his siblings regarding paint finishes, curtains, floor waxing, upholstery, and the placement of furniture and prints—along with exhortations to "reclaim" family pieces from estate sales, including works that had never belonged to The Grange (whose overfurnished rooms began to resemble an estate sale themselves). When in 1923 Dorothy and Hugh bought a *pied-à-terre* in Boston, a strike for independence made possible by Sarah's death, Codman directed its decoration just as insistently. If the siblings were given too free a rein at 5 Marlborough Street, he believed, Boston might endanger their ability to "remain faithful to Lincoln."[185]

To ensure his directives were dutifully carried out, and also to restrict heirlooms from migrating to Marlborough Street, Codman frequently demanded "kodaks" of the interiors at The Grange. The images his siblings sent him, devoid of human figures and often inexpertly shot, project a haunting quality. In these empty interiors, scholar Ellie Reichlin has noted, we see "the family's truest portraits," an assemblage of objects standing proxy for the offstage Codmans.[186] These documents allowed Codman to recall multiple generations' worth of family members' possessions, and only by extension the men and women themselves. (In one letter to Dorothy he traced the decades-long history of a set of fruit knives, a recitation that included every portrait of the knives' owners.)[187] In some instances, Codman's memories of his family's homes defy historical logic. Speaking of his grandparents' house at 34 Beacon Street, for example, he could describe its layout from periods well before his birth—and once explained he couldn't fully recall certain furnishings at Lincoln without first recalling where they had stood at 29 Chestnut Street, a home he had never known.[188]

In the early 1920s, likely after Sarah died, the family decided to transfer The Grange to SPNEA upon the death of the last sibling. The idea likely originated with Codman, who was friendly with SPNEA's director William Sumner Appleton, although the men's initial discussion might only have been spoken (the earliest documentary evidence for the SPNEA plan appears in Ahla's 1923 will, which confirms her agreement to the plan).[189] The donation made sense from a practical standpoint because this branch of the Codman family had no heirs, but in a deeper way it served as an emotional stopgap to the family's litany of losses. (These included the disappearance of John Codman's last mulberry tree; long propped up on the house's second terrace, it came down the year of Sarah's death.)[190]

Codman's thoughts about the scheme may be gleaned from a 1937 comment to his cousin, Martha Codman Karolik. Advising her to turn her Codman-designed Washington, DC, home into a house museum rather than donating its contents to Boston's Museum of Fine Arts, he explained: "Museums like the one in Boston are quite passés, and seem to me *mere cemeteries* for beautiful furniture and objets d'art that were created to embellish private houses."[191] By donating The Grange (or the Codman Estate, as it would be known) to SPNEA, Codman could not only preserve the original context of its contents but also arrest the period in which he had the greatest control over its appearance—a factor that may explain the urgency of his decorating-by-remote.

For the first half of the 1920s Codman led an expatriate life of little substance, if one accompanied by glamorous surroundings and company. He spent his days, and sometimes entire nights, playing Mahjong with a circle of older women that included Consuelo Vanderbilt Balsan, her mother Alva Belmont, and Lady Orr-Lewis. He occasionally still saw Wharton, as well, who had moved permanently to France in 1911; the pair's tumultuous, on-again-off-again friendship had by 1920 settled into a friendly détente that lasted until her 1937 death. In 1924 Codman exchanged Corbeil-Cerf for the Château de Péthagny in Calvados, France, an eighteen-bedroom home he airily described to Tom as "pleasant but not grand."[192] His frequent letters to Lincoln, when not filled with lectures about glazed chintz or petit point, contain a great deal of grousing about money and its lack. (Hoping to outfit Péthagny in his own style, Codman wrote his siblings, "now I have bought a Hispano-Suiza there is no money to spend on unnecessary luxuries, so the curtains, chandeliers, and lots of other things will have to wait.")[193]

If Codman had spent his earlier life attempting to live up to the legacy of John Codman—stewarding Lincoln's legacy by reimagining its past—then in his final decades he seemed determined to live down to the example of his "Bad" Uncle Richard. After years of scheduled payments, in 1918 he at last acquired Richard's Copley portrait from his Uncle Dick. (As Codman explained to Ahla, their grandfather Charles Russell Codman had named Dick for his scandalous uncle only on the condition that his aunt, Parnell Codman Savage, would leave his son the portrait.)[194] Paying his uncle the considerable sum of $4,000 for the painting—the equivalent of about $80,000 today—he hung the portrait center stage at his New York City townhouse. "Uncle Richard's portrait by Copley is a great improvement to my library," he crowed to Dorothy in 1919; "I think it a very splendid picture myself."[195] When he sailed to France in 1920 he left behind nearly all his New York furnishings—including Leila's portrait—but insisted on bringing the Copley. As Oliver Wendell Holmes Sr. once declared, a "family portrait . . . of one's great merchant-uncle, by Copley," was an essential badge of the Boston "man of Family"—and certainly this is how Richard's image functioned for him.[196] But as the sole ancestral representative in Codman's home, Richard was not a particularly good chaperone.

In France Codman was drawn to any place associated with Richard, particularly the châteaux his great-great uncle had briefly owned. Years before he initiated his châteaux cataloguing project—and indeed, likely inspiring its creation—Codman made pilgrimages to these sites, beginning in 1894 with the Château de la Thuilerie at Dammartin. He brought Leila back to Dammartin on their honeymoon, and in 1908 they leased their rue de Varennes apartment partly due to its proximity to Richard's Hôtel de Créqui. Speaking as if he had personally known his ancestor, Codman wrote Sarah that simply seeing Créqui made him feel "much at home."[197]

In 1919 he began transcribing Richard's letters from the 1790s while creating a standalone study of his French homes (a document that included several properties Richard had never owned). Between 1923 and 1925 Codman made several attempts to purchase the Château de la Thuilerie, despite the fact that (as he wrote Tom) "the house has lost all its looks" along with the "jardin anglais" Richard had created.[198] How Codman could have understood the home's appearance under Richard's ownership is a mystery— Richard's communications with John had been necessarily vague—but it was typical of him to channel Richard in this way, and even to defend his reputation (in 1906 Codman claimed to have discovered documents exonerating Richard for the firm's financial losses in France).[199] Codman's archival investigations increasingly blurred the distinction between his ancestor's era and his own. In writing to Lincoln he sometimes enclosed eighteenth-century letters along with his own; and in describing his new secretary Francis White to Tom, he claimed White was "a very nice boy . . . like the young men of Uncle Richard's day."[200]

Unable to secure one of his ancestor's properties, in 1926 Codman purchased the seventeenth-century Château de Grégy at Brie-Comte-Robert. Grégy was in some respects a French equivalent to The Grange. A stylish country home about as far from Paris as

Lincoln lies from Boston, the château had received its own substantial makeover in the eighteenth century—a period that ended less happily in France than in Massachusetts (as Codman enjoyed pointing out, its tenant in the 1790s was guillotined the month of Richard's arrival in Paris).[201] When Codman completed his own renovation of the château the following year, "restoring" its eighteenth-century appearance just as he had at Lincoln, he reserved its grandest room as a shrine to his ancestor's portrait.

In May 1926, Codman installed the Copley painting in Grégy's Grand Salon.[202] Initially it constituted the *only* work of art in the room, flanked by two mirrors and facing a third above the opposing fireplace. Codman had often used mirrors to create illusionistic space within his rooms—in *The Decoration of Houses* he and Wharton wrote that opposing mirrors created "an air of unreality"—yet in this instance the illusion was as historical as it was spatial.[203] If Codman were seated on the couch below Richard's portrait, the mirror opposite him would frame the pair together; and if he stood at the mantel, he would appear in the mirror as if grafted onto the Copley painting. For a man of Codman's enormous self-regard—and also one who greatly admired male beauty, whether in art or life—this arrangement would have had a powerful effect. As Codman's great-great-uncle James Russell once said about his father's Copley portrait:

2.14
Château de Grégy (ca. 1620), Villefranche-sur-mer, France, seen in 1927. Codman Family Papers, courtesy Historic New England.

I think sometimes I can almost see the lips move. They are the last thing I look at at night and the first things I look at in the morning. . . . It is impossible to describe the satisfaction and comfort.[204]

As if to frame this familial consummation at Grégy, Codman wallpapered the Grand Salon in a chintz pattern recalling one from his grandparents' Beacon Street home—the site of his birth—and lined its windows with curtains taken from his paternal grandfather's house at 29 Chestnut Street.[205] On the adjoining wall to Richard's portrait Codman installed an ancestral mantel from the May family, a hard-won relic from his Aunt Alice's estate. And yet for all these trappings, assembled in a home "not 100 kilometers from [Richard's] own Château de la Thuilerie," as Codman marveled, he insisted to Tom that he loved Grégy precisely because it had "no associations with the past to sadden me."[206] He could never banish the past from Lincoln, but at Grégy he could reshape it to his own design.

If Richard's portrait at first bestowed a blessing upon Codman's expatriate life, then it soon summoned a family curse. Within three years of the portrait's installation at Grégy, Codman embarked on a project that uncannily recalled—and even surpassed—Richard's ruinous real estate ventures of the 1790s. Since 1920, Codman had annually rented a summer villa in Cannes, the Villa Francesca, but by the end of the decade he decided to construct his own home there. Not content with mere bachelor lodgings, he aimed to create nothing less than the grandest palace ever built on the Riviera—a project funded largely by his inheritance from Leila, whose estate still remained theoretically in trust for her surviving son. The eighteen-acre property he purchased in February 1929, situated in Villefranche-sur-mer, had once belonged to King Léopold II of Belgium. Between 1929 and 1931 Codman crowned this steep hillside property with a sprawling, neo-Palladian palace along its crest. In a nod to the site's erstwhile royal ownership, he christened the home "La Villa La Léopolda."

A colossal, forty-five-room structure spread over two grand terraces, La Léopolda integrates the exterior elevations of no less than three historic villas: the Château Borély (1778) in Marseille, the Villa Belgiojoso Bonaparte (1796) in Milan, and the Villa Melzi (1808) on Lake Como (the last two designed by the same Swiss-Italian architect, Giocondo Albertolli).[207] For the first floor of his villa Codman created a regal suite of "Gala Rooms," including a dining room, library, *Salon de Famille*, and "Italian Ball-room" (in a later prospectus for the house, Codman called this series of spaces "an endless vista of immense decorative value").[208] Describing the ballroom to Wharton, he claimed that it represented "the most magnificent room to decorate of my architectural career."[209] A thirty-foot cube rising two stories at the center of the house, it was lined with "Turkish Blue" imitation marble, trimmed in bright yellow and violet stone, and lined with mirrors.

In its garish ornamentation, the ballroom constituted a kind of Continental antipode to Lincoln's southeast parlor (see figure 2.10, p. 64), the room Codman once considered his North Star of good taste. La Léopolda's magnificence painfully clashed, as well, with contemporary European design—whose postwar practitioners condemned such bombast as visually and morally bankrupt (consider the home's exact French contemporary, LeCorbusier's minimalist masterpiece the Villa Savoye). To paraphrase Wharton's damnation of the Vanderbilts, Codman's last and grandest design revealed him entrenched in a *thermopylae* of Gilded Age excess from which no force on earth could dislodge him.

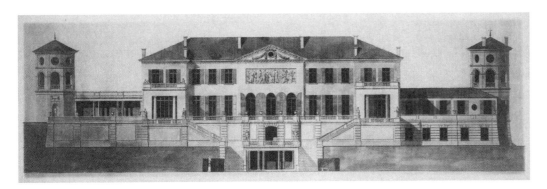

2.15
ABOVE: Ogden
Codman Jr., La
Léopolda, rear
elevation drawing
(1929).
BELOW: La
Léopolda's "Italian
Ball-room." Codman
Family Papers, courtesy
Historic New England
(both images).

2.16

Ronny Haddow
(left) and Codman in
Cannes, France
(ca. 1929). Detail.
Codman Family Papers,
courtesy Historic New
England.

For a single man who rarely entertained, the scale of La Léopolda and its regal elaboration defy rational explanation. (As *The Decoration of Houses* insists, a grand ballroom is "never meant to be seen except when crowded.")[210] For Codman, however, La Léopolda appears to have functioned purely as a dream space. Speaking of the project to Tom, he sighed, "I shall have a place so beautiful that it seems like a fairy tale, and I feel somehow it cannot be true"; similarly, he described the grounds as "make-believe" spaces.[211] His entire career had been founded upon such stagecraft, yet at La Léopolda he enacted Richard's particular fantasy: the New Englander who wakes up to find himself a French count. Indeed, as if to perfect the illusion of a generational pedigree at La Léopolda, Codman purposely mismatched Louis XVI and Louis XV styles in his bedroom suite. Explaining in his later prospectus for the house that "the changes made by successive owners [have] result[ed] in unexpected harmonies" between differing periods, he implied he was simply the home's most recent—rather than its only—owner.[212]

Construction at La Léopolda had been underway for just a few months when the Wall Street Crash of 1929 occurred. Writing Tom eleven days after Black Monday, Codman did not initially appear worried about his assets. "My stocks shrunk about a million dollars," he explained, "but there [are] still about four millions left, and it will not affect my income at present."[213] What he could not see coming was the market's continued slide (within days of his letter, the Dow lost almost half its worth), nor did he foresee that Roosevelt would take the United States off the gold standard in 1933—a move that instantly reduced his income by more than 40 percent.[214] Even without these losses, it must be said, La Léopolda's final costs of over $800,000— the equivalent of about $13 million today—consumed nearly a quarter of his original capital assets. Most of the remainder was now frozen in real estate.

As late as the following spring Codman was more worried about mismanagement by his contractors, a situation he believed his secretary-companion, Ronny Haddow, had created. In outlining the situation for Tom, Codman revealed that Haddow had been the principal driver behind the project from the start; "it is curious," he wrote, "that his persuading me to buy this place should be his undoing."[215] Alarmed by their rift, Tom advised, "I do hope you won't be too hasty with him . . . you have been so long intimate," but in the end Codman banished Haddow from Cannes.[216] ("Ronny clung to me like a limpet," he told Tom, "and I finally had to get my lawyer to get rid of him.")[217] In Codman's litany of complaints about Haddow's bottomless sense of want—hotel rooms, a fine wardrobe, a sportscar, and ultimately a palace on the Riviera—we see the designer himself rather uncannily reflected. Codman admitted he would miss the young man.

Haddow's intended room at la Léopolda, nestled within the so-called Bachelor Wing—a lavish suite of rooms occupying nearly half the second floor—would now stand empty. So, too, would Codman's own bedroom. By the time of La Léopolda's completion in 1931, Codman's financial outlook had considerably worsened. He wrote Tom in anguish:

> It is too awful here, although the house is faraway better than I expected, but I have tied too much money in it, and shall have to sell it and Grégy too I fear. . . . Most of the villas here are closed, everyone has cut down to the bone. There is no one anywhere, all the hotels are empty. All my shares are steadily going down; it looks as if I should have to take the job of caretaker at Lincoln for next winter.[218]

Faced with the prospect of losing La Léopolda before he even moved in—and perhaps Grégy as well—Codman moaned, "it is like poor Uncle Richard all over again." Ultimately he managed to hold onto Grégy, and intermittently to find renters for La Léopolda. At first living in the "Villino," a small home on the La Léopolda property, Codman was by 1934 forced to rent even this space and relocate to "the tiny house on the road leading from my lower gate," as he wrote Wharton.[219] "I shall have to content myself with having created, but not finished a work of art," he continued; "fools build houses for wise men to live in (though sometimes it is the other way round)."

What, in the end, are we to make of La Léopolda? The villa is often held up as a Master Class drawn directly from the pages of *The Decoration of Houses*: its proportions, historical sourcing, materials, and spatial arrangements represent the very consummation of Codman and Wharton's philosophy. Yet the home also reflects their approach in another, more profound way—for when they wrote that "any *trompe l'oeil* is permissible . . . if it gives an impression of pleasure," they seem to foreshadow Codman's masterwork on the Riviera.[220] La Léopolda fools the eye in every inch of its dazzling surfaces. There is no family in the *Salon de Famille*, no ball in the ballroom, and no bachelor in the Bachelor Wing. It is a monument to wealth resting upon an empty bank account.

Ultimately more fable than fairy tale, La Léopolda stands like a warning about the limits of desire itself—not just Codman's need to please a handsome young man, but his wish to demonstrate he had at last vanquished the humiliation of Dinard. Fables end with punishments, and it was Codman's fate to gaze upon La Léopolda without crossing its threshold. This he did from the windows of the Villino or by gazing into the stereoscopic photographs he commissioned of his villa—images that cast the illusion of a three-dimensional space small enough to hold in his hands.[221]

In 1934, Codman admitted to Tom that, although now forced to economize, he was "glad I have not many years to face doing it."[222] He would live another seventeen years. The end of his life was marked by profound loneliness; aside from Tom's occasional visits he appeared to see no one, and frequently complained of his isolation. Now living primarily at Grégy he spent his days and nights in the company of the dead—poring endlessly over his genealogy notebooks—while sustaining himself on a steady diet of chocolates. (It is something of a Codman family legend that Codman missed the entire Second World War engrossed in his research. In truth, Grégy was occupied by German troops who confined him to his bedroom.)[223]

Tom's letters to the family in Lincoln, written during a series of trips to Grégy in the mid- to late 1940s, paint the portrait of his brother's long and painful decline. Codman is toothless, incontinent, howling for chocolates, and—perhaps most tragic of all for this inveterate cataloguer—robbed of his memory. (In 1947, Tom wrote Hugh and Dorothy that their brother had become "impossible and quite gaga.")[224] By this date Codman had lost Richard, as well. Fearing the death duties that would be levied against his estate, he asked Tom in August 1946 to bring the Copley portrait "home" to Lincoln, where it hung for the first time—to a now-diminished audience of Codmans. (Less than a month after the painting's transfer, Hugh died in the children's former nursery.)[225]

Codman lay mostly bedridden for his last five years at Grégy, tended by his secretary Francis White. He died at the château on January 8, 1951, missing his eighty-eighth birthday by eleven days. For a man who spent a lifetime collecting genealogies and death records, assiduously connecting family lines across generations, Codman's French death certificate is shockingly spare. Under the line "known relatives or friends," White's name appears alone.[226]

The subsequent sale of Grégy and La Léopolda proved insufficient to cover the debts held against Codman's estate, and so Dorothy lost 5 Marlborough Street—and with it, her independence from Lincoln. Two years after her return to Tom and the family home, in 1954, her brother was declared mentally incompetent; when Tom died nine years later she became The Grange's last and sole occupant. Mindful of preserving the home's principal rooms as a future museum, Dorothy lived her final years in the servant's ell at the rear of the house. A Codman to the last, she spent her days creating a series of inventories and biographical indexes. (Undoubtedly succumbing to some form of dementia herself, she appended one list with a legal question, asked of no one in particular: "Where to sign, as unmarried [?]")[227] Like her family before her, too, she collected: shells, blank postcards, and, toward the end of her life, boxloads of "Dennis the Menace" cartoons carefully cut from each morning's newspaper.

When SPNEA acquired the property after Dorothy's death in 1968, the organization initially planned to preserve the home as it appeared when they first took ownership. Within a few years, however, the decision was made to turn back the home's "bell jar" moment to circa 1920.[228] Codman's departure for France, it turned out, had stopped The Grange's clock forever.

Copley's portraits of John and Richard Codman today hang in separate rooms at the Lincoln. Codman once envisioned his ancestors' portraits hung together as pendant works, writing Tom they might form the nucleus of a "Codman Room" at Boston's Museum of Fine Arts.[229] In effect, the two portraits transform the entire Codman Estate into a Codman Room—a constellation of objects standing as the sole proxy for, and primary legacy of, five generations. Presiding over this Memory Palace, the portraits embody the twinned tensions that shaped this family—a persistent double vision marked by homesickness and wanderlust, pride and insecurity, momentary pleasures and the comforts of the past. Nowhere is the symmetry Wharton and Codman promoted better illustrated than in the faces of these two men. Together, they form the very reflection of Ogden Codman Jr.

THREE

THE BARD OF BEACON STREET

The Proper Bostonian did not just happen; he was planned . . . to fit into
a social world so small that he could not help being well defined.[1]
—Cleveland Amory, *The Proper Bostonians* (1947)

A bachelor never quite gets over the idea that
he is a thing of beauty and a boy forever.[2]
—Helen Rowland, *A Guide to Men* (1922)

On a sunny March morning in 1936, a photographer at Miami's Roney Plaza Hotel
captured sixty-one-year-old Charles Hammond Gibson Jr.—published poet, lifelong
denizen of Beacon Street, and final scion of a storied Boston family—dressed to the
nines and conducting a flock of flamingoes. On the reverse of the photograph its subject
recorded for posterity, *Gibson—Flitting Among the Flamingoes + Peacocks.* (Discounting the
man himself, no peacocks appear in the image.) Snapped near the conclusion of Gibson's
"state visit" to the South, as he put it, the tableau fittingly illustrates what he and his inner

3.1
*Gibson – Flitting Among
the Flamingoes + Peacocks*
(March 1936). Gibson
House Museum,
Boston, MA.

circle only half-jokingly referred to as the nascent Gibson Movement of the 1930s.[3]

Gibson's turn as an Alpha Flamingo could have been lifted directly from Carl Van Vechten's jazz-age novel, *The Blind Bow-Boy* (1923). Speaking of his new love interest, the book's youthful Duke of Middlebottom describes the older man as "a silver flamingo . . . glowing, glamorous, shining—and strange, aloof; he d-d-d-does not mate with the rose flamingoes."[4] On the same day Gibson posed with his flock in Miami he received, himself, the adulation of a young male admirer. Thanking him for his picture and expressing regret at not finding Gibson at his hotel, despite repeated attempts, his fan wrote: "I will certainly be over in Boston and hope to see you."[5] Fame hungry and deeply insecure about his vanished youth—the last time Gibson had been the object of romantic pursuit had been the 1890s—the poet found himself in 1936 suddenly, almost magically, in demand as an author and personality. Contracted to read his sonnets and trade witty banter on radio broadcasts throughout that spring (programs with daffy titles like "The Gibson News Flash" and "The Gibby Gibby Gibby Bedtime Hour"), Gibson ignored the clownish nature of these spots as resolutely as he avoided his own reflection.[6]

That spring Gibson had every reason to flit. With the death of his mother the previous year he had assumed the role of paterfamilias—a familias that ended with him—and inherited his family's imposing townhouse in Boston's Back Bay. Only months after taking its ownership he hatched the scheme that consumed his remaining years: the transformation of his birthplace into a shrine to his literary career. Placing his home and himself under a virtual bell jar, Gibson declared to the *Boston Herald* in 1950 that he "died" sometime around 1940 (indeed, even during his triumphant 1936 tour, Gibson traveled with his own coffin and an "undertaker-in-ordinary"—his driver—as a precaution).[7] In the end he would live fourteen years beyond his self-proclaimed termination date, penning endless sonnets as remarkable for their poignancy as for the poverty and narcissism of their verse (such was the man's charm).

On Christmas Night 1944, he composed "The House of Gibson" for an audience of one:

> With all of them gone, I am so alone,
> I am like an old dog that has lost its bone.
> Like the last leaf on a family tree,
> Withered and worn, as you can see.
> Alas, for the head of the House of Gibson!
> (Vulgarians pronounce it Jibson)
> Alas, for a head, without any tail,
> That must live alone and its fate bewail!
> All Boston wails and must bemoan,
> The fate that he lives all sole alone.[8]

In truth, few Bostonians—vulgarian or otherwise—gave the man or his family much thought in 1944. By the time Gibson entered his seventies, both he and the once-fashionable district of Boston's Back Bay had devolved into an anachronistic symbol of Boston's fading "Brahmin" elite. To arrest this decline would require a performance more demanding, and far campier, than his Miami stunt.

OLD MONEY, NEW LAND

A string of deaths, and hopes for a marriage, led Catherine Hammond Gibson to build 137 Beacon Street in 1859. Twenty-one years earlier, she had lost her sugar merchant husband, John Gardiner Gibson, at sea. She buried her father six months later. For the next two decades Catherine and her two sons shared her widowed mother's grand, if crowded Beacon Hill home (dubbed the "elastic house" by family members for the number of relations living there).[9] When she reached her fifties, history cruelly repeated itself. In 1856 her eldest son, twenty-one-year-old John Gardiner Gibson Jr., died in a maritime accident—followed three years later by the death of her mother. With the financial freedom her inheritance granted her, Catherine determined to leave Beacon Hill for the "New Land"—as the Back Bay district was then known—and launch her surviving son, Charles Hammond Gibson (later Sr.), on the Boston marriage market. She was not the last in the family to feel its bloodlines slipping through her fingers, nor the only one to see in 137 Beacon Street the promise of immortality.

3.2
Edward Clarke Cabot: 137 Beacon Street (1859), Boston, MA. Courtesy John Woolf, Gibson House Museum, Boston, MA.

The New Land's six hundred acres had emerged from the muck of Boston's once-tidal Back Bay. Starting in 1857 this decades-long landfill project doubled the traditional boundaries of Boston while also stretching the limits of its social fabric. Old Boston families like Catherine's, whose networks of intermarried cousins criss-crossed the narrow streets of Beacon Hill, looked upon this new district with equal parts excitement and suspicion. Here rose perhaps *too* fashionable brownstones, built in the latest French and Renaissance Revival styles and boasting every modern convenience: indoor plumbing, built-in closets, high ceilings, service yards, and sophisticated ventilation systems. And yet like an olfactory symbol of the district's dubious novelty, Back Bay was also plagued until the 1880s by a powerful "Venetian odor"—a polite phrase resident William Dean Howells used to describe the area's chronic failures of sewage disposal.

Howells's celebrated novel *The Rise of Silas Lapham* (1885) chronicles Back Bay's physical and social upheavals through its title character, a household paint baron whose grandiose Beacon Street townhouse serves as a foil to the venerable, portrait-lined home of blueblood Bromfield Corey. Howells might have been telling a version of Catherine's story. Leaving behind the patrician milieu of her mother's house, she—like the fictional Lapham—was among the first to build south of Boston's Public Garden. Standing in a treeless, muddy landscape, 137 Beacon Street was in its first years virtually neighborless and surrounded on all sides by the havoc of construction. (Howells describes Back Bay in this period as a landscape of "blossomed weeds" in vacant lots, its air resounding with the sound of hammers by day and crickets by night.)[10] The startling newness of this district concealed its residents' veneration for the past. More so than in any other American city, Boston's social scale relied upon the faithful stewardship of ancestral ties, a totemic reverence for family crests, and the occasional infusion (sometimes at odds with these aims) of new sources of capital. Ensconced in the walnut-lined interiors of her new home, Catherine sought a daughter-in-law with the fortune of a Lapham and pedigree of a Corey.

From its beginning, 137 Beacon Street formed one half of two wholes. Fashionable architect Edward Clarke Cabot, designer of the new Boston Athenaeum (1847) and a distant cousin of the Gibsons, created 135 and 137 Beacon Street as twin structures. Catherine's nephew Samuel Hammond Russell built 135 Beacon—indeed, it was likely he who persuaded her to invest in the New Land. Though he lavished more money on his home's interior, Catherine proved the greater stage manager of the two. In a novel reorganization of the period's standard two-room entryway, she directed Cabot to create an undivided hall the full width of her house. Centered on a sweeping staircase and framed by three massive arches, the space suggested a home of far grander proportions than a typical Back Bay townhouse—an architectural maneuver fairly engineered to attract a suitable bride. Howells describes Lapham's home in similar terms. Determined to capture "the whole width" of the house for his first floor reception room, Lapham spurs one Boston matron to speculate the choice was made to benefit his unmarried daughters ("Aren't they ambitious," she sniffs).[11]

The other complement to 137 Beacon Street lay on Nahant, a peninsular near-island fifteen miles northeast of Boston. Here Cabot built Catherine a summer home even larger than her Back Bay townhouse, christened Forty Steps for the home's adjacent beach stairs. Constructed the same year as 137 Beacon Street, Forty Steps stood on older land. First established as a summer retreat in the early 1810s, Nahant featured regular

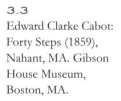

3.3
Edward Clarke Cabot:
Forty Steps (1859),
Nahant, MA. Gibson
House Museum,
Boston, MA.

steamship service from Boston by the end of the decade and a seasonal population that included Catherine's father, an early investor in the area. In 1827 one Nahant newspaper characterized the resort as nothing more than an extended Beacon Hill drawing room—and by the 1860s, the summer colony constituted a powerful distillation of both Beacon Hill *and* the emergent Back Bay.[12] As a consequence, when Boston elites shuttered their city homes from May to September Nahant received a "tidal wave . . . of young eligibles."[13] By building 137 Beacon and Forty Steps in tandem, then, Catherine extended the matrimonial hunting season over the entire calendar year. As it happened, her future daughter-in-law turned out to be the girl next door.

Rosamond Warren had always summered on Nahant—her father, Jonathan Mason Warren, owned the property next to Forty Steps—but given her youth she would not initially have struck Catherine as a prospective bride. (Around the time Catherine built 137 Beacon Street, her twenty-two-year-old son ushered at his cousin's wedding to Rosamond's older sister; junior bridesmaid Rosamond was then twelve.)[14] Though frequently thrown together in their small Boston circles, Charles and Rosamond did not announce their engagement until a full seven years after her 1864–1865 debut. They married in December 1871.

Catherine's patient plan for her son, then in his late thirties, succeeded beyond her own high expectations. Not only was Rosamond descended from a storied line—her great-great uncle, General Joseph Warren, was the hero of the Battle of Bunker Hill—but she was also connected by blood or marriage to nearly everyone in their Boston set, including the Crowninshield, Cabot, Mason, Quincy, Shaw, and Longfellow families. And as grand as the reception hall at 137 Beacon Street might have been, it was no match for the Warrens' home at 2 Park Street—a Beacon Hill landmark designed by Charles Bulfinch, complete with an ancestral Copley portrait over the mantel.[15] With her dynastic mission accomplished, Catherine ceded her third-floor bedroom at 137 Beacon Street to Rosamond and retreated to a smaller

3.4
The first generation at 137 Beacon Street. TOP: Catherine Hammond Gibson (1804–1888). MIDDLE: Charles Hammond Gibson Sr. (1836–1916). BOTTOM: Rosamond Warren Gibson (1846–1934). Gibson House Museum, Boston, MA.

suite upstairs. Over the next half-decade the nursery across the hall welcomed Mary Ethel Gibson, born in 1873; Charles Hammond Gibson Jr., born in 1874; and "little" Rosamond Gibson, born in 1877.

The arrival of Charles and Rosamond's only son, known for the entirety of his life as Charlie or even "Little Charlie," coincided with Back Bay's social triumph—and also the first signs of its decay. Christened in Richard Morris Hunt's magnificent new Trinity Church, its main sanctuary still under construction, Charlie entered a social milieu dominated by Boston's profoundly insular "Brahmin" class (a label Oliver Wendell Holmes Sr. coined in 1860). By the time of Charlie's birth much of patrician Beacon Hill had moved to Back Bay, and yet this is precisely the moment H. G. Wells later identified as the beginning of Boston's cultural stagnation:

> The capacity of Boston, it would seem, was just sufficient but no more than sufficient, to comprehend the whole achievement of the human intellect up, let us say, to the year 1875 A.D. Then an equilibrium was established. At or about that year Boston filled up.[16]

Eventually even Howells knew the jig was up. Moving to New York City in 1889, he claimed Boston's problem was not its absence of life but rather the city's congealed atmosphere of "death-in-life."[17]

Divided between Beacon Street and Nahant, Charlie's childhood was typical of his era and class: he attended a private schoolroom, lived in two fully staffed homes, and wore the clothing of a miniature adult. Shot through his early years, however, are the threads of his later eccentricity. From an early age he loved the artifice of theater. On Nahant he enthusiastically participated in *tableaux vivants*, plays, and musicales, often assuming the star roles of enchanted princes. (At fifteen, according to a visiting cousin, Charlie hammed it up as "a young lady very fond of dancing . . . too funny.")[18] Charlie showed an early interest in fashion, as well, reporting in a detailed letter to his mother that "Melle (Mary Ethel) is dressed in a grey suit with satin and plush trimming."[19] He was then seven.

Most pronounced of all was Charlie's love for home. This passion first attached to the colossal dollhouse he shared with his sisters at 137 Beacon Street. Rosamond's mother Annie Crowninshield Warren commissioned the work for her four daughters in 1852; designed by Salem cabinetmaker Israel Fellows, the four-storied structure stood six feet high and mirrored, however coincidentally, the layout and furnishings of Rosamond's later Beacon Street home.[20] In her privately published memoir, Rosamond relates that her children held the dollhouse "more or less sacred," furnishing a second cupboard for their dolls to live in while preserving the Fellows house as a place "where their dolls could make visits and have parties and weddings."[21] In his final years Charlie treated 137 Beacon Street with similar reverence.

When in 1887 Rosamond sent Charlie to St. Paul's School in Concord, New Hampshire, she worried about her twelve-year-old's excessive attachment to home. She confided the move was "a wrench for me, as [Charlie] was not very strong and had never been away."[22] When he returned two years later to resume his studies with a tutor, the house had entered a new—and, one might argue, final—era with the 1888 death of his grandmother Catherine.

Within a year of Charlie's return, and a respectful two years' distance from Catherine's funeral, Rosamond initiated a transformation of the home's interiors. Though she had made small interventions at the house since her arrival there—her family passed along a number of paintings and other works from 2 Park Street—her mother-in-law had closely controlled the arrangement of its interiors. The house was now Rosamond's to manage, and the flurry of changes she carried out indicate how eagerly she must have anticipated this moment. First turning her attention to the home's Stair Hall (as Catherine herself had), she papered the walls in a bold Aesthetic Movement pattern, a high-relief composition of gilded vines, flowers, and fruit meant to evoke seventeenth-century stamped leather. With this dramatic change she converted the space from a staid if elegant hall into one that reflected the latest fashion.

To assert her ascendancy even more emphatically in this space, whose very proportions had been designed to attract her lineage, she installed *The Pedigree of Warren*—a three-foot-high genealogical chart cataloguing twenty-nine generations of her family from a "Danish Knight" (said to be the great-great-great grandfather of William the Conqueror) to Rosamond's parents. Commissioned in 1878 and likely first hung at 2 Park Street, this extraordinary, fantasy-laden chronicle served as a kind of directory for all visitors to 137 Beacon Street. By the time of his inheritance in the 1930s, Charlie considered it the very founding document of his family. (As the writer Wallace Stegner once noted, "gentility is inherited through the female line like hemophilia, and is all but incurable.")[23]

3.5
Stair Hall at 137 Beacon Street. Courtesy Mary Prince, Gibson House Museum, Boston, MA.

Just as Charlie's birth coincided with Boston's "equilibrium" moment, Rosamond's renewal of 137 Beacon Street occurred at a time when, in the words of historian Bainbridge Bunting, the city "began to rest on her oars," retreating into a long era of nostalgic resistance to change.[24] Driving this conservatism was Boston's slowing economy, characterized by stalled industrial production, shrinking development, and a social elite whose fortunes lay primarily tied up in trusts. Brahmins viewed growth itself with suspicion. Beyond this attitudinal shift (one later so closely associated with Boston that it bears remembering it was not always so) were the more specific challenges presented by the Panic of 1893 and subsequent recession, developments that only further hampered innovative investment. However ironically, then, the rigid conservatism Charlie would later embrace—his resistance to change in any form, whether social, literary, architectural, or sartorial—first developed in a home whose chatelaine enthusiastically embraced the new.

By the mid-1890s nearly every space at 137 Beacon Street reflected Rosamond's touch. She papered the dining room in a fashionable faux burlap, the library in burnished gold, and replaced Catherine's more sedate geometric paper in the private stair hall with a lush botanical print. Carpeting the entirety of the first floor and main stairs with wall-to-wall crimson cut-pile, she created a regal passage to her favorite space within the house: the Music Room. Here she painted the original dark walnut wainscoting white, added hardwood flooring, and introduced pale pastel upholstery. Though mostly acquiescent in his wife's redecoration schemes, Charles Sr. insisted upon controlling two spaces within the home: his bedroom and the library, the latter of which served as a masculine foil to the more delicate Music Room. Retaining the outdated, tufted "Turkish" furniture of these rooms, he seemed to predict his son's later, equally conservative taste.

Assisting Rosamond in the makeover of 137 Beacon Street was the new Boston interior decorator Ogden Codman Jr. It is unclear which individual elements Codman undertook—the Music Room suggests his style more than any other space in the house—yet records indicate Charles Sr. paid him in the fall of 1891 for "material," "painting," and a decorating commission.[25] The Gibsons and Codmans were cousins by marriage, and Codman appears to have socialized with both Rosamond and Ethel (at twenty-eight he lay generationally between the two). Yet at the time of his commission for 137 Beacon Street, Codman's primary interest there lay with seventeen-year-old Charlie.

"THE *JUICIEST* LOOKING BOY I EVER SAW"

In the summer of 1891 Codman wrote Arthur Little from Newport that "Big Chicago Sam Dexter and Little Charlie Gibson are here."[26] Given the raunchy tenor of the men's correspondence in this period, and the flavor of their later references to Charlie in particular, Codman's aside was intentionally wolfish (Little responded with the creepy exclamation, "[Charlie] would be a nice little boy to know!").[27] As they and others now noticed, Charlie had blossomed into a striking young man—the very embodiment of Holmes's original description of the Boston Brahmin ("altogether too good-looking . . . [and] commonly slender, his face is smooth, and apt to be pallid, his features are regular and of a certain delicacy").[28]

No one was more aware of his charms than the young man himself. In his later satirical poem "On Myself" (1899), Charlie—let us now promote him to Gibson—

describes, "This youth who flits across the page / Of Life, precocious though he's underage," a "popinjay" whose songs are "sweeter, they seem to me, than paltry goods."[29] Calling himself a "fellow of a certain wit / Upon whose head no bridle e'er would fit," the poet asks, "Is he a lover or a leached hound?" Wilde once quipped that "to love oneself is the beginning of a lifelong romance"; while this was true enough for Gibson, there is no record among his papers of any external romantic interests in these years.[30] For these details we must return to Codman and Little. It turns out Gibson was nothing if not "precocious . . . though underage."

Peppering Codman and Little's correspondence in the 1890s are references—some oblique, others direct—to Gibson's sexual partners, starting around the time he turned seventeen. The identities of these men are in some cases no longer known, but at least one later became a fixture of Boston society and several were Gibson's cousins (in his circles it was difficult to find anyone who *wasn't* his cousin). "Have you seen Willie Beal?" Little asked Codman in December 1891, referring to a former conquest of both men; "*And 'little Charlie'*? Sometime I must ask if he really does!"[31] In spring Little returned to this theme, writing, "think of the Gibsons coming to Swampscott—I shall have a good chance to investigate 'Little Charlie' now and his ways and see if there is any truth to the wild accounts Willie Beal has given!"[32] Little later heard from the subject himself: "Charlie was here yesterday, he has about given up on Brady [?] and Willie Beal 'only goes downtown when he wants to'!!"[33]

Nor were theirs the only tongues wagging about the handsome teenager. In January 1892 Codman relayed that Gibson's cousin Mason Hammond (another of the men's mutual conquests) had told him: "Charley is a bright boy with very little to him really just feeble impulses."[34] Little replied by explaining, "Mason has 'had' 'little Charlie' and therefore discourages you about him"—adding that Gibson was "principally interested in his clothes and in Samuel Hooper Hooper."[35]

Hooper, then twenty-three to Gibson's seventeen, appears to have been Gibson's first long-term beau. Living with his elderly aunt two doors down from the Gibsons at 141 Beacon Street, Hooper eventually made his fortune in investment banking and real estate. Never married, in his later years he organized the Boston Assembly society balls and was in 1936 proclaimed "Boston's senior dandy" (a title that doubtless rankled his ex, who in the 1930s brooked no rivals in this category).[36] "How funny [Gibson] and S. H. Hooper must be together!" Little exclaimed in February 1892, "Anywhere but mostly in a bed!"[37] By May Codman was scheming to break up the pair, writing: "Charlie is nice but I don't see him as much as I should like to . . . we must cut out Samuel Hooper Hooper this summer."[38] Neither Codman nor Little, it appears, succeeded in bedding Gibson. As late as 1919 Little would sigh, "Charlie was always the *juiciest* looking boy I ever saw."[39]

3.6
Gibson at seventeen (ca. 1891). Gibson House Museum, Boston, MA.

It was in this overheated period that Gibson met the man who became the love of his life. Although their affair was relatively brief, its intensity fueled much of his early writing and seems to have emotionally sustained him well into the 1940s. The effects of the scandal it created were just as enduring.

Maurice Maria Talvande, the self-styled Comte de Mauny of France (aka Maurice du Mauny-Talvande), arrived in the United States in December 1891. His reputation landed the month before. As Codman wrote Little in November, "de Mauny and his mother are coming here in December, he has got rid of Count Rudolph . . . it seems that de Mauny's name is something else and his father was queer."[40] The twenty-five-year-old de Mauny—a worldly rake known by name, at any rate, in Boston circles—had fled to America to avoid a family scandal. His father Felix Talvande, former director of the Banque Talvande in Le Mans, France, had been convicted in 1889 of financial fraud and sentenced to prison.[41] The following year his wife sought legal separation from him while his son distanced himself with the new surname "de Mauny," taken from his mother's side, later styling himself with the fictive title "le Comte de Mauny."

Gibson and de Mauny met immediately after the Frenchman's arrival in December 1891, but their orbits appear to have crossed only a few times in the early part of the decade. In these years de Mauny traveled between London, Paris, Boston, and New York, marketing himself in America as a lecturer on French history. For his part, Gibson had his hands full with Beal, Hooper—and college. In the fall of 1892 he entered the Massachusetts Institute of Technology (MIT); "they wanted to make me an engineer," he later claimed, but in his brief tenure at MIT he appears to have spent more time socializing than studying. Years later Gibson's MIT classmate and Delta Psi fraternity brother R. E. Lee Taylor wrote him: "I trust that your life is now a *pure and moral one*, and that you bear constantly in mind that you are in the great city, beset by the temptations of the flesh-pots."[42] Taylor concluded the letter by asking Gibson to "turn one more pirouette extra for me" the next time he danced the "Habinera," signing, "I am yours in the old way."

Gibson's departure from MIT after only a year may have stemmed from the Panic of 1893, a crisis that hit Charles Sr.'s cotton brokerage especially hard. Writing his mother Sarah that year Codman claimed:

> Charley Gibson [Sr.] has lost *all* his money, poor Rosie [Rosamond] what a hard time she does have he is *too* stupid. Little C[harlie] has been living on some people named Kelly all summer.[43]

Rudderless and temporarily homeless, Gibson had two strokes of fortune in early 1894. In February the *Boston Evening Transcript* published his first sonnet—a leaden treatment of the season of Lent. The following month, likely with the help of his cousin Edith (*née* Russell, now Lady Playfair), he landed a secretarial position with Alfred Harmsworth, 1st Viscount Northcliffe, who was then planning the Jackson-Harmsworth Polar Expedition to the Arctic Ocean. Gibson likely had no plans to accompany the expedition, nor did he long remain in Harmsworth's employ, but in this role he gained a lifeline to Europe and access to other, more sympathetic men. Chief among these was de Mauny.

On the eve of his departure for England, Gibson catalogued for Little the full range of extra-Harmsworthian opportunities that lay before him. To Codman, an amused Little wrote:

He's expecting to go to England [and] has "a fine literary offer"! the present Earl of Chatham wants him to catalogue the correspondence of his ancestor Fox!! Fancy Charlie doing that—he has also been asked to visit the Countess of Essex!!! And a French chateau!! . . . Really you would have gasped if you had heard it all—I hope it will amount to something and it may but you would have been amused if you had heard it all. . . . What a funny boy he is . . . I shall be curious to hear how Charlie gets on in England and what he *does*."[44]

What Gibson did that spring seemed to include very little secretarial work. "I have just got a long letter from Charley Gibson who is staying with the Playfairs and having a splendid time," Codman reported to Little at the end of March, "I wonder where he gets the *money* to do so?"[45] (Earlier, Codman censured Gibson's parents for refusing to support his life in London; "I never heard of such fools as the Gibsons, their doings with Charley beat the Dutch.")

Older admirers made up for Gibson's lack of parental support. In the spring of 1894 he became involved with an English peer whom Little identifies only as "Beaumont" (possibly Miles Stapleton, the Baron Beaumont, a man twenty-four years Gibson's senior). By May, Little reported he "had a letter from Charlie . . . from Augustus Hare's house, he is having a good time and will apparently stop there indefinitely—France for the summer, etc. etc."[46] Hare, a dandified, sixty-year-old bachelor, writer, and preservationist—as meticulous about his Hastings home as he was about his person—constituted the very model of the future Gibson (Somerset Maugham once dubbed him "the Last Victorian").[47] Years later Hare wrote Gibson, "I have got your portrait framed and hung up in the room you were in," a sign of genuine affection from a man who curated his home so painstakingly.[48]

Beaumont and Hare's overlapping patronage soon gave way to a new liaison. As Little wrote Codman in June:

> Your letter from Charlie must have been funny. I doubt he ever comes home. He had better lay up treasures in the Bank as I suppose the other thing won't last forever. So he is going to be with de Mauny!! I wonder if Beaumont is running dry! I would give a lot to know *everything*! Wouldn't you?[49]

The gossiping pair would have to wait until the winter of 1894–1895 to learn more about the Gibson–de Mauny affair, yet Gibson himself recorded its operatic beginning in a curious document. Titled "Etching," this two-page manuscript bears the credit line, "from the French of Maurice du Mauny [as] translated by Charles H. Gibson Jr."

The operatic love scene that "Etching" recounts is undeniably by Gibson's hand. Not only is the style unmistakably his own, but the manuscript—which he copied out sometime in 1894 or soon thereafter—survives in two different drafts, belying any notion of its translation. The text begins:

> Is it heaven, or is it earth? Truly it is heaven when I gaze into thy dear eyes—A heaven of that deep blue that is so like the sea; and your eyes, as dark, seem to take the colors of the things that roll beneath its depths. Be it sea or sky, my being loses itself in them and seems to escape from its mortal frame.[50]

In the following passages the narrator, who lies alongside his beloved on a stormy summer night, describes torment ("what if you did not love me?") followed by ecstasy ("a flash of lightning from thine eyes lights up the darkness: It says—what does it say?—'I love you'"). It is at this point that the—er—storm is unleashed:

> Another flash of lightning—but not from you this time. It comes from without. It tears the very elements and from afar the thunder follows close upon it. It lightnings it thunders; the storm approaches—it is here—the rain and the hail beat against the window-panes . . . crushing down the wheat like so many bullets. The pregnant tops bend beneath their load so that the ripened seeds are shaken down by the rain over the ground.

In closing, the narrator asks, "And do you dear one do you remember that first kiss, sealed by a thunderbolt?"

It is easy to wince at the purple prose of this ventriloquized love letter, or even to doubt the veracity of the scene itself. But for a young man who had experienced more than his share of physical relationships, Gibson records here for the first time his deep emotional attachment to another man. He had fallen in love—and also, with the very idea of love. And yet however clearly Gibson declares his own feelings, his sleight of hand regarding the work's authorship begs the question: Was this a one-sided passion? It appears not. In de Mauny's later memoir, *The Gardens of Taprobane* (1937), he describes an early encounter with an unnamed youth who sounds for all the world like Gibson himself in this period:

> He was a very pretty, perhaps too pretty, and very young individual . . . a vision in white. Wavy hair, golden, brushed from the forehead; china-blue eyes, shaded by long curled lashes; plucked eyebrows, very red lips, and perfect features . . . I could hardly tell, at first sight, whether the vision was male or female. It proved to be male, of kinds: exceedingly good-looking, and with the charming manners of the world. I could not help observing him, as one would examine a museum piece.[51]

De Mauny goes on to explain that this mysterious young man, "though rather full of his ancestors," had been cast off by his family for "vice had ceased to be vice for him; it was only the natural sequel of desire, and desire was an irresistible compulsion." No man in Boston was more "full of his ancestors" than Gibson, of course, nor were there many in his youth who matched his embrace of "vice." And while not cast off by his family when the two men met—Gibson's extended European travels were more escape than exile—de Mauny knew, from the perspective of 1937, that the young man's break with his family was imminent.

Gibson's similarly revealing essay, "On Affection"—undated, but likely also written in the summer of 1894—uses the Old Testament example of Jonathan and David to argue that

> in this case the affection for the mind was so blended with that of the body, as to create a great love, one for the other. . . . Whether this were a perfect condition, according to man's interpretation of nature's law and order, is

difficult to say. . . . [But] it is a natural thing . . . when these qualities have once adhered to form an affection of this kind . . . a love stronger than man's will.[52]

Boston, it would turn out, had no difficulty declaring whether such a love represented a "perfect condition."

Following an idyllic summer and fall in the French countryside, primarily in the region of Touraine, Gibson and de Mauny returned to America in November 1894 for the Frenchman's new lecture tour. Gibson served as his tour manager. In New York, this professional façade appears to have gone unquestioned, but in Boston the pair quickly became an object of scandalous fascination. The men's sleeping arrangements caused "much interest" in town, Codman wrote his mother (at 137 Beacon Street Gibson had given de Mauny the bedroom adjoining his own), as had de Mauny's bogus title:

> Lunched with Herbert [Browne] and Arthur [Little] to hear all the gossip— mostly about Charley Gibson and his French friend. They have been talked about in Boston, Mrs. Amory Lawrence having called him an imposter. Frank Peabody was sent her as a lawyer by the Gibson-de Mauny faction, this shut her up . . . young Edward Crowninshield spread awful tales of Ct. de M. when in Boston Xmas which tales have grown as such things do. . . . Really one cannot be too careful with such people.[53]

The situation only further deteriorated by the spring. Writing his mother again in March, Codman related: "Frank Crowninshield and others tell me that the men in Boston think the worst of Charley Gibson. Poor Rossie [Rosamond] they have had a hard time this winter. All Boston has been talking about them in a horrid way. . . . I am sorry for her she is kind, if stupid, and I suppose she adores Charlie."[54]

In April, the Gibsons asked de Mauny to move to a boarding house.[55] By this date history itself conspired against the men, for on April 3 the first of Oscar Wilde's trials began—weeks that produced shock waves on both sides of the Atlantic, tearing the veil from male "friendships" once quietly tolerated. As a character in Beverley Nichols's novel *Crazy Pavements* (1927) later claimed, "I was a young man in the 'nineties, but I have no use for an age in which one could gain a bad reputation merely by wearing a flower. A bad reputation was . . . abominably easy for people in those days."[56] In his poem "A Prayer for Love," written that June, Gibson beseeches God to "Let the barriers of this World which do harass my communion with the souls of other mortals fall away."[57]

Gibson and de Mauny's relationship survived another two years, through the support of sympathetic figures like his Beacon Street neighbor, Isabella Stewart Gardner—whose circle always included a number of gay men—and the anonymity of foreign travel. Gardner welcomed the couple to her home in November 1895, when no other Boston matron dared to receive them, and kept track of their travels abroad through a mutual friend, Count Carlo Emo.[58] Writing Gardner in June 1896, Emo reported he had seen "Charles Gibson and de Manny [*sic*]" together in London, adding, "I suppose Mrs. Gibson is very sorry to have her son away for so many months."[59] Gibson would in fact remain abroad for much of 1896–1897—a period spent, in part, researching the architecture of French châteaux. These travels later informed his writing and lecture tours and offered him a welcome repeat of his previous summer with de Mauny.

The affair appears to have come to an end by 1897. Never a stranger to maudlin poetry—in his 1894 Beaumont/Hare phase, Gibson had penned "Lines Written in Dejection"—his verses in 1897 constitute a litany of despair unusual even for him. Poems titled "To Be Without," "Envy and Discontent," and "So Young and Yet So Old" catalogue a powerful love gone sour, due in part to his diminishing youth. Even more upbeat titles like "Life" and "Happiness" descend quickly into abjection ("Life is dull pain and wretchedness and hate," "Happiness, why has thou flown away?").[60] Most telling of all, because written entirely in French, is Gibson's "Rêve d'Amour" ("Dream of Love") from August 1897. Here he returns to the reclining lovers of "Etching," yet mourns "it is only flesh that attaches us" and concludes the scene not with a kiss but with the grim reality of an empty bed.[61]

Drifting back to Boston in 1897 at the age of twenty-three—a time when most of his peers had already established careers—Gibson printed up business stationery with the aspirational letterhead, "Real Estate and House Furnishing."[62] His plan to launch himself as a dealer/designer had once involved a partnership with de Mauny, it seems, for in the fall of 1896 Codman wrote his mother: "Charley Gibson [is] going into interior decoration! I hear de Mauny is to be foreign agent."[63] No clients appear to have materialized. Gibson remained something of a social pariah, it seems, even despite de Mauny's absence; when he attempted to organize two "subscription dances" after his return, he was forced to cancel both for lack of response.[64]

In June 1898, Gibson learned that de Mauny had married Lady Mary Byng, daughter of the Earl of Strafford. Following their wedding the couple rented the magnificent Château d'Azay-le-Rideau—a choice that must have further pained Gibson, who knew the site well from his travels with de Mauny. The newlyweds were soon joined by a dozen teenaged boys. De Mauny planned to turn the château into an invitation-only finishing school for the sons of English peers, yet the school's apparent lack of any academic program and its cadre of suspiciously handsome, dandified students soon raised eyebrows. (As one local journalist claimed, this was "a very peculiar university where . . . the students are so well behaved that the sight of women, even in low-cut dresses, does not present any danger to them. How surprising!")[65] Amid mounting rumors that de Mauny made sexual advances to his fellow students, the nineteen-year-old son of the Duke of Westminster confronted de Mauny "with the result that, all we suspected of him is true, he owned up that it is so."[66] De Mauny's "university" closed in December, his lease to Azay summarily revoked.

Whatever *schadenfreude* Gibson might have felt about the Azay scandal, he continued to dwell on the ideal of his great love. In July 1899, he penned the following diary entry:

> Reviewing all the past, of years . . . now gone, how much wells up in the heart—like a turbulent sea. Ah! Beloved One! You are here in the midst of this sea, this tempest, this Heaven—I cannot count the moments, the seconds, minutes, hours, months that it has taken to build you . . . inch by inch, stone by stone, until then you were a human being—a soul—a God. . . . I have lost a part of myself while you are gone—for thou art me and I am thee—and we are one—and yet two—Two, so distant that we may never join . . . never to be able to bridge that awful chasm which divides us—which makes it impossible to fly each to the others [*sic*] arms and join the spirit with the flesh—Ah Never—and Yet?[67]

And yet . . . indeed. Although the two never met again—their connection now reduced, in Gibson's words, to "a somewhat hampered correspondence over many thousand miles"—in 1899 he and the god he had so painstakingly constructed would reunite in his first novel.[68]

"THE COMING OF GENIUS"

Given the whiff of scandal that still attached to his affair, the title of Gibson's debut novel, *Two Gentlemen in Touraine* (1899), was a bold choice—despite the protection his pen name ("Richard Sudbury") might have offered. This thinly veiled *roman à clef* recounts the travels of an American narrator who joins his "intimate friend," the dashing, older Comte de Persigny, for a tour of the French countryside. The journey begins with the narrator's long-awaited stay at the Count's château: "Was there ever a more romantic spot for lovers to meet. . . . Was there ever a more perfect setting for a poet's fancy?"[69] Architectural history provides the novel's literary pretext—Gibson's research on French châteaux is in full evidence here—yet the principal story lies in the relationship between the two men.

"We had been attracted to each other" for several years, the narrator explains, "an intercourse of two minds . . . out of the ordinary range of friendships."[70] However different their natures—the Count's "Latin spontaneity impressed itself upon this Anglo Saxon"—the men are "kindred souls," "joined together in immaterial marriage."[71] Impressed by the Count's title, fortune, and intellectual brilliance, the narrator details even more fully the man's physical qualities: his athletic body, deep-set eyes, wavy hair, and even the perfect temples framing his forehead. Nor is the narrator's admiration restricted to the Count alone. Upon meeting the Prince de Gourmet, the narrator admires the prince's "resplendent" calves, exclaiming, "Ah, Cupid! Cupid! Where would you not lead us?"[72]

Gibson completed the first draft of *Two Gentlemen in Touraine* in February 1895, the same month Boston first learned of his affair with de Mauny. Although this draft differed little from the final version, in June 1895 Gibson added a revealing section later expunged from the published book. Titled "l'Envoi" ("the sendoff"), the fragment appears to eulogize his relationship with de Mauny well before its actual conclusion:

> Our friend the Count is now far separated from us. . . . That life which we had looked forward to seeing for a little space with so much longing and which, at the time, seemed to have no room for thoughts of any others, has nevertheless vanished from us. It has passed, like a watch in the night, like a dream from which we have been awakened.[73]

It is possible that at this early stage in the book's creation—a time when their romance was still in full swing—Gibson intended these words more as a farewell to his novel than to his Count (indeed, an "envoi" is the literary term for such an ending). Yet by 1899, this goodbye likely cut too close to the bone for him to retain it.

Although the book was a relative commercial success, *Two Gentleman in Touraine* received only tepid critical praise; its narrative was described as "pleasant if not stimulating," "dreamy and fanciful," and "written in the style of half a century ago."[74] As for those who knew the real-life figures behind the book's protagonists, verbal gymnastics were required to avoid addressing its subject matter. A friend of Rosamond's wrote to apologize for not yet having read the book, congratulating her instead on the "sumptuous garb" of its leather binding; similarly, Augustus Hare—who might have been expected to comment on the book more fully, both as a writer and de Mauny's predecessor—wrote Gibson only that "I was astonished to see such a large, beautifully got up volume" before changing tack to address de Mauny's recent school scandal.[75] Even Lady Playfair, whose opinion Gibson valued more than most, wrote simply, "the book is beautifully got up. . . . It is easy to open and light to hold, [with] excellent type."[76] Gibson learned his lesson. Not only would he never again write so transparently about one of his romantic relationships, but—in contrast to the reams of manuscripts and literary fragments he would later save— he preserved not one of du Mauny's letters from this period.

However deflated Gibson might have felt by such nonresponses to his novel, his mood at the century's turn was decidedly optimistic (consider his self-referential 1899 poem, "The Coming of Genius"). In January 1900 he wrote in his diary:

> There is at the outset of every year, as there is at the outset of every life, an uncertain desire to succeed in something; as if we were about to enter some great race. . . . The fountain of life flows early in the year. . . . We look not for the end of things while the freshness of life is upon us and we feel its vigor and its youth. O, take not from us this blessing of our soul. O grant us an eternal youth, full of happiness, for all time.[77]

For the moment Gibson felt young, desirable, and full of purpose; in the 1900 census he listed his occupation for the first time as "author." Over next two years his "fountain of life" would flow at full tilt. Returning to Europe for an extended period beginning in the summer of 1900, he sat for two portraits during a stay on Lake Como and commissioned another the following year in London—where he appears to have struck up yet another relationship with a titled nobleman.

In 1901, Gibson received a letter from Rodrigo de Saavedra y Vinent, aka His Excellency the Marquis de Villalobar. The dashing, thirty-six-year-old Villalobar was serving at the Spanish Embassy when he and Gibson met in London the year before. Identifying himself simply as "Rodrigo," the Marquis addresses Gibson as "my dear babe" (he was ten years Gibson's senior) and thanks the younger man for naming him in the will Gibson forwarded him—an extraordinary step for Gibson to have taken, not only given his youth but also considering the apparent newness of the men's acquaintance.[78] Inspired to reciprocate, as Gibson no doubt anticipated, Villalobar assures him: "I have been clever in leaving you things that will please you, to be sure," including articles of jewelry, lace, and pressed "flowers and leaves that *once* meant something" to them both.[79] Villalobar may have been nothing more than a romantic footnote for Gibson—this single letter is the only evidence of their likely affair—yet the exchange is a telling measure of his powers of attraction and an indication of the heady international set he ran with, however briefly.

Villalobar closes his letter to Gibson expressing he is "sorry to hear you are worried by your family, that whish [*sic*] you to go back home. I'm sure you believe 'there is no place like home' but I see you try to stay away from it." There is no doubt Gibson's peripatetic lifestyle stemmed from the desire to avoid his family, whose emotional and financial support had dwindled considerably in recent years.[80] By the time of his return in fall 1902, his relationship with his father had irretrievably deteriorated—a rift reflected in Gibson's mournful sonnet composed that year, "The Spectre Lord," which contains the lines, "Oh but to know a father's love / And feel his kindly glance!"[81] Still smarting from the scandal of his son's affair with de Mauny, Charles Sr. had doubtless also heard dark rumors of Gibson's activities abroad. One mysterious episode, which Gibson referred to only as the "affair Versailles," was serious enough to warrant a series of letters to Lady Playfair, begging her not to mention its details in her letters home.[82]

Nowhere was this break more clearly demonstrated than in Gibson's departure from 137 Beacon Street. Throughout his years of traveling he had always maintained the family home as his Boston address. Following his 1902 return, however, he moved to the first of a series of bachelor's apartments in Back Bay—an exile from 137 Beacon Street, whether self-imposed or dictated by his father, that lasted until the 1930s.[83] This was not the only door that shut for him in 1902. Whether due to his loss of parental support, the waning of patronage from older foreigners, or some combination of the two, Europe was now closed to Gibson, as well. After nearly eight years of transatlantic escape, he would remain the rest of his life in Boston.[84]

Around the time of Gibson's final return from Europe, profiles of the young writer displayed more interest in the man than in his work. In February 1902, the *Boston Daily Paper* described Gibson as "an agreeable conversationalist . . . addicted to the refinedly intellectual," who "some years ago . . . was the host of M. de Toilland [*sic*], a member of a noble French family, who enjoyed some vogue here."[85] For those who might not recall the dubious nature of this connection, the article's author pointedly describes Gibson as "decidedly blond"—code in this period for a young gay man.[86]

In a similar vein, a 1904 *Boston Journal* profile described Gibson as a "debonair and well groomed" author of "clever work in prose and verse," one of the city's "society bachelors who keep apartments apart from the female shrine."[87] Having concluded his summer season in Nahant, the article continues, Gibson marked his return not by squiring eligible young women about town but "by giving a tea for his bachelor friends at his den on Charles Street." If Gibson later chose the early 1900s as the end date for his home's significance, then it appears Boston fixed the same period as the starting point for his new public persona: the swishy Brahmin bachelor. The pariah of the 1890s, it seems, had become a charming curiosity—a caricature whose appeal increased with its ever-deepening anachronism. This shift in perception, and the power it offered him, was not lost on Gibson.

The *Journal*'s aside about Nahant was another form of shorthand, meant to confirm its subject's place within the city's social firmament. Like Gibson's emerging image in the Boston press, Nahant, too, would become an important tool in his self-fashioning—not just for the patrician cachet the place carried (although this, too, played a part) but more specifically for the elaborate tea gardens he cultivated at Forty Steps. Starting around 1900, the Gibsons allowed their son free rein to arrange the family's grounds on Nahant. Acting as a kind of coregent there with his mother (his father, like most of the colony's family men, was primarily a weekend visitor), Gibson developed a love for Forty Steps that equaled, and in some respects even surpassed, his attachment to 137 Beacon Street. As a child he associated Forty Steps with theater, make-believe, and a welcome release from Back Bay's rigidity. As an adult he created a world unto itself there, a "fairyland," to use one journalist's words, of scented flowers and fantastic topiaries. Like a reversal

3.7

Gibson at Forty Steps
Beach, Nahant, MA
(ca. 1905). Gibson
House Museum,
Boston, MA.

of the biblical narrative, Gibson's expulsion from 137 Beacon Street had driven him *into* the garden.

The intensity with which Gibson cultivated his rose gardens serves as a parallel to, rather than a repression of, his sexual appetites. (As Codman and Little continued to gossip, Gibson's liaisons only increased with the new freedom of his bachelor quarters.)[88] For Gibson as for Marcel Proust's character the Baron de Charlus, the two activities appear to have whetted one another. "For the best of us," the highly sexed Baron explains:

> Gardens are all mere ersatz, surrogates, alibis. From the depths of our tub, like Diogenes, we cry out for a man. We cultivate begonias, we trim yews, as a last resort, because yews and begonias submit to treatment. But we should prefer to give our time to a plant of human growth.[89]

Gibson appears to have made this connection between gardening and eroticism early on. Writing Little in 1894 from Hare's manicured estate—likely a model for Forty Steps' gardens—he made a lewd joke about installing garden statuary that Little repeated to Codman: "Charlie reports much excitement *over the erection* (not A. H. he adds!!)."[90]

Gibson second novel, *Little Pilgrimages Among French Inns* (1905), reads like a sanitized version of the love story in *Two Gentleman in Touraine*. In the novel's preface he explains— now under his own name—that this loosely constructed narrative, based upon "several summers in picturesque parts of France," is intended merely as an invented "excursion by a number of types."[91] First among these is the distinguished figure of Count Romeo di Pamponi. An older man with an eye for a pretty lad ("That is what I call a *joli garçon*!" he exclaims at one point), the Count is safely quarantined from the novel's young American, George van Cortland, who romantically pursues fellow traveler Gladys Wilton. Describing George and Gladys's blossoming romance, the narrator strays into the dubious territory of *Touraine*: the couple's love is "subject to different laws and impulses. . . .

They are maddened with desire, with ideals unfulfilled, a promise of happiness held not by Nature . . . they are, indeed, to be pitied."[92] Clearly still pining for the life he once envisioned with de Mauny—and dreading the future his father expected of him—Gibson includes this soliloquy from the party's otherwise unnamed Frenchman:

> [Americans] have no temperament. They go to their office in the morning and think of nothing but business all day, and in the evening are too tired to do much of anything . . . how much more brilliant is the life of an American who marries a Frenchman![93]

If Gibson hoped *Little Pilgrimages Among French Inns* might serve as a corrective to *Two Gentleman in Touraine*, he was disappointed by the novel's near-universal dismissal. Critics found the book "gossipy," "tiresome," "exceedingly clumsy," "awkward," and written "in a most unfortunate literary style" that was "in dire need of condensing" (even favorable notes were restricted to remarks that the book was "daintily attired" and "prettily designed").[94] More damning were reviewers' responses to the concocted love story between George and Gladys, cited as an "inane plot of supposed love interest" with only a "slightly drawn heroine." (As the *Philadelphia Telegraph* perceptively noted, "the love-story part has the appearance of being lugged in rather against its will.")[95]

For Gibson a number of factors outweighed the book's negative reviews. First, however critics might have carped about it, the book was a commercial success (like *Two Gentlemen in Touraine*, it would go into a second printing). Second, his own circle had this time responded more positively to his work—from Rosamond, whose copy Gibson inscribed in thanks for her support and encouragement, to a host of Boston matrons who arranged private readings. Perhaps most gratifying of all was the extensive *Boston Sunday Globe* feature that *Little Pilgrimages* prompted. Titled "Writes of French Inns," the piece had little to say about the novel but much to share about the author himself. Its description of this "society man," descended "from the most essentially New England stock" captures Gibson in microscopic detail:

> He was young, say a year or so past thirty; erect, but cast in a fine mold, his head well shaped, nose straight, eyes clear and direct in their gaze, hair light brown and growing thin on top; a hand firm in its clasp of greeting, with the fingers long and sensitive. Nervous force was evident, and his speech was clear-cut, yet unlike the spoken language of New England—the speech, one would say, of a citizen of the world, who had partaken somewhat of the old-world style of speaking.[96]

The article goes on to dissect Gibson's fashionable clothes and numerous club memberships, the refinement of his bachelor lodgings, and the details of his illustrious Warren lineage—ultimately concluding that "so *unliterary* was his appearance, and so suggestive of the training and atmosphere of social Boston, that the visitor was at a loss to find an approach to the common ground of literature." Gibson, it seems, was too refined to be *simply* a writer. As he offers in the interview himself, "I enjoy society as a diversion and as a means of meeting friends, but I have many other interests and am obliged to engage in business. My business is that of a broker." (In profiles from this period until

3.8
James E. Purdy's 1904
portrait of Gibson,
taken a year before the
publication of *Among
French Inns*. Gibson
House Museum,
Boston, MA.

the 1920s, Gibson insisted he worked for a brokerage. Aside from managing—poorly—his own inherited stocks, there is no evidence for the claim.)

By 1905 the Portrait of the Writer as a Young (-ish) Man was complete. James E. Purdy's studio portrait of Gibson, taken the year before, perfectly captures this handsome, supremely confident, and well-dressed "society leader"—a man who trades by day and writes by night, without a whiff of bohemianism. (The photograph remained Gibson's favorite image of himself.) And yet in the *Globe*'s insistence upon its subject's "graceful, delicate, and earnest" style, along with its aside about his affected speech patterns, the newspaper gave the same wink to readers the *Boston Sunday Herald* had a few weeks before. Equally fulsome in its praise for Gibson's social credentials, the *Herald* ends by openly speculating on his bachelor status (as for marriage, "Mr. Gibson maintains a grim silence on the subject").[97] While it's true that Gibson brooded about many things, his lack of marriage prospects never appeared to bother him. Like Jane Austen's Emma Woodhouse—who declared "it is poverty only which makes celibacy contemptible"—he believed his social position obviated the need for a spouse.[98]

When Gibson published *The Spirit of Love and Other Poems* in 1906, readers of his novels might have seen this collection as a literary departure—yet poetry had been, and would remain, the mainstay of his writing. Much of *The Spirit of Love* constituted warmed-over (if disguised) reflections on his affair with de Mauny, yet the collection includes many works written before and after their relationship, as well as poems devoted to a variety of other themes: tributes to historic (most royal) personages, reflections on his fleeting youth, and ruminations on nature, music, and death. The earliest date to 1893, when the nineteen-year-old Gibson began to compile his "Green Book of Early Poems" (a notebook whose very title suggests visions of future glory); the latest belong to the watershed year of 1902, when his residence in Boston became fixed. In all, this privately published work includes 111 poems, five "letters in verse," and fragments of his unfinished play "Hamelin Plantagenet," a fictional account of his Warren ancestors at the court of Henry II.

Gibson dedicated *The Spirit of Love* "To Thee who lov'st, yet never hast known / Where thy true love hath strangely grown." Most strangely grown of all was the book's central epic, a sprawling 270-line poem titled the "Amatoryad, or The Spirit of Love." Written in the years immediately following his breakup with de Mauny, this meditation on the futility of love not only serves as the book's title poem but also proclaims a new literary genre (at the book's start Gibson refers to the entirety of his *oeuvre* as "my Amatoryad"). Critics were quick to condemn both the poem's pretension ("how dare you risk such a word as 'Amatoryad'?" Thomas Wentworth Higginson fumed) and the difficulties its "flamboyant" diction presented.[99] Indeed, it is hard to soldier through such exhortations as:

> Let us run the lover's race,
> Bees, or butterflies, to chase,
> Hither, thither, through the air
> Seeking honey everywhere.

What critics most consistently faulted in Gibson's work was its anachronistic style, a charge he would have considered high praise. (He pointedly included in *The Spirit of Love* his "Odes After the Style of Anacreon," a tribute to the Greek lyric poet whose use of archaic Ionian style provides a parallel to his own insistently Victorian mode.) Though he considered himself a standard-bearer for Boston's illustrious literary past—Lucius Beebe once quipped that "every Boston family in the nineteenth century boasted either a potted palm or an author"—by the turn of the century writers like H. G. Wells were declaring the city's literary scene long dead.[100] "The central figure of [Boston's] literary world," he railed, "is that charming old lady of eighty-eight, Mrs. Julia Ward Howe," a woman who led "an authors' society that is not so much comprised of minor stars as a chorus of indistinguishable culture."[101]

For others—including, no doubt, his father—Gibson's work was simply the wrong *kind* of writing. Within Brahmin circles, acceptable modes included historical scholarship and literary fiction; Bostonians of an earlier generation might have celebrated Henry Wadsworth Longfellow's sonnets, yet critics in this post-Wilde era viewed male poets with suspicion. Condemned for the feminine exploration of their own emotional landscapes, "men of a poetic temperament"—as one writer implied—were "to a great extent unqualified for association with women."[102] Gibson's tendency to turn at once inward *and* backward not only suggested a dangerously effeminate sentimentality but also an inability to navigate the world outside the home.

Gibson was no more worried about his poetic calling than by his continued bachelorhood. Doubling down on the sentimental nature of his earlier poems, in 1908 he produced *The Wounded Eros: Sonnets*, a collection of new works that adopted unrequited love as a universal theme. Privately published again, *The Wounded Eros'* 128 sonnets cast Eros (aka Cupid) as love's instigator, object, and tragic hero ("What winged boy hath caught again my heart," Gibson writes, "inspiring this strange longing?"). In his introduction to *The Wounded Eros*, poet William Stanley Braithwaite explains that Gibson's project examines "the ancient and immemorial love of man for woman."[103] Yet in a rather pointed disclaimer, Braithwaite adds: "I am convinced of [the work's] origin in the imagination—that is to say, there being no likelihood that the story is of an actually known experience." Regardless of the love object's gender in these sonnets—only two of which mention a "maid"—Gibson is far more focused on his own emotional state, underscored by a forest of exclamation points, than on the qualities of his beloved. The *Chicago Evening Post* declared the work "disastrous," its maudlin verses like "too many jewels upon the chain . . . [and] of too personal a nature."[104]

Upon reading *The Wounded Eros*, Gibson's friend Isabelle Metcalf wrote him in concern. The sonnets "are very beautiful my dear boy," she wrote, "but do you know, such a wave of depression sweeps over one on the perusal that one longs for the next volume when you will be lifted up and into something attainable and cheerful."[105] She offered Gibson her "hope that you may regard me as one capable of sympathy and friendship," confiding that she herself had "been obliged to resort to psycotherapy [*sic*] to free myself from the hypnotism of depression." As she intuited, his wretchedness in these sonnets was more than just a poet's melancholic pose. Continuing to mourn the life he might have led with de Mauny and now exiled from 137 Beacon Street, as well, he feared the loss of the two things that mattered most to him: his youthful looks and social standing.

In his twenties Gibson began to pen annual birthday poems chronicling his fading attractions (his "Sonnet on Reaching the Age of Twenty-Four" bemoans "my dying youth [that] I fain would mourn!") and even clipped antiaging secrets from the *Boston Globe*'s Women's Page.[106] However deeply he believed his family tree's roots to be planted, moreover, he struggled to maintain his club memberships and agonized over the correctness of his inherited—and, as he surely realized, mostly invented—heraldry. As one Boston matron of this period said, "few people can live in Boston, and not sooner or later have an inferiority complex—it is in the air."[107]

Financial insecurity only compounded Gibson's anxieties regarding his age and pedigree. As the narrator in *Two Gentlemen in Touraine* noted, "we are not our own masters when first the poetic view . . . takes hold of us"; to "grow up and rub against the world" meant to be "engaged in work . . . for which we are often wretched."[108] To supplement his income in these years he tried his hand at a number of different jobs, including interior decoration (his business card from this period advertises "special attention given to French rooms"), real estate (following a lucrative sale, Little wrote Codman that Gibson's commission was "more paying than what he generally handles!"), and in at least one instance he served as a commissioned shopper for women's dresses and furs.[109]

The most visible work Gibson undertook in this period, if not the most lucrative, paid in book sales and social dividends. Taking a page from de Mauny's book, he made scores of bookings for lectures on literature, travel, and French culture starting in the early 1900s. In most cases these events served as pretexts to read his own work and give illustrated accounts of the art and architecture he had encountered on his European travels. In 1907 alone, he sent lecture prospectuses to no less than seventy-two clubs in Massachusetts, New York, Connecticut, Maryland, Pennsylvania, and Washington, DC—yet his greatest successes in this arena took place in Boston's "smart houses," where Brahmin hostesses arranged invitation-only readings of his fiction and poetry.

In its coverage of one such gathering in 1907, the *Boston Globe* described the setting for this "poet of society":

> Mrs. Burr's drawing room, with its walls hung with crimson damask and gilded furniture was a most delightful place to listen to Mr. Gibson as he read selections. . . . [Among those] who attended were Mrs. Winthrop Sargent, whose dashing style of beauty was well set off by a costume of dark blue velvet with which she wore a hat to correspond trimmed with shaded blue plumes.[110]

For the assembled guests at these salons, the chatty young poet was likely more admired for his family background and sartorial style (matched by that of the attendees) than for his verses. Like his contemporary, Florence Foster Jenkins—the wealthy, would-be opera singer noted more for her passion than her ability to sing—Gibson, too, appears to have mistaken his elite audience's *esprit de corps* for an endorsement of his talents.

It was Gibson's love of architecture and gardening, rather than writing, that landed him his first full-time job in 1914. He was then forty. That year Boston Mayor James Curley appointed Gibson as Boston's new parks commissioner, responsible for overseeing all city parks, public squares, and city beautification projects. Hired through his connection to city benefactor George Parkman, the new commissioner was touted by the *Boston Globe* as "an engineer and landscape architect" with a real estate business at 121 Beacon Street (in fact, the address of his rooming house).[111] Charmed by Gibson in spite of himself—the son of an Irish scrubwoman, Curley had no love for Brahmin elites—the mayor later fondly reminisced about the poet-commissioner in his 1957 memoir. Noting Gibson's "wry sense of humor" and campy affect, Curley tells the story of "Sir Charles" (his nickname for the commissioner) entering a Boston bar filled with beer-drinking longshoremen. Ignoring the "snickers and disparaging remarks from the boys," Curley writes, Gibson proceeded to order an elaborate, rainbow-layered cocktail called a Pousse-Café—and never blinked when the bartender handed him, instead, a whiskey with beer chaser.[112] As if to play up to the fey caricature his boss delighted in (likely *because* Curley loathed the class Gibson represented), the new parks commissioner took no salary, wore a fur coat to the office, and requested an open touring car with a driver.[113] Within weeks of assuming his new position, Gibson wrote Princess Eleanore of Bulgaria to offer her a tour of Boston's parks (her secretary declined on her behalf).[114]

What might otherwise have been an uneventful—if colorful—tenure for Gibson at the Parks Department erupted in controversy in 1916. In a months-long battle that played out before an amused Boston press, Gibson declared war on the Boston Art Commission— over a public restroom. In a scathing letter to the *Boston Globe* in January 1916 ("Gibson Attacks Art Commission"), the parks commissioner condemned the "highly undesirable structure being forced on the Parks Department" at Boylston and Tremont Streets, a building both "hideous in appearance [and] a grave danger to respectable citizens who have a right to use a public convenience station on the Common."[115] The design forced upon his office, however, was merely an alternative to the public restroom Gibson himself had proposed: a costly pink granite temple modeled on Marie Antoinette's music pavilion at Versailles. What made perfect sense to Gibson (didn't every Bostonian deserve a public toilet from the ancien régime, planted on the Boston Common?) left most in the city as perplexed as the bartender he'd asked to make a Pousse-Café.

Gibson's primary objection to the alternative facility—to be situated, however coincidentally, across from the Hotel Touraine—was that it would have invited "bands of thugs . . . inviting opportunities for assault and *blackmail*" [italics mine].[116] A bathroom palace on the Common was not only a more elegant solution, Gibson believed, but unofficially it was a more discreet one, given the park's active cruising scene. (As the parks commissioner knew better than most, Boston police had in the 1910s dramatically increased arrests of gay men for "lascivious behavior" in city parks.)[117] In the end Gibson managed to build a small, octagonal convenience station on the Common in nondescript gray granite. A tasteful if easily overlooked monument to his time as commissioner—he resigned in the spring of 1916—the building is today a snack concession named The Earl of Sandwich.

During Gibson's tenure as parks commissioner his father's health rapidly declined, as did apparently Gibson's relationship with the rest his family. In 1914 he removed 137 Beacon Street from the insurance policy he held for his personal belongings; though he had lived elsewhere for twelve years at this point, his decision indicates the removal of everything he stored at the family home, as well.[118] Of the Gibson children it was only Ethel who had so far fulfilled the expectations of her family and class. In 1911 she married Dr. Freeman Allen, moved to her own home at 200 Beacon Street, and five years later welcomed a son. (However different the two men were, Allen once shared with Gibson Codman's leering attentions. Upon seeing a photograph of Allen at Boston's Camera Club in 1892, Codman wrote Little about "a photo called the 'bathers,' i.e., Frank Curtis & Freeman Allen *naked* . . . their cocks were hidden by their *legs*—I want a copy awfully.")[119]

When Charles Gibson Sr. died on April 21, 1916, he left 137 Beacon Street to Rosamond for the remainder of her life and thereafter to their daughters. Still in mourning later that year, "little" Rosamond married her cousin Charles Gibson Winslow and settled on nearby Marlborough Street. The only sibling who still needed a home at this stage—their father's namesake and only son—had been disinherited. It was a blow from which Gibson never recovered; as he wrote in 1934, "my life has been an extraordinary experience, owing to an infirmity put upon me by my father, mostly hell, with glimpses here and there of heaven."[120]

In the decades after his father's death, Gibson's life settled into a kind of dress rehearsal for his final years at the family home. He wrote incessantly but published no more books (in the 1930 census he recorded his occupation as "none"). He worried constantly about money, and in one much-talked-over case in Boston, sought an inheritance from a wealthy paramour—a cousin of Codman's named Phillip Bradlee Stone. ("I think Charley Gibson earned his legacy???" Codman wrote his brother Tom; "I do not believe in his blackmailing him. P. Stone was probably quite willing to *pay* for what he *wanted*.")[121] Gibson drank too much in these years and rattled off letters to luminaries he'd never met, including a remarkable 1928 letter to the boxer Jack Dempsey (seemingly written while intoxicated). "Say Jack your all right," he wrote, "Youra regular guy, as Van Dyke says in the book [W. N. Van Dyke's serialized *Daredevil Jack*] . . . I couldn't find any nudes, but the pictures of you in the rings are arl right."[122] That same year Gibson collected the business card of a young man named Jimme "Fairbanks" Hindson, shown reclining in boxing shorts and offering "health services" to gentlemen.[123]

If his much feared loss of youth was now coming to pass—in a 1929 poem Gibson mourned, at fifty-five, that he was *mid-way* "upon the stream of life"—this appears to have had little effect on the traffic coming through his apartment.[124] As Little wrote to Codman:

> Went to a party . . . Charlie Gibson was there and looks very different from what he once was[,] he seems to have fattened up considerable. I can't see how if what Fernald tells is true of the amount of men visitors he has at night and in the early A.M.![125]

Little's letter indicates the extent to which Gibson remained an object of gossip in Boston—leading him, at one stage in 1918, to bring a $50,000 libel suit against a man in their circle for "defamation of character."[126] The 1920s were no kinder to him in this respect than the winter of 1894–1895. Writing his brother Tom in 1925, Codman brutally confided: "Poor Charley Gibson, every body seems to despise him. . . . Thirty years ago or is it forty? He used to be rather amusing at Arthur Little's."[127]

His father's death did allow Gibson, at least, to shore up his relationship with Rosamond—even if her protracted grief highlighted his own shortcomings as the family's default patriarch. Three years into her widowhood she continued to wear full mourning, and in the memoir she wrote in the late 1920s—with Gibson's help—she eulogized her husband in ways that only demonstrated the stark differences between son and father.[128] "He was always a strong, well, handsome man," she wrote, a financially acute businessman "devoted to outdoor sports, horses, riding, hunting, sailing, and bicycling, tennis, and ending with golf."[129] However hard it had been to face his loss, she was at least consoled by the presence of "my little pair of grandsons." She does not mention her son.

In 1933 Gibson moved back into 137 Beacon Street to care for his ailing mother. On September 22, 1934, he recorded in his diary: "My Beloved and Devoted Mother passed into Eternal Life at 9:15. The saddest day of my life."[130] For a man whose wretchedness often came across as a poetic pose, there is every reason to believe Gibson was gutted by Rosamond's loss. For nearly sixty years she had provided him an enduring, if not always effective, shield—from his father, Boston, and even his own less generous impulses. If her death stripped him of a lifelong defense, however, it also offered him an unprecedented opportunity.

3.9
Gibson in his early sixties, around the time he inherited 137 Beacon Street (ca. 1935). Gibson House Museum, Boston, MA.

A LONG NIGHT AT THE MUSEUM

It is a measure of Gibson's expectations that, on his sixtieth birthday in November 1934, he cut short his annual dirge about the march of years (writing in his date book only, "How soon hath time, the subtle thief of youth, etc.") to record the more momentous line: "2:30. Distributions Estate R.W. Gibson."[131] It was likely at this meeting that his sisters announced their decision to transfer ownership of 137 Beacon Street to him, for a rough draft of the agreement was drawn up the following day. It was a generous act—Gibson had already inherited Forty Steps in his own right, and Ethel was now a widow—yet it was not without acrimony. He later complained that his sisters "ramsacked [sic]" the house following Rosamond's death, an imagined pillaging that he claimed cost him "five years of continuous and laborious work" to bring the house back to its former glory.[132] As late as the year before his death Gibson continued to dwell on the pain of his original disinheritance, telling a journalist, "my father did everything for my sisters, you know."[133]

Leaving his things at 121 Beacon for the time being, Gibson entered the house from the start as its conservator.

Adopting Rosamond's bedroom as his own, he explained to an interviewer in 1953 that it had always been his wish to sleep in the "bed in which he was born" (to others, he confided this was also the bed in which he intended to die).[134] Leaving the room essentially undisturbed—according to Gibson's later estate appraisal, even Rosamond's silver dressing set never moved—he made two significant additions. Across the bed he placed his Grandmother Warren's lace spread, and over his bureau he hung a framed, black-edged photograph of the Gibsons' plot at Mount Auburn Cemetery.[135] Taken the day of Rosamond's funeral, the image features the graves of four family members but reads on reverse only: "Grave of My Mother."

If Gibson's aim was to memorialize his mother's arrangements at 137 Beacon Street—last updated in the 1890s—then his approach to the two spaces most associated with his father, his former bedroom and library, represented the opposite strategy. Effectively removing the paternal bedroom, Gibson transformed this space into a writing den he named the Red Study (initially "the Pink Bed Room," named for the poppy-colored carpet he installed in May 1935).[136] Here he recreated the décor of his bachelor apartments, rooms described by the *Boston Globe* in 1905 as "furnished in an old-fashioned key . . . adorned with pictures and bric-a-brac proper to the shadow of Beacon Hill."[137] These elements included prints of his Warren ancestors, family coats of arms, framed letters from royalty (or rather, letters from their representatives thanking Gibson for his

3.10
The Red Study at
137 Beacon Street.
Courtesy John Woolf,
Gibson House
Museum, Boston, MA.

unsolicited tribute poetry), along with numerous photographs of himself as a younger man. Over his desk and the room's center table Gibson scattered his ever-growing collection of manuscripts. While he left his father's library essentially intact, Gibson made one transformative addition. Over the mantel he hung a triptych of himself—the three portraits he had commissioned in 1900–1901. Capturing him at the moment of his greatest dandified beauty, and on the cusp of his final rift with his father, this gallery suggested Dorian Gray's portrait in reverse, a tableau of Charlie Before the Fall.

By reimagining his father's rooms, Gibson created shrines within this larger temple to his youthful, literary persona. As Virginia Woolf observed in her 1932 essay "Great Men's Houses":

> It would seem to be a fact that writers stamp themselves upon their possessions more indelibly than other people. Of artistic taste they may have none; but they seem always to possess a much rarer and more interesting gift—a faculty for housing themselves appropriately, for making the table, the chair, the curtain, the carpet into their own image.[138]

Even the home's interstitial spaces now reflected Gibson back to himself. The walls of the upper stair hall proclaimed more than he likely realized about his campy range of passions: here prints of French châteaux jostled for wall space with a pinup of boxer Joe Louis and publicity shots of actress Maude Adams. As a visitor to the house in the 1940s noted, "Mr. Gibson had a lot of 'funny' photographs and things hanging there," adding, "I never asked him about Joe Louis."[139]

The curatorial approach Gibson adopted in the first months of his return led, on the morning of May 22, 1935, to an epiphany. Putting up the house in preparation for his annual removal to Nahant, he started a new line in his diary: "Gibson House—Gibson Museum / for 1 or 2 years Marking Everything."[140] This passion project of his later years—to transform both 137 Beacon Street and Forty Steps into public museums—offered Gibson the possibility to arrest time at these houses, and in doing so, to preserve his identity. Cast in amber, the interiors at Boston and Nahant would reflect the presumed "Golden Age" of his class; his rose gardens at Forty Steps, forever maintained as he designed them, would provide a horticultural complement to his poetry; and most important of all, his writing—unpublished for decades—would be safeguarded for future audiences. By formally establishing the homes' period of significance as 1859 to 1900, moreover, Gibson erased his years of exile from the family home. 137 Beacon Street would forever reflect the environment of a newly published, twenty-six-year-old author.

Despite this 1900 cutoff date for the houses' (and his own) period of significance, Gibson considered his literary production to be evergreen. With his manuscripts now scattered throughout his family home—a collection he referred to as early as 1931 as his "literary archive"—he believed his museum could, by a kind of alchemy, transform these dog-eared typescripts into new publications long after his death.[141] Yet if 137 Beacon Street provided Gibson the vehicle for this conversion, then it also became his most important muse.

The idea to spend "1 or 2 years Marking Everything" soon became its own literary enterprise. The process lasted more than two years. Not only did Gibson craft elaborate labels for objects in the house ("at this desk and with this pen the sonnets of 'The

Wounded Eros' were written by me at my rooms at 9 Charles Street in 1904, Fourth Floor") but he also drafted detailed room guides for future docents.[142] In these he speaks conversationally of himself in the third person ("On this piano Mr. Gibson used to compose symphonies. . . . His performance, at times, was compared by music critics to that of a professional, his touch being especially delicate") and issues commands to an invisible curatorial staff (the cover of one guide warns, "Never to be loaned or handled by order of Charles Hammond Gibson").[143] In some passages he invites readers to imagine the home, himself, and his social milieu through *absent* stage props. Describing a "most valuable and delicate set of Chinese rugs" collected in the 1920s, Gibson confides they "are not always exhibited," for

> when on the floor they are never walked on, except in Chinese slippers, an example of which, worn by Mr. Gibson at a famous Chinese Ball at Marble House, Newport, Rhode Island, given by the late Mrs. Oliver Belmont for her daughter the Duchess of Marlborough in 1915, may be seen. These are kept on the lower shelf of the Treasure Cabinet on the left.[144]

Gibson's room guides examine the home's wallpapers, upholstery, and architectural elements like archaeological strata, sometimes offering wholly invented backstories for these elements. Referring to the staircase in the entry hall, for example, he makes the absurd claim: "The Grand Staircase, covered with a crimson carpet, is sometimes called the Ambassador's Staircase, because it was here that Ambassadors and other distinguished guests were received."[145] Today one of the most frequently repeated stories about Gibson involves this staircase, if not its use by invented ambassadors. In order to preserve the home's rooms intact, the writer is said to have served bathtub gin on the stairs to bewildered guests, barring them from the "public" rooms with velvet ropes. The story may be apocryphal, but it captures his curatorial rigor—a restrictive attitude once applied, in miniature fashion, to Rosamond's sanctified dollhouse.

However many room guides, sonnets, odes, and essays continued to flow from Gibson's pen, his writing style—like his house—came to a full stop at 1900. His dated literary form had always drawn criticism, from *Two Gentlemen in Touraine* onward, but with his museum project Gibson was now forced to defend the anachronistic character of his environment. His contemporaries did not look upon the Victorian period with fondness. In her 1913 manual *The House in Good Taste*, decorator Elsie de Wolfe wrote presciently, "I fancy the furniture of the mid-Victorian era will never be coveted by collectors, unless someone should build a museum for these freakish objects of house furnishing."[146] For his part, comic novelist Beverley Nichols perceived Victorian interiors as a kind of visual punchline. In his 1927 novel *Crazy Pavements*, the flamboyant Lord William pronounces, "If I were Prime minister I should issue an order that everybody possessing Victorian drawing-rooms should be forced to preserve them intact, because of the inroads which good taste is making upon them. Nothing is so shattering as to live in an era of really good taste. It stultifies the soul."[147] Not to be outdone, within a year of Gibson's museum epiphany, *New Yorker* cartoonist Charles Addams introduced the Addams Family—macabre characters defined, in large part, by their home's spooky Victorian interiors.

Gibson, however, was in it for the long game. Writing his lawyer about the museum scheme, he insisted: "I would like to make a prophecy to you, that by the year 2000 a

Victorian museum would be a very unique, very important institution."[148] To preserve a patrician home—especially one that epitomized a bygone era—was for him a form of *noblesse oblige*. Indeed, in *Two Gentlemen in Touraine* he directly linked the notion of a public museum with the homes of European nobility. Of the Château Azay-le-Rideau, the book's narrator writes, "year after year of taste and care have made it, at last, a perfect museum of artistic and historical ornaments," a didactic model of "distinction, elegance, [and] breeding . . . acquired with centuries of blood."[149] No special effort was required, then, to transform Gibson's house into The Gibson House (as he would later style 137 Beacon Street). Like Azay, by his reasoning, its generational strata of taste, bloodlines, and cumulative history were now fully formed. The work ahead lay only in *resisting* change at the house. Yet no amount of velvet ropes could preserve 137 Beacon Street from the changing fortunes of Back Bay.

Gibson and his Boston milieu had always moved forward, and halted, in lockstep. The year of his birth in 1874 marked the peak of Back Bay's ascendance, its avenues lined by mature trees and its townhouses filled with patrician and parvenu elites. By the time he inherited his family home, the district—and, it must be admitted, the man himself—had entered a period of marked decline. In the mid-1930s few of Back Bay's townhouses housed families of wealth; rather, they were carved into apartment buildings, rooming houses, doctor's offices, academic institutions, and middlebrow shops. In his elegiac *Boston and the Boston Legend* (1936) Lucius Beebe described the area's demise in Wagnerian terms: Back Bay was witnessing nothing less than the *Götterdämmerung* ("Twilight of the Gods"), he claimed, its patrician class replaced by "shabby apartments and trade."[150] Not only had the district been hard hit by the years of the Depression, but it had also been transformed by the rise of the streetcar and automobile—developments that spurred the exodus of wealthy families to the suburbs. By 1940, only five years after Gibson assumed the title of 137 Beacon Street, only five houses in Back Bay belonged to descendants of their original owners.[151]

If Howells's *The Rise of Silas Lapham* had announced Back Bay's emergence as a Boston power base, then John L. Marquand's Pulitzer Prize–winning novel, *The Late George Apley* (1937), served as the district's obituary. Published two years after Gibson initiated his museum scheme, *The Late George Apley* is a trenchant satire of old-money Boston. Apley, a Boston Brahmin born in 1866 and raised in a townhouse on Beacon Street, is both "late" in the sense that his class was itself entering an obsolescent phase—the hour was late for them all—and also "late" in the sense that he represents a kind of walking dead man.

Trapped by the constraints of his class, hemmed in by inherited furnishings, and haunted by an early love affair thwarted by his family, Apley writes to his son at the end of the novel: "these conventions in someway have stepped in between me and my life. . . . They were designed to promote stability and inheritance. Perhaps they have gone a little bit too far."[152] Like Gibson's, Apley's life is structured by a tribal Boston worldview and paralyzing reverence for the past. (His parlor, too, remains "just as it had been when Grandmama arranged it.")[153]

It is tempting to believe Marquand based his character directly on Gibson—the two would appear together in a feature for *Life* magazine in 1941—yet it is more useful to consider the ways Apley and Gibson represent a similar and moribund type, one that even a non-Bostonian could recognize. After reading advance proofs of *The Late George Apley*, Upton Sinclair wrote Marquand's publisher:

> I started to read it and it appeared to me to be an exact and very detailed
> picture of a Boston aristocrat. . . . But finally I began to catch what I thought
> was a twinkle in the author's eye. . . . I hope I am not mistaken in my idea that
> the author is kidding the Boston idea. It is very subtle and clever, and I am not
> sure that Boston will get it.[154]

In his home, writing, and eventually in his person, Gibson was himself subtly "kidding the Boston idea"—and Boston did not get it.

On January 18, 1936, Gibson called to order the first meeting of the newly christened Gibson Society, seven individuals—mostly friends and cousins—charged with directing the museum's "historical and literary mission."[155] He left immediately thereafter for a months-long visit to the mid-Atlantic and South, a trip that served both as an exploratory tour of house museums and also a dry run for the celebrity he believed his home promised. Traveling with a female friend and driver, Gibson first visited the Crowninshield Gardens at Winterthur in Delaware—a home then in its own early stages of development as a house museum (Winterthur's owner, Henry Francis du Pont, was his cousin by marriage). He then proceeded to visit Colonial Williamsburg, recently restored by John D. Rockefeller; paid homage to Edgar Allan Poe's grave in Baltimore; attended a reception at the White House; and continued on to Georgia and Florida, where he performed in campy nighttime radio spots and mingled with (read: stalked) Russian royalty at posh hotels.

Lacking the resources of a du Pont or Rockefeller, Gibson in April 1938 sought an external partner for his scheme: The Society for the Preservation of New England Antiquities (SPNEA), an organization founded and directed by his cousin William Sumner Appleton. At Gibson's invitation Appleton assembled a committee of eight to tour the house and assess its proposed donation to SPNEA. Setting aside just thirty minutes for this visit on May 4—and warning Gibson that several of its members could only come for half this time—Appleton showed little enthusiasm from the start. Writing to one committee member he offered: "You may not want to come to the house at all, and there isn't the slightest necessity for doing so."[156]

Undeterred by Appleton's lukewarm response, an eager Gibson wrote him—twice—on the day before the committee's visit, outlining his plans for

> a literary shrine, the framework, in an unusually complete condition, of a
> New England writer, in the setting of a family background representative
> of the history, culture, and standards of Boston during the last half of the
> nineteenth century. . . . It represents the higher standards of American letters,
> the arts, and the arts of living.[157]

Writing as if the museum were already fully institutionalized, Gibson referenced his Manuscript Department, Department of Textiles, and (most endearingly) his Silver and Bric-a-Brac Department, explaining which of these were likely to be open at the time of the committee's visit. Like the Treasure Cabinet that held his historic Chinese slippers, these "Departments" consisted of bureau drawers stuffed with articles awaiting tags, or boxes filled with crumbling, onion-skin typescripts—all requiring more attention than a fifteen-minute tour would have allowed.

Writing Appleton the day after the committee's visit, Chair Thomas Frothingham declared its members "convinced that it would be a great mistake to maintain that house as a memorial to Mr.Gibson . . . it is a thing we should stay out of, absolutely!"[158] The back channel exchanges that occurred over the following week—the group would not meet for an official vote until May 11—are notable for two particularly damning elements. First, there is no discussion of Gibson's proposal to create a literary shrine. Not once, in fact, is his profession as a writer mentioned. Second, in considering the architectural merits of 137 Beacon Street—the sole criterion the committee addressed—members insisted that, while they were not opposed to preserving a mid-Victorian home, they believed "the Gibson house [always a lower-case 'h'] . . . is not at all a first-class" example of its type, nor was it "so outstanding that we might not get another as good."[159] In a terse letter to his cousin on May 13 ("Dear Sir"), Appleton informed him of the committee's rejection. Years later when Gibson asked him to join the Gibson Society board, Appleton wrote a colleague, "I should much prefer having nothing to do with it."[160]

However shielded Gibson might have been from the rawness of the committee's private reactions—their conclusion that 137 Beacon Street was simply too banal to warrant preservation might have broken him—their official denial undoubtedly stung. Fortunately, Forty Steps continued to provide him the solace and admiration Boston did not. Indeed, in the 1920s and 1930s his elaborate rose gardens at Nahant were only just entering their full maturity, prospering as if in indirect proportion to his shrinking world in Back Bay. One 1932 profile of his gardens, open to the public every July, proclaimed them "one of the show places of the North Shore."[161] The article goes on to exclaim: "Mr. Gibson has accomplished a horticultural stunt in producing his beautiful rose gardens," using only a palette of "white, pink, and wine-colored" blooms and combining grand displays with a number of "petite, dainty, and delicate" tea gardens.

Like his poetry and his Boston home, his rose gardens—"laid out in a curious composition," according to the *Boston Herald*, "of the French and Italian formal styles, with a Yankee casualness"—belonged to another era.[162] Chief among his floral "stunts" at Forty Steps was the garden's centerpiece, a Victorian arrangement of Evangeline roses thirty feet in diameter "growing in a goblet shape and ascending into a complete ball at its tip almost ten feet from the ground."[163] Alongside this floral chalice was an arrangement of Tausendschon pink rose bushes, trained "to resemble two perfectly shaped rose baskets." While 137 Beacon Street rarely saw visitors, Gibson estimated that his annual "Festival of Roses" drew tens of thousands by the 1930s—a group that included "presidents, cardinals, princes, dukes, singers actresses, and various celebrities."[164] Even allowing for Gibson's characteristic hyperbole, press coverage of the gardens and Gibson's correspondence with those who visited there—including, indeed, Cardinal William Henry O'Connell, Archbishop of Boston—confirm the site's tremendous appeal. [165] (Inspired perhaps by the Cardinal's visit, Gibson signed one letter from this period "First Epistle of Charles the Horticulturalist.")

The gardens at Nahant offered Gibson more than just a source of public adulation. It is worth remembering that he spent nearly half the year at Forty Steps, where his gardening constituted a vital complement to—and in the summer months, a substitute for—his writing. ("I only wanted to create beauty," he once told a reporter, "through my verse and my garden.")[166] Nearly as much as 137 Bacon Street, moreover, the gardens of Nahant constituted a kind of mental scaffolding for him—a place that contained, as

3.11

Commercial postcard
of rose gardens
at Forty Steps,
Nahant, MA (1926).
Photograph by Charles
Hammond Gibson,
Jr. Gibson House
Museum, Boston, MA.

he once put it, the "fragrance of memory."[167] In a telling letter from 1939, Gibson told a friend he had "drempt [*sic*] that all the family arrived to stay" at Forty Steps (Ethel had died the year before, and "little" Rosamond was then living in California).[168] No sooner had they arrived than "the gardeners took my best potted plants and emptied them into the gutter, [and] drunken trespassers came and sat on my hydrangeas. . . . When I tried to placate them by offering them hospitality in the house I looked and saw a burglar putting on my best English flannel trowsers [*sic*]. I moaned." The memory of his humiliation in the 1890s, it seems, cast its shadow even over his beloved gardens.

Between 1941 and 1945, Gibson's nightmare about Forty Steps came true, to a certain degree, when the United States Navy commandeered his land for military exercises. Despite the damage the sailors wrought on his rose gardens—the landscape at Forty Steps never fully recovered—he felt compensated, at least, by the presence of handsome naval officers. In his 1945 poem "To My Honorary Gardeners," he confirms that the connection between gardening and eroticism remained strong even for this septuagenarian. Speaking of the men assigned to tend Forty Steps' grounds, he wrote, "I even might arise at dawn / And from my window watch you roll the lawn / But if I could for once employ all three / My soul might reach a stage of extacy [*sic*]."[169]

Gibson's romantic yearnings in this period were not limited to ogling sailors—for after many decades, de Mauny had reappeared in his life. Between 1939 and 1941, the men exchanged a number of touching letters, and while it is possible the two had never lost contact, this remains their only surviving correspondence. In 1925 de Mauny, then many years estranged from his long-suffering wife, had purchased a small island off the coast of Sri Lanka (then British Ceylon). There he built an Art Deco villa named "Taprobane" and surrounded it with elaborate tropical gardens. It might well have been de Mauny's publication of *The Gardens of Taprobane* (1937) that brought the men back together, for in his earliest letter from this period de Mauny references having sent Gibson the book's prospectus. (Echoing Gibson's own boasts, the brochure describes the many "kings, princes, duchesses, Prime Ministers . . . and humbler mortals" who made pilgrimages to Taprobane.)[170] Though Gibson might have been forgiven for envying his old flame—de Mauny had managed to publish his gardens, after all—he graciously responded, instead, by offering de Mauny his "Ode to Taprobane," a poem that imagines their reunion on the island ("I fly, I fly! See how I fly—to Taprobane!").[171]

In January 1940, de Mauny wrote "Dear old Charles" that he'd read his ode "over and over again," confiding it had awakened many old memories: "How often do I think of 137 Beacon Street. . . . It seems only yesterday and I feel quite sad."[172] Writing similarly the following October, he confessed to Gibson: "I often think of 'le petit Pontvallain' [a village in Touraine]. They were our happiest days were they not?"[173] Tempering his wistfulness with a sense of urgency, de Mauny asked Gibson: "When shall we meet? How few [years] are left. I am nearly seventy-four and probably will go first."[174] Repeating his invitation in 1941, he added in a postscript: "Why are you not here? We might share expenses and live like fighting cocks."[175]

As both men realized, their homes and gardens had long ago replaced the need, or possibility, for a romantic partner. (In *The Gardens of Taprobane* de Mauny asked, "The friend of friends eludes me . . . where am I to find him, whose beautiful soul and body should not only complete but surpass the beauty that surrounds me?")[176] Gibson's responses to de Mauny reveal that he, too, now focused his attentions primarily on his homes, yet in his final letter to de Mauny he closed with the poignant, "Yours till death takes us."[177] Eleven days later—on Valentine's Day, in fact—Gibson's prior letter to de Mauny, dated November 28, was returned unopened and stamped: "DEAD—RETURN TO SENDER."[178]

Gibson's inscrutable remark to the *Boston Herald* in 1950, claiming he had "died" a decade before, is more understandable when we consider his world in the early 1940s. Not only had he lost de Mauny but also, for the foreseeable future, Forty Steps. And while he had made a lifelong habit of bemoaning his fading looks, he now faced the grim reality of aging. On turning sixty-five in 1939, he recorded he was losing his teeth and his stomach ached ("my spirit is yet young, but in fact I begin to wilt").[179] In this period too, his dwindling financial resources—always his greatest anxiety—appeared to have reached an all-time low; his last letter to de Mauny included the confession, "Ruined? My dear boy, we are beggared beyond description!" (One visitor to 137 Beacon Street at this time recalled his host serving "soup" made by boiling a beef bone in water.)[180] In 1940 Gibson let the last of his household staff go, now taking his meals at the nearby Hotel Brunswick—and in the winter months he rented a room there, too, to avoid heating 137 Beacon Street.[181] Putting on a brave face for *Life* magazine when asked to join John Marquand for a March 1941 feature ("Marquand's Boston: A Trip with America's Foremost Satirist"), Gibson gamely posed in his library with the novelist; caught in the camera's glare he appears like a waxwork figure, a visual punchline to Marquand's writing. (In one uncharitable caption, *Life* offered that Gibson's home "reflect[ed] an era when great prosperity gave Beacon Street homes a massive ugliness then considered good taste.")[182]

By the 1940s, 137 Beacon Street had devolved into more than just an example of

3.12
Novelist John L.
Marquand (left) and
Gibson in the library
of 137 Beacon Street,
1941. Note triptych of
Gibson's 1901–1902
portraits over the
mantel. Photograph
by Otto Hagel for
Life magazine. Otto
Hagel Archive at the
Center for Creative
Photography,
University of Arizona.

outdated style. In 1942 its moth-eaten carpets, sprung upholstery, and faded wallpaper received a funereal blanket of oily soot when Gibson's boiler exploded (even before the accident, a cleaning woman described the home's interiors in a state of "gross neglect").[183] Covering most of the home's surfaces, too, were the manuscripts he continued to churn out. Writing his literary agents in 1945—or rather, the men "I regard as my literary agents"— he admitted: "all I can do now is write . . . an enormous accumulation has submerged me here at Gibson House, which is now a Literary and Historical Memorial—a sort of pre-museum awaiting my death."[184] (Gibson later told a journalist his writings appeared "like the droppings of pigeons all over the house.")[185]

What might have been the setting for a truly Gothic tale—a moldering house whose rooms ultimately madden its final inhabitant—was, for Gibson, an environment in which he appeared to thrive. Much like the narrator in *Two Gentleman in Touraine*—who asked, "could you imagine anything more romantic than living in a ruined castle?"—he appeared to find nobility in his home's decay. Writing a friend in 1943, Gibson declared: "The house is peaceful—almost too peaceful. . . . I do not mind the shortages of food and clothes. The House is simply heavenly."[186] To another, he wrote that he was "often laid low with all manner of delightful deseases [*sic*] . . . and my roof leaks like seives [*sic*] but Gibson House is delightful."

Above all, he loved his home for the protection it offered from the rapidly changing world—and snickering—that lay outside his door. As writer Mary Bookstaver confided to a friend in 1896, "freedom consists in being protected . . . see how happy is the little canary bird in its gilded cage! I defy anyone to say it is not free. Were the door opened, some ravenous cat would eat it."[187] Gibson envisioned just such a cage in a 1900 diary entry, announcing his "uncertain plan" in time "to build me a mansion—a palace—from whose windows I may look down upon Evil, and from within whose walls I am to be conscious only of that which is good and of the beautiful."[188]

When he did leave the house, his antiquated clothing functioned like a kind of deep sea diving suit—sustaining him in the outside atmosphere until he could safely return to the parlors his mother had decorated. Like Evelyn Waugh's character Ambrose Silk in *Put Out More Flags* (1942), Gibson "caused time to slip back to an earlier age . . . leav[ing] his persecution downstairs with his hat and umbrella."[189] Far from suffering a shortage of clothes, as he wrote his friend during the war, he had made a conscious decision to wear nothing made after the 1930s. When asked in the 1950s where he bought his suits, he insisted, "I have my clothes, why should I buy any? I have a suit or two from every year from 1892 to 1937" (and showed a preference for formal outfits from 1890s, right through the mid-twentieth century).[190] The pose of the dandy is always a form of defense, yet in Gibson's case his clothing—like his house, his poetry, his gardens, and even his diction—placed him safely in another era, notably the one in which he had been desired.

Marquand's George Apley claimed, "there are familiar enough eccentric types [in Boston], but even these conform to a pattern of conformity."[191] Gibson's particular genius, however, was his sendup of conformity itself—a caricature of the "Boston idea" so subtle in its campy sensibility that it was like a funhouse mirror held up to the city's fading elite. It is no wonder, then, that his eccentricities placed him socially beyond the pale. (When Cleveland Amory published his encyclopedic study of old Boston, *The Proper Bostonians,* in 1947, he ignored the Gibson family entirely.) No stranger to pariah status, Gibson was by this time better prepared to face off with his tribe. Indeed, the persona he created in the final decades of his life constituted his greatest achievement in fiction—a figure that became, by the 1950s, a kind of foolish if beloved local character. Not only was Gibson in on the joke, he was the one scripting it.

Two Gibson profiles near the end of his life reveal the delight mid-century journalists took in parading this living Boston relic. The first, written by Lawrence Dame for the *Boston Herald* in 1950, identifies Gibson as a "Proper Bostonian" (despite Amory's snub), a "Victorian . . . minstrel" and "aesthete" who harkened back "to the dandies of Beau Brummel's day . . . a small man, almost frail in appearance, but with a nimble if somewhat cantankerous physique."[192] Despite Gibson's regal affect—"his butler calls him 'Sire,'" the piece begins—Dame reassures his readers the poet is an "indefatigable conversationalist . . . [who] sparkles with humor." Gibson's irony-laden pronouncements range from his gardens to politics to cocktails, but occasionally he lapses into more serious meditations. ("I am a disembodied spirit," he offers over a martini; "often I think of myself as Renaissance, and again as Greek or Eastern. I was born to be an individualist.") Though he nods to his subject's writing career, Dame rightly concludes that Gibson "is quite as remarkable in himself as for anything he has done."

Three years after Dame's article appeared, Harvard professor Frederick C. Packard Jr. invited Gibson to record nineteen of his sonnets for posterity.[193] The recordings are remarkable not only because they preserve Gibson's eccentric diction and delivery but also because they pull back the curtain on his Brahmin minstrel performance. For in addition to reading his poetry—to what sounds like an audience of two appreciative friends—he also reads portions of Dame's profile aloud. In multiple instances he and his audience erupt in laughter over Dame's descriptions, and at one point Gibson confesses, with a chuckle, how performative his remarks to the journalist were: "I talk too much, you see . . . this is me as a humorist."[194]

If Dame's piece presented Gibson as a witty raconteur, then *Boston Post* columnist Grace Davidson offered him as a kind of Brahmin clown-for-hire. In her 1953 column titled "About People," Davidson begins: "When a distinguished visitor to our city asks to meet a Bostonian who dramatizes the Boston legend, the anxious-to-please hostess telephones Charles Hammond Gibson."[195] She insists that "he never fails to turn in an expert performance at lunch, tea, or formal ball . . . and he is easy to find: he is listed in the telephone directory." Held up as a figure of high camp, Davidson's Gibson is a "small, lean . . . seventy-eight-year-old prototype of John Marquand's George Apley," a "frail bachelor . . . [who] sleeps in his late mother's handsome bed" and hosts "wonderful tea parties" at tables set "with pink china the way it was a hundred years ago." Apparently ignorant of Gibson's writing career, despite the piles of manuscripts she describes seeing at 137 Beacon Street, she offers that he "has just written his first volume of sonnets."

Gibson's late recognition as a walking performance piece . . . worked. As his guest books from the 1950s attest, the year before his death saw a significant rise in the number of dinner parties and other celebrations at 137 Beacon Street. Between 1950 and 1952, no more than forty visitors appear annually; in 1953 alone, Gibson welcomed ninety-one guests.[196] Significantly, many of the entries in these books indicate guests encountering the poet and his house for the first time ("Charming Personality!" "A most charming visit," "I step into another world!").[197] And as "frail . . . and cantankerous" as he was reported to be, Gibson appears to have attracted a circle of young men to his home in these years, including a group of Harvard graduates who met there to play Mahjong with "Uncle Charlie," as they called him. Kenneth MacRae (Harvard class of 1945) later fondly remembered, "the Mahjong club never got to Mahjong, but spent . . . evenings over one winter socializing, having cocktails, etc."[198] Gibson "cut quite a figure" at these gatherings, MacRae recalled, "very much the center of attention and center of conversation."

The year before Gibson's death, writer Susan Nichols Pulsifer attended a dinner at 137 Beacon Street. Though a stranger to her host, her subsequent letter to him demonstrates an unusually perceptive understanding of the man and his home. In Gibson she saw neither Marquand's relic nor Dame's minstrel, but rather, a man who had achieved something of value and permanence—if not with his writing (though she touchingly asks if she might speak to the *New Yorker* on his behalf) then in the way he orchestrated time itself. She wrote:

> I know just how you feel when you say that you enjoy today looking through the lovely long "vistas" of your old rooms; for here you do not only look through space,—you look through time itself,—a more meaningful vista and dimension, which I think we can only see into as we get older: you look through these vistas of rooms, of time,—back to your youth, your childhood,

even possibly back to another generation. . . . You see I am one who believes that time cannot truly be said to pass or disappear; time merely *extends*, in my belief. . . . Am I right?[199]

Pulsifer was right. Gibson never consigned history to a position remote from himself—rather, he collapsed his past into an ever-living present. (As William Faulkner famously put it, "The past is never dead. It isn't even past.")

The last gathering Gibson hosted at 137 Beacon Street, appropriately enough, was a celebration of Queen Elizabeth II's coronation in June 1953 (Gibson had for many years engaged in a one-sided correspondence with the future Queen). Yet it was one of the guest book's final entries, penned by a friend from the Hotel Brunswick, that recognized the occasion's true monarch: "Long may *he* reign!"[200] Four days shy of his eightieth birthday that November, Gibson was dead. As if to prepare for this moment—indeed, when had he *not* been preparing for this moment?—he had ended his Harvard recording the year before with his 1938 sonnet "Remembrance":

> Oh, I would have you once remember me,
> Not as I am, with suffering that mars
> The countenance and seared with countless scars.
> But as I was, a youth of twenty-three,
> Fresh fashioned for the life that was to be.[201]

THE FALL—AND RISE—OF THE HOUSE OF GIBSON

If Gibson's 1950s profiles winked at his self-fashioning, then his obituary in the *Boston Herald* laid the game bare. The piece appears at first glance to confirm his carefully cultivated image ("Charles Hammond Gibson Dies / Poet, 79, Was 'Proper Bostonian'") and lifts wholesale some of the more colorful sections of Dame's and Davidson's profiles.[202] Yet it also includes qualifiers that suggest its subject was delusional, foregrounding his lists of social accolades and literary accomplishments with the caveats, "His self-written obituary said" or "Gibson claims." And rather than naming him outright as a fixture of Boston society, the newspaper offered only that he "delighted in being designated as a 'Proper Bostonian.'" Not once is his plan to establish a museum mentioned in the obituary, which simply ends: "Mr. Gibson died in his home at 137 Beacon Street, which he called 'Gibson House.'"

For their part, the appraisers of his estate did not mince words. Their twenty-six-page report is in its own way more damning than anything Appleton's SPNEA committee might have said in 1938.[203] Though Gibson happily confided to friends in 1946 that "an inventory of my estate . . . has exceeded its original book value" (he claimed to have spent $15,000 to restore his mother's interiors), appraisers now pegged the worth of Gibson's collection, in Boston and Nahant, at just over $3,000 in total.[204] Appraisers assigned the qualifiers "obsolete" or "no commercial value" no less than 225 times in the document, accompanied by descriptors like "poor condition," "overstuffed," "worn," "very badly worn," "all broken," and "as-is." The contents of Gibson's famous wardrobe appear here only as "miscellaneous old clothing," while his beloved typewriter and Rosamond's *The*

Pedigree of Warren held "no value." Even the Chinese slippers from the Vanderbilts' ball fell under the heading, "small pieces of bric-a-brac (no value)."

To their credit, the Gibson Society—an all-new board, given that five of the original 1936 cohort had died and two were too old to serve—understood that "obsolete family portraits," overstuffed furniture, and the intact collection of three generations held a value no accountant could fully measure. Taking seriously their charge to open Gibson House as a public institution, while recognizing the limits of its small endowment, they made the difficult decision in 1957 to let Forty Steps go—and along with it, Gibson's dream to present his poetry and rose gardens as the marriage of his accomplishments. It took three years after his death to prepare even the neglected 137 Beacon Street to receive the public, but on June 11, 1957, the Gibson House Museum officially opened its doors.

In press coverage of the opening, the 1950s' disdain for the Victorian period was on full display. The *Boston Herald* offered there was much in this home to "startle visitors," who had only to ring the bell to "enter the world of Victoria" and experience a series of interiors so spooky they "would make a perfect second-act setting in the theater."[205] Under the headline "Era of Black Walnut and Clutter," Boston's *Panorama* magazine announced: "Here at last is the long awaited museum—one you can completely cover in a short period of time—that is, unless you get lost among the clutter."[206] Local journalist Elizabeth Bernkopf repeated this warning, describing "the immense clutter of functionless objects" at Gibson House, whose "stiff," "formal," and "imposing" character was not for everyone.[207] Her review ends with a quote from Mark Twain: "People who like that sort of thing will find it just the sort of thing they like."

One man who certainly "liked that sort of thing" was Gibson's longtime friend Gerard B. Ladd, anointed by him as the museum's first curator. Though seventeen years Gibson's junior, he was struck from the same mold. The two had met in 1920 at the Trinity Church Men's Club, when Ladd was a handsome young twenty-nine-year-old; by 1957 Ladd had himself become an aging bachelor-aesthete known to favor a Victorian frock coat.[208] From the start the board was reluctant to present the house as a reflection of the men's dandified, Wildean world—and doubtless, they worried over winking press coverage that Ladd had celebrated the museum's opening with "pink tea and cucumber sandwiches."[209]

The solution they landed upon was to present the home not as a literary shrine to Gibson, or even as a museum devoted to his family, but rather as a "center of Victoriana" for the study of *any* material related to Victorian Boston, whether connected to the Gibsons or not.[210] Announcing a call for "gifts of theater and concert programs of the era between 1837 and 1901," as the *Boston Herald* reported, the museum sought to create a research library devoted to this era with the house as its primary exhibit.[211] Beyond collecting Victorian ephemera, the museum in its early years also accepted—much to the confusion of later curators—Victorian furnishings that had never belonged to the house.

At the time of the museum's opening audiences not only considered Victorian interiors cluttered but downright unnerving, evoking the "second-act setting" the *Boston Herald* described. The Addams Family's creepy Victorian home had entertained *New Yorker* readers for as long as the Gibson Society existed, its style an intentional reversal of "normal" American family life. Yet with the tremendous success of Alfred Hitchcock's thriller *Psycho* (1960), just three years after Gibson House opened, we see reflected not one but two optics problems for the museum. As Hitchcock fully realized, postwar American audiences viewed Victorian interiors with a distaste that bordered on panic. (It bears noting how uncannily the entry hall of Norman Bates's home resembles 137 Beacon Street, even down to specific decorative details.) Beyond this, the director also knew that Bates's failed heterosexuality—his disordered relationship with his dead mother, his obsessive preservation of the family home, and inability to bed Janet Leigh's character—provided its own, arguably greater source of terror. The museum's board therefore faced a Bates problem as much as it did a Wilde one.

Later Gibson Society board member Marjorie Drake Ross claimed that, in the museum's first decades, there was a concerted attempt by the board and surviving family members "to eradicate Charles Hammond Gibson Jr.'s presence from the house."[212] Yet whatever protection the museum might have gained from his "mixed reputation . . . because of his 'personal life'" (as a one-time Gibson acquaintance put it in 2007) came at the expense of public interest.[213] By shrinking from its more colorful and recent past, Gibson House resolved into the very anodyne model of a mid-Victorian home SPNEA had spurned in the 1930s. As former Gibson Society board president Edward Gordon recalls, the museum remained a fairly "closed society" well into the 1980s.[214]

All of this changed with the arrival of Catherine Seiberling, who served as Gibson House's resident guide from 1986 to 1988. During her tenure, "Charlie" (as he became affectionately known once more) returned with a vengeance. Indeed, if the board's suppression of Gibson's story owed in part to the 1950s' "Lavender Scare"—a period of widespread persecution of gay men—then we might place Seiberling's efforts, in turn, in the context of 1980s' AIDS-related Queer activism. Not only did she embrace Gibson's eccentricities and sexual identity, but in some ways she magnified the caricature of his later years—an approach that coincided, perhaps not coincidentally, with a more than doubled number of annual visitors to the museum by the mid-1980s.[215] In her Gibson House *Study Report* (1991), the first comprehensive study of the house and its collections, Seiberling noted that Gibson "liv[ed] a somewhat flamboyant and unorthodox homosexual lifestyle," smoked sweet cherry tobacco, and reportedly "walk[ed] around town in silk pajamas."[216] The pajamas story, which has no basis in surviving contemporary accounts, soon took on a life of its own. Not only did it appear in several 1990s articles about the museum's founder, but as late as the early 2010s his "silk pajamas" had mutated into "a pink kimono" on house tours.[217]

The year Seiberling's *Study Report* appeared, Gibson House received a more public boost with the publication of Steve Gross and Susan Daley's sumptuous *Old Houses* (1991)—a love letter to the "shabby chic" aesthetic that emerged in these years. "Like ancient pieces of pottery unearthed after centuries of repose," the book offered, "cracked, faded, and broken—these houses possess a beauty and truthfulness more real and valuable than any replica could ever be."[218] In a lavish twelve-page spread devoted exclusively to Gibson House, the book gloried in the home's moth-eaten rugs and faded upholstery, celebrating the very ruin that 1954 appraisers had condemned. Connected to this aesthetic, of course, was the period's fascination with patrician wealth and disdain for the new, epitomized by the frayed collars and duct-taped Topsider loafers Lisa Birnbach catalogued in her immensely popular *The Official Preppy Handbook* (1980).[219] That Gibson so presciently forecasted these trends—writing about the "remains of rank" and "air of artistic decay" he admired in the ruined homes of the French aristocracy—is perhaps unsurprising.[220] As collector David Dietcher has said, "I've long considered that gay men hold a special franchise on this dismal sense of beauty."[221]

3.13
The Red Study's
romantic disarray,
seen in Steve Gross
and Susan Daley's *Old
Houses* (1991). Image ©
Steve Gross and Susan
Daley.

When curator Wendy Swanton arrived at Gibson House in 1992, the museum's interpretative focus turned back to the extended Gibson family and away from the more outlandish stories and Brahmin minstrelsy of Gibson himself. In her twenty-five-year career at the museum Swanton weeded the house of its non-Gibsonian Victorian elements and produced valuable studies of Gibson's parents' and grandmother's generations. But she also effectively placed the museum's founder back in the closet. Speaking to *Harvard* magazine in 2015, Swanton offered:

> [Gibson] was a very eccentric lifelong bachelor, a poet and an author; we have no proof or documentation that he was gay. In a way, I feel we should respect his privacy and let others draw their own conclusions as they wish.[222]

To be fair to Swanton, Codman and Little's correspondence regarding Gibson's sexual liaisons had not yet surfaced—but even in the absence of this material, the genie was already out of the bottle. Invited to create a collection of imagined "family portraits" for Gibson House in 2010, artist-in-residence Hannah Barrett reclaimed the poet as a Queer icon. Her dreamlike *Tales from the House of Gibson* series includes the surreal portrait *Lord Charles and Lady Marbletop*, a meditation on the nested worlds Gibson inhabited. Barrett's monumental figure fuses the writer's formal Purdy portrait with a candid shot from Nahant (see figures 3.7 and 3.8, pp. 96 and 98), juxtaposing the muscular legs of his youth with the arched formality of a woman's plumed hat. The painting's title constitutes its own gendered hybrid: a mixture of Gibson's regal guise with the name of a character he developed for an unpublished novel, likely based on his cousin Lady Playfair.[223] It is in the figure's split environments that we see his complex persona emerge most clearly. Straddling the rocks of Forty Steps Beach and the Red Study at 137 Beacon Street—a room filled with the appurtenances of a dandy—he is a dazzling chimera.

In June 2019 Swanton's successor at Gibson House, Meghan Gelardi Holmes, launched a new house tour for Boston's Gay Pride month: "Charlie Gibson's Queer Boston," the first museum-sponsored program to seriously address his sexuality. Speaking of her decision, Holmes explained:

> You cannot understand the Gibson House without understanding that Charlie Gibson was a gay man. The project of preserving his family's home was a deeply personal one, and his choice to do so is tied up with his sexuality. He was interested in memorializing Back Bay's Gilded Age past, which was also a time when he was young and desirable and participating in a thriving queer subculture in Boston.[224]

3.14
Hannah Barrett, *Tales from the House of Gibson: Lord Charles and Lady Marbletop* (2010). Oil on linen (60" x 40"). Courtesy Hannah Barrett and Childs Gallery, Boston.

And so we find Gibson, at last remembered at the house "as I was at twenty-three." But as he knew better than anyone, it is impossible to fix him at this—or any—age, for he is at once the "juiciest boy" Boston ever saw, the moonstruck lover of a French Count, the poet declaiming in Mrs. Burr's drawing room, the tireless curator, and the wizened relic of Marquand's satire. "We do not have to *do* these things anymore," Gibson once reflected on the events of his life, "they are all still there as we remember them, and almost as vivid as when they first took place."[225] It is the combination of these experiences that forms the "disembodied spirit" he believed himself to be—and that ultimately constitutes Gibson House's most valuable collection. For as the poet's epitaph reads, "Only the Spirit Lives."

FOUR

LOVE AND MAGIC ON EASTERN POINT

If one wished to see a coxcomb expose himself in the most effectual manner, one
would advise him to build a villa, which is the *chef d'oeuvre* of modern impertinence, and
the most conspicuous stage which Folly can mount to display herself to the world.[1]
—Francis Coventry, *The World* (1753)

Every spirit builds itself a house, and beyond its house a world,
and beyond its world a heaven.[2]
—Ralph Waldo Emerson, *Nature* (1836)

It started with an invitation to Red Roof. Twenty-eight-year-old Henry Davis Sleeper—
"Harry" to his friends—first met the home's owner, Harvard professor A. Piatt Andrew,
at an April 12 dinner party in Boston. Joining Andrew six days later at his Gloucester,
Massachusetts, retreat, he arrived for lunch only hours after the Great 1906 Earthquake
toppled the city of San Francisco. Sleeper's heart was next.

    In the words of one local, Red Roof—like its master—exuded "an aura of immutable
bachelorhood."[3] Perched on a granite shelf overlooking Gloucester Harbor and tucked
behind a hedge-topped wall, the house
was virtually invisible from the rutted road
that formed Eastern Point Boulevard.
Intimate and lined with books, the home
featured exposed brick, boxed timbers,
and nook-lined fireplaces—Andrew
would have lit a fire that cold spring
day—as well as a soaring, third-floor suite
outfitted with a personal gymnasium.
Red Roof was both a private hideaway
for the thirty-three-year-old professor
and a home made for entertaining: its
indoor and outdoor dining rooms linked
to a hidden kitchen, its terraces featured
piped-in music through an elaborate
system of plumbing, and its living room
could transform from a quiet reading
room into a theater in the blink of an eye.

4.1
Red Roof (1902)
in Gloucester, MA
seen from Eastern
Point Boulevard in
June 1903. Red Roof
Archive, courtesy
Historic New England.

The home's allure owed in no small part to its bachelor creator. (As one guest signed Red Roof's guest book, "Here's to you, adorable little house. But you have nothing on your master A.P.A.!")[4] A graduate of Princeton and Harvard, Andrew was a brilliant economist with keen interests in theater, literature, and music—and yet he defied his period's stereotype of the meek, Ivory Tower academic. This professor was blessed with matinée-idol good looks, a deeply charismatic personality, and a passion for all forms of athleticism—tennis, swimming, golf, jogging, rowing, and horseback riding—preferably in the company of handsome young men. Following his lunch with Sleeper, Andrew hosted recent Harvard graduates Edgar Rust, Tom Beale, and Ray Atherton for the night. The next morning found Atherton and Andrew nude sunbathing in his canoe.[5]

It is difficult to imagine a man less like Andrew than Sleeper. Shy, constitutionally frail, and possessing no formal education—though known for his sharp wit—Sleeper led a quiet life in the Beacon Street home of his widowed mother. Unlike the highly sexed Andrew, moreover, it appears he had enjoyed just a single romance: a years-long relationship with poet and satirist Guy Wetmore Carryl, who died under tragic circumstances exactly two years to the month before Sleeper's first visit to Red Roof. It seems Carryl came up in the men's conversation that day, for in the note he wrote Andrew the next morning, Sleeper enclosed an article by the late writer along with an invitation to dinner in Boston ("just ourselves").[6] As he later confessed to Andrew, he had "never expected the good fortune again of finding anyone possessing the characteristics that made [Carryl] what he was."[7]

Sleeper's infatuation with his host grew over the next year with Andrew's encouragement. The professor sent him multiple pictures of himself ("I'm glad you didn't make me choose between them," Sleeper sighed, "I might have ended by politely accepting one . . . and then stealing the other") and he closed one early letter to Sleeper

4.2
Andrew and Sleeper around the time of their 1906 meeting at Red Roof.
LEFT: A. Piatt Andrew (1873–1936) shot in his preferred profile mode. Photograph by Harris & Ewing. Cape Ann Museum Library & Archives, Gloucester, MA.
RIGHT Henry Davis Sleeper (1878–1934). Courtesy Historic New England.

with such "subtle flattery," as its recipient observed, that he found himself "caught . . . with keen pleasure."[8] In turn, Sleeper sent him frequent lunch and dinner invitations, along with tickets to the opera, plays, and the exclusive Myopia Hunt Ball. Following a shopping trip to Philadelphia he mailed two "gay cravats" to Red Roof accompanied by the plea, "is it any use for me to ask you not to write a note? Your letter about the opera was sufficiently nice to answer for this—and the next ten occasions."[9] Most significant of these was the anniversary of their first lunch—a milestone he marked, as Andrew noted in his diary, by descending upon Gloucester "with many presents. Iron box, Lincoln autograph, etc. [Sleeper] spent day and night here."[10] Writing after this visit, Sleeper told Andrew he wished only for two things: "*First:* That the anniversaries to come may . . . each bring you a new measure of happiness. *Second:* That I may have the satisfaction of living to witness the same! My love to you."[11]

Given his taste for athletic young men, it is unlikely Andrew returned Sleeper's love in the same way. Yet it is worth noting that he saved Sleeper's letters from this time and clearly valued his friend's opinions, sending him drafts on financial policy that Sleeper read with keen interest (in a flirtatious note, Sleeper confided how much he admired Andrew's "attractive form"—of writing).[12] Yet for all the depth of their friendship, he surely knew he had little hope of holding Andrew's romantic attention. Indeed, in 1906–1907, Andrew appeared to be juggling no less than three serious relationships, all more than likely sexual, with former students Frank Storey and the aforementioned Beal and Rust. (Rust—whom Andrew took to Europe following the young man's 1904 graduation—had by the time of Sleeper's arrival become something of a cohost at Red Roof.) And while Andrew often invited Sleeper for overnights, he failed to include him in the raucous, days-long stag parties he hosted at Red Roof in these years, gatherings that included as many as a dozen worshipful Harvard students— among them, the twenty-year-old Franklin Delano Roosevelt.

Expressing concern one year that the Easter holiday and Harvard's spring vacation might not align, Andrew wrote a friend that he nevertheless hoped "to get some lads from college . . . and have a real Red Roof party."[13] As his guest books attest, a "real" Red Roof party involved all-day athletic contests, scrambling over the rocks, and "frightful roughhous[ing]" (in Andrew's parlance).[14] At night there was often a good deal of drinking—one pair of images shows guests in varying states of sobriety, labeled "A.M." and "P.M."—along with a variety of staged photographs. (These included a series

4.3
A Harvard house party at Red Roof, May 1907. TOP, L to R: Piatt Andrew, Edgar Rust ('04), John Tuckerman ('04), and Roger Poor ('06). BOTTOM, L to R: Piatt Andrew, Joseph Husband ('08), Richard Eggleston ('09), Crawford Burton ('08), and Candler Cobb ('07). Red Roof Archive, courtesy Historic New England.

documenting such ersatz Red Roof "teams" as the Red Roof Riding and Driving Club, Debating Team, and Musical Team.) In one 1904 diary entry, Andrew notes he "played tennis all day" with three Harvard men whose locker room names he records as "Stinkfoot" (J. Willard Wheeler, '05), "Wooly Bottom" (Harold F. Mason, '05), and "Stallion" (Rust, who had recently returned from their European trip). Speaking of himself in the third person, "Doc"—as his students called him—records his own new nickname: "Smut."[15]

Sleeper's chief rival for Andrew's heart, however, was not one of this rambunctious crew—"Doc's" romantic affairs were typically short lived—but rather, Red Roof itself. The house dated to the first generation of vacation settlers on Eastern Point, a narrow, picturesque peninsula alongside Gloucester Harbor. In 1887, a group of investors purchased and subdivided the former Thomas Niles farm into 250 plots; within two years eleven Queen Anne–style cottages sprouted up on the Point, and by 1904 this stretch of land once considered beyond civilization featured the colossal, three-hundred-room Colonial Arms Hotel. The son of a wealthy banker, Andrew was in 1901 a young professor with rooms in Harvard's Russell Hall—and it is a truth universally acknowledged that a single man in possession of a good fortune must be in want of a . . . home. His choice of Eastern Point likely derived from his sister Helen's recent marriage to Isaac Patch; the son of an old Gloucester family, Patch would build the couple's own home here. In February 1902, Andrew shared his plans for Red Roof with the Patches, and that summer he watched, spellbound, as the house rose on the harbor. After one visit to the construction site, the laconic professor recorded, "My interest intense."[16]

Andrew set up housekeeping at Red Roof that September, every detail of the home carried out to his own wishes ("the house is *really a wonder*," he marveled).[17] Like a moonstruck lover he endlessly photographed the new home—a record that eventually expanded to hundreds of images, all carefully pasted into bursting guest books. At first Andrew struggled to find a suitable name for his new love. (The eventual "Red Roof" did not emerge until a year later, when he painted the home's sweeping, Arts and Crafts–style roof its signature color.)[18] For this first season he tried out "The Shanty," and in one telling entry he simply referred to the house as "my wife."[19]

By the time of his lunch date with Sleeper, Andrew's devotion to his home had only grown. Half in love with Red Roof himself, Sleeper became a frequent guest there and in later years eagerly accepted any invitation to serve as its caretaker in Andrew's absence. The only way to guarantee invitations to Red Roof in perpetuity, however, was for Sleeper to build his own home on Eastern Point. And so on August 13, 1907, he bought Lot 101 from George Stacy, developer of the Colonial Arms Hotel next door. (The fact that such a choice harbor-side lot remained available was likely due, in part, to its uncomfortable proximity to the sprawling, three-year-old behemoth.) For Sleeper the location could not have been more desirable. The closest available property to Red Roof, it lay separated from Andrew's home by just one owner, Caroline Sinkler, who became a close friend to both men. In her own nod to Red Roof's gravitational pull, she had named her house "Wrong Roof."

When Sleeper completed his home in 1908 he christened it "Little Beauport," a nod to Samuel de Champlain's 1606 appellation for Gloucester Harbor, "Le Beau Port."[20] Yet in a deeper sense the name also conjured the figure of a "beau" or dandy—a romantic aspirant. However modest this "little beau" might have first appeared, and however mild mannered its owner, both would eventually exert a powerful influence on Andrew, Eastern

4.4
Little Beauport (1908)
in 1910. Photograph by
Thomas E. Marr and
Son. Courtesy Historic
New England.

Point, and the very arc of American interior design. Indeed, like a portent of the home's future sovereignty, on New Year's Day 1908 the towering Colonial Arms Hotel burned to the ground. Sleeper's home, still under construction, lay unscathed.

Growing from an initial twenty-six rooms to a staggering forty-six (Beauport would lose its diminutive along the way), Sleeper's home became one of the most published properties of the twentieth century—a phenomenon that shows no signs of slowing in our own time. Its first full-length feature, published in the *Gloucester Daily Times* in 1909, rightly predicted that the house "has a charm and attractiveness that it would seem would never pall"; nearly a century later, the UK-based *World of Interiors* featured Beauport on its September 2006 cover under the banner: "Style Pioneer's East Coast Fantasy."[21] (When the magazine's American editor Mitchell Owens hosted a lecture on Beauport in 2023, he regaled the standing-room-only crowd with the desperate calls he had received from designers without tickets to the event—men and women who claimed Beauport as their "favorite American home," yet many of whom, he chuckled, confessed they had never seen it in person.)[22] Indeed, it is a measure of the home's peculiar powers of attraction that the typically sober National Park Service named Beauport a National Historic Landmark in 1976 for the significance of its "playful" interiors—a criterion never before (or since) applied by the agency.

4.5
Beauport's entrance
façade today.
Photograph by
Matthew Cunningham.
Courtesy History New
England.

To say that Beauport has been widely published, however, is not to say that it is widely understood. In fact, the common thread linking most of its profiles is the repeated declaration of the home's inscrutability. It has been hailed as "provocatively unusual," "improbable," "impish," and "syncopatedly disheveled"; it is a "cock-eyed . . . domino game," "a riddle with a different answer for anyone who tries to solve it," and even, in the words of poet Kate Colby, "a Chinese ivory orb of inter-suspended, concentric worlds."[23] The home appears to have confounded even the director of the Society for the Preservation of New England Antiquities (SPNEA), William Sumner Appleton. An architectural historian not generally drawn to the provocatively unusual, he declared Sleeper's house in 1934 "the greatest antiquity in New England."[24] The house was then just twenty-six years old.

Beauport's ineffable attraction is frequently ascribed to its "magical" qualities. It is a "house of enchantment," an "Ali Baba's cave," "the magic house of East Gloucester," and a "fairy tale home" pulled straight from the story of Hansel and Gretel (Henry James even went so far as to declare Beauport "miraculous").[25] In his 1951 guidebook to Beauport—theatrically titled *Beauport at Gloucester: The Most FASCINATING House in America*—author Paul Hollister declared that any reader crossing Beauport's threshold will "find the magic is real."[26] Enchantment assumes the figure of a magician, of course—or even the dark arts of a sorcerer.

The home's frequent comparisons to Hansel and Gretel's cottage naturally summon the witch who built her house as a temptation; as Hollister warns his readers, "every room [at Beauport] is a mild ambush and a trap . . . leaving departing visitors hypnotized and covetous."[27] Perhaps to encourage such occultish comparisons, Sleeper installed in his home colored glass spheres known as "witches' balls" and told *Country Life* in 1929 that a secret passage at Beauport recalled ancient New England "refuges from witch searchers."[28] No New England house in this period, *Country Life* cautioned, was safe from "charges of wizardry."

Beauport's famous inscrutability inevitably leads critics, with apparent relief, to simply throw up their hands. Its charm is a mystery no one can solve, a fairy tale that too much daylight might destroy. Yet for historians like Douglass Shand-Tucci, this critical abdication illuminates the discomfort surrounding the home's unacknowledged Queerness—reflected both in its undercurrents of camp and theater, and its creation by a man whose sexuality lies beyond the pale of polite conversation. "Beauport is a riddle," he writes, "whose explanation need no longer be avoided."[29] The answer to the home's enigma lies, he believes, in its Queer reclamation of the Arts and Crafts Movement and Colonial Revival styles—an aesthetic he refers to as "gay Gothic."

Shand-Tucci is perfectly right about the home's critical force field—to claim Beauport's depths simply cannot be plumbed smacks of a "Don't Ask/Don't Tell" policy—yet the house's mystery lies deeper than any gay aesthetic that might be identified in its rooms. To comprehend Beauport's curious appeal we must first acknowledge that we are not Sleeper's primary audience. The house is an architectural geisha performance for which we hold no ticket, and whose curtain fell more than a century ago. Andrew was the only figure ever capable of fully solving the house's riddle, and it's unclear if he ever tried. The fact that the residue of this magic remains—we feel, quite genuinely, that our host is intent upon charming us—is a testament to the longevity of Sleeper's powers.

In the wake of the men's first meeting, and well before Beauport's completion, Sleeper commissioned a work that announced his transformation from a grieving, introverted Mama's Boy into the romantic beau of Eastern Point. Painted in late spring 1906, Wallace Bryant's monumental portrait of Sleeper is in its own way as charming and baffling as its sitter's future home. Composed in an unusual horizontal format, the portrait presents Sleeper in a regal, carved Bishop's chair; smartly dressed and coiffed, he gazes at the viewer with a brooding expression, his face half in shadow. Although Bryant presents Sleeper at nearly life size, his visual weight is matched by the gleaming vase on the table beside him. The painting is a dual portrait of a man and his collection.

Manifesting the same color harmony for which Beauport would become famous—Bryant likely found him a demanding client on this score—the work is a symphony of reds. From his oxblood vase to the dusky red damask of his throne, and from his scarlet tie to his rosy lips, Sleeper brandishes Andrew's signature color in this work with the grace of a matador. In the tender leaves that emerge from the vase's tumescent form we see reflected all the optimism of new love—and the promise of reinvention.

4.6
Wallace Bryant, *Henry Davis Sleeper* (1906). Oil on canvas (60 7/8" x 66 ¼" x 2 ¼"). Gift of Stephen Sleeper, 1941.1703. Courtesy Historic New England.

FOGLAND FAMILY

Taking his great-nephew aside in the early 1930s, Sleeper pointed to a golden spoon in his collection and told the puzzled boy that in 1878 he was born with the utensil in his mouth.[30] While not strictly a Boston Brahmin, Sleeper hailed from a well-heeled family with wide social connections and a prestigious address in Back Bay. His grandfather Jacob Sleeper rose from an impoverished orphanhood to make a sizable fortune in wholesale clothing and real estate; retiring at forty-eight, he supported a range of religious and educational institutions, chief among them Boston University, which he cofounded in 1869. His son Jacob Henry Sleeper would earn the rank of Major in the Civil War—likely clad by the family's textile firm, which secured lucrative government contracts to produce Union uniforms.[31] After his marriage to Maria Westcott in 1867, Major Sleeper joined the family business and, in 1873, moved to 295 Marlborough Street with their four-year-old son Jacob. Two more children followed the family's move to Back Bay: Stephen Westcott Sleeper in 1874 and Henry Davis Sleeper four years later.

The Sleepers' youngest son was born a "blue baby," a condition stemming from infantile oxygen deprivation. His inauspicious birth foreshadowed a lifetime of poor health. Too frail for the schoolroom and likely unexpected to reach adulthood, he was privately tutored at home. (Posthumous accounts that he later studied architecture at the Ecole des Beaux Arts in Paris, a wishful fabrication first printed in the 1950s, have no basis in fact.)[32] By the age of ten Sleeper was spending his summers in Marblehead Neck, where architect Arthur Little designed a summer home for the family. Not strong enough to engage in the rough-and-tumble circle of his brothers—or perhaps simply uninterested in the world outside his family's homes—he constructed a series of elaborate dollhouses from his sickbed in Boston, and at the Marblehead house assembled a miniature Japanese garden atop the family's billiard table.[33] The creation of these miniaturized worlds appears to have been consolatory for Sleeper, an emotional outlet he undoubtedly relied upon when, in 1891, he lost his father at the age of thirteen.

We know little about Sleeper's teenage years, aside from cursory references to his travels in the American West.[34] Although this uncharacteristic burst of activity suggests improvement of his health, it might just as well indicate the reverse. The period's so-called West Cure, which sought to treat nervous exhaustion in "overcivilized," effete young men by exposing them to the bracing environment of the great outdoors, was the masculine equivalent of the era's indoor "rest cure" for overfatigued women (famously explored in Charlotte Perkins Gilman's classic 1892 short story "The Yellow Wallpaper").[35] Always more comfortable indoors than out, in 1899 the twenty-one-year-old Sleeper moved from his childhood home to 336 Beacon Street—a house he shared with his mother and, for the time being, his older brothers. Around this time Jacob and Stephen launched their careers in diplomacy and real estate, respectively, while Sleeper occupied himself primarily in "pleasant searching with mother among old shops and houses," a shared passion for antiquing reflected in the overstuffed rooms of their home.[36] Much of this collection eventually made its way to Beauport, yet these objects—like the man himself—would present quite differently in their Eastern Point setting.

Sleeper's decision to create a summer home in 1907 recalibrated his family dynamics and allowed him to forge important new relationships. Although he assumed his mother's residency at Beauport from the start, the home was always his own (he secured a $10,000 loan to purchase the property) and its construction, decoration, and entertaining schedule his exclusive domain.[37] Indeed, from the first summer she occupied Beauport until her death nearly ten years later, Maria Sleeper formed a shadowy, if beloved, figure in her youngest son's life—a development due partly to her failing health (as early as 1907 she was often bedridden) as well as to the ascendance of his new circle. For along with the construction of Beauport, Sleeper had adopted a family of his own choosing.

To better understand his place within this new constellation, centered as it was on the figure of Andrew, we must return to the man who first captured Sleeper's heart. Sleeper met Guy Wetmore Carryl not long after Carryl's 1901 return from Paris, where he served as a foreign correspondent. Several years older than Sleeper, he was urbane, handsome, bookish, and passionate about his home—in other words, he embodied all the qualities Sleeper later recognized in Andrew. Today Carryl is primarily known for his mildly risqué collections of verse, *Mother Goose for Grownups* (1900) and *Grimm Tales Made Gay* (1902), but he was a writer of wide-ranging talents, authoring plays, satires, and stories for a number of popular American magazines. When Carryl built his shingle-style bachelor's retreat in Swampscott, Massachusetts—a humorist to his fingertips—he christened the home "Shingle Blessedness." Sleeper described life there as idyllic, and Carryl himself as a man "of poetic instincts . . . a genial and most communicative companion."[38]

4.7
Guy Wetmore Carryl at
Shingle Blessedness in
1903. Courtesy Historic
New England.

On March 4, 1904, an electrical fire at Shingle Blessedness left Carryl critically wounded. Four weeks later, he was dead. In its coverage of the popular writer's death, the *Boston Globe* noted that Sleeper, "perhaps his closest personal friend," remained with him until the end. The physical extent of their relationship may never be known, but Sleeper's emotional attachment to Carryl is clear. He kept framed photos of the writer at 336 Beacon Street, collected several volumes of press clippings about his work, and was on intimate terms with what the *Globe* called the writer's "most romantic bungalow."[39]

Carryl's homosexuality, at least, appears beyond doubt. The *Globe* hints at another of his possible liaisons—a young Italian protégé named Reuben Pierre—and Philip Hayden has discovered epistolary evidence of Carryl's unrequited love for a man named John Randolph Mordecai.[40] Certainly, Carryl's unpublished poem "Estrangement"—saved by Sleeper, but perhaps written to Mordecai—leaves little to the imagination. (The poem pines for its subject's "tender manly heart," celebrating "The holiest passion known to life's brief span— / The heart to heart pure love of man for man!")[41] It would be tempting to see in Sleeper's relationship with Carryl a foreshadowing of his later crush on the romantically unavailable Andrew. And yet the writer's enigmatic dedication to Sleeper in his posthumously published novel, *Far From the Maddening Girls* (1904), suggests at least some form of reciprocation: "In furtherance of an unfulfilled intention," it reads, "this book is dedicated to the author's dear friend and comrade, Henry D. Sleeper."[42]

Far From the Maddening Girls likely found its publisher through Sleeper (the *Globe* confirmed that he "had charge of [Carryl's] business" in the writer's final weeks). The novel appears to have drawn inspiration from his own happy experience as a confirmed bachelor, a lifestyle the grieving Sleeper would seek to emulate. A witty apologist for the single life, the book's narrator, Mr. Sands, distinguishes bachelors of circumstance from those for whom the state is a sacred calling. "A bachelor proper," he writes, "is the product of his inclinations, not of his restrictions. He is magnificent in his isolation."[43]

Practically applying his philosophy, Sands demonstrates the pleasures of homemaking in the absence of a wife. Charting the design and exquisite outfitting of his bachelor retreat, "Sans Souci" ("Without Care"), Sands identifies the home as a "temple to celibacy" while implying a kind of consummation between man and house. Lovingly poring over the plans for his home, he declares them "too large to kiss" and confesses that their "edges were frayed with too much fondling" (later, he declares his impatience "to get upon terms of intimacy with my rooms").[44] Rather unconvincingly, at the novel's end Sands falls for his neighbor, Miss Berith, whose proximity and eligibility feel like looming threats throughout the book. Although reviewers tended to hail this ending with relief ("Darkest Celibacy to Brightest Matrimony," the *Minneapolis Journal* summarized), few readers—and certainly, not Carryl himself—likely believed Sands wasn't more magnificent in his isolation.[45]

When Sleeper first encountered Andrew and Red Roof, he surely felt—among other emotions—that he had stumbled upon the real-world incarnation of Carryl's protagonist and fictional home. Here was a man who perfectly fulfilled Sands's philosophy, exploiting all the rich possibilities of bachelordom without the specter of an eligible female neighbor in sight. Indeed, as he soon realized, when Andrew wasn't scrambling over the shoreline with his Harvard beaux he could be found in the company of a charismatic set of older, unmarried women with homes on Eastern Point—a group that not only posed no romantic threat but one that offered a profoundly satisfying, and rare, form of companionship.

Playfully reclaiming a colloquial term for an untidy woman, or "dab," the original members of this all-female group declared themselves the community of "Dabsville."[46] When Andrew and Sleeper joined their circle, "Dabs" transformed into a four-lettered acronym drawn from the first letters of the friends' surnames. In addition to the two men, this group included the celebrated Philadelphia painter Cecilia Beaux, who had vacationed in Gloucester since the 1880s and built her own home, Green Alley, to the south of Red Roof in 1905; Joanna Davidge, the director of a New York City girls' finishing school, whose 1903 home, Pier Lane, lay between Red Roof and Green Alley; and Caroline Sinkler, the neighbor between Andrew and Sleeper, who in 1905 purchased the home she named Wrong Roof. (Alternately known as "The Enchantress of Philadelphia" and "The Lavender Lady," Sinkler was known for the mourning weeds she'd worn since the death of her fiancé in 1895. She and Sleeper shared the final "S" in the group's collective acronym.)

As a set the Dabsvillians were lively, witty, creative, and intellectually curious—a kind of seashore Algonquin Round Table before the fact. Snobs regarding personal merit rather than social standing, they were frequent and hospitable hosts yet could also be clubbish and insular. (Rebuffing "two snobs I know in Philadelphia," Sleeper wrote Andrew, he told the hopeful visitors that his circle primarily included "middle-aged, unmarried women.")[47] Childless, financially independent, and devoted to their homes, they were, in the best Carrylian sense, the sum of their inclinations rather than their restrictions. Not surprisingly, such freedom did not entirely escape censure. According to local historian Joseph Garland, clucking neighbors dubbed this unusual community of bachelors and "old maids" (on average, the women were nearly twenty years older than Sleeper) collectively as the "She-Shore" of Eastern Point.[48] Unbothered by—indeed, typically disdainful of—outsiders' views, this unconventional family of friends appears to have discovered a cure for the terrible disease of loneliness.

In 1907, Dabsville's ranks grew significantly, if only by one. Though she owned no property on Eastern Point and never lent her surname to Dabsville's acronym, Isabella Stewart Gardner—the iconoclastic art collector and so-called Seventh Wonder of Boston—would become, after Andrew, the group's most colorful figure. As early as 1875 one Boston newspaper described the thirty-five-year-old Gardner as a "millionaire Bohemienne":

> She is the leader of the smart set, but she often leads where none dare follow. . . . She imitates nobody; everything she does is novel and original. She is as

brilliant as her own diamonds, and as attractive. All Boston is divided into two parts, of which one follows science, and the other Mrs. Jack Gardner.[49]

The connection began with Beaux, who knew Gardner through collecting circles. In April 1903, the painter brought Andrew to the newly opened Fenway Court, Gardner's home and museum; receiving a personal tour of the collection from "Mrs. Jack," Andrew was charmed by this sixty-three-year-old widow ("delightful experience," he recorded in his diary) if less impressed by her great friend, the painter John Singer Sargent ("a very businesslike unaesthetic burly man").[50] Four more years would pass before Gardner accepted an invitation to Red Roof, once again under the aegis of Beaux. "What fun all this will be for me," she wrote Andrew in anticipation of her September 1907 visit.[51] Like Sleeper the year before, she had little idea what lay in store for her—yet unlike him, she was not a figure so easily impressed.

In her breathless note to Andrew after this visit, Gardner appears instantly to have understood Dabsville's appeal. Writing from her Brookline estate she observed:

> In a few hours what a change! The land change does not make one into something rich and strange—alas! Your village is Fogland with the sea's white arms about you all. Don't let others crawl in—Only me! For *I* care. I love its rich, strange people, so far away. . . . I shall expect you and Mr. Sleeper at midday on Saturday. Then perhaps I can *say* a bigger thank you than I can write.[52]

4.8

A. Piatt Andrew and Isabella Stewart Gardner at Red Roof, Gloucester, Massachusetts (October 6, 1910). Photograph by Thomas E. Marr and Son. Isabella Stewart Gardner Museum, Boston.

It is worth noting that Andrew and Gardner's profound connection—following this September exchange of visits the two became close and lifelong friends—caught fire only after her introduction to "Fogland," where the "rich, strange" milieu of Dabsville clearly cast him in a new light.

With her plea to let no "others crawl in" Gardner not only acknowledged the group's exclusivity but also recognized Andrew as its beating heart(throb). By January 1908, the pair had adopted nicknames for one another, Gardner becoming "Y" for the archaic spelling of her name ("Ysabella") to Andrew's "A." She could not have devised a more fitting reminder than this, that Andrew—the quintessential alpha male—would always come first (indeed, in one instance she referred to him as "A. No.1").[53] In spite of his prolonged absences from Eastern Point beginning in the 1910s, Andrew's primary position within the group never wavered—nor did the group ever question who his primary acolyte might be. Gardner reveled in Sleeper's friendship ("as for Harry Sleeper, there are no words!") but in the end, as she acknowledged to Andrew, Beauport's owner "loves *you* best in the world, we all come lagging behind."[54]

In the complicated dynamics of Dabsville, it is also worth noting Beaux's unusual position. Although she was eighteen years Andrew's senior—a fact she disguised by shaving eight years from her birthdate—her close friendship with him was more flirtatious than Gardner's. Beautiful and charismatic, Beaux comes across in Andrew's photographs like a puckish progenitor of Rosalind Russell. Celebrated for her talent as a portraitist but often unfairly labeled the "female Sargent," she occupied a similarly ambiguous space in terms of her sexuality. Clearly drawn to handsome, unavailable gay men—as with Gardner, Andrew was the primary but not the sole such figure in her circle—the never-married Beaux was likely either bisexual or lesbian. (In 1906 she ended an intense, apparently romantic, five-year relationship with Dorothea Gilder, a woman twenty-seven years her junior.)[55] Her competition for Andrew's affection could take playful forms, as when she and Gardner argued over the wreaths each made to celebrate Red Roof's "settlement anniversary," but it could also manifest itself in a less sympathetic light. After a 1908 visit with Andrew and Sleeper in New York, Beaux recorded in her diary that, however much she enjoyed seeing the men together, "I have to remember the one appalling FACT."[56]

Less than a week before Sleeper purchased his property on Eastern Point, Andrew suggested a field trip with Sleeper and Beaux. On August 6, 1907, the friends drove sixty miles north to tour the Jonathan Hamilton House in South Berwick, Maine—a grand eighteenth-century country estate then owned by Emily Tyson and her stepdaughter Elise (later, Elise Tyson Vaughan). After acquiring the house in 1898 the women worked for two years with Arthur Little's professional partner, architect Herbert W. C. Browne, to restore the home and create an extensive Colonial Revival garden. The Tysons' ambitious renovation projects would have keenly interested their visitors, yet in the end it was a small garden pavilion at Hamilton House that captured Sleeper's attention.

To understand his epiphany at South Berwick we must, as this trio did, make a detour en route to the Tysons'. Stopping in Essex, Massachusetts, at the start of their trip, Andrew brought Sleeper and Beaux to the William Cogswell house. Built in 1728 as an imposing country seat, the house had by 1907 fallen into a state of neglect. Exploring this romantic near-ruin—its roof nearly collapsed and most of its windowpanes shattered— Sleeper particularly admired the home's intact interior paneling. It was with these rooms fresh in mind that the Dabsvillians encountered the Tysons' novel garden folly later in the day, a small cottage completed earlier that year.

To create the interiors of the "Doll's House," as they named it, the women had hauled wagonloads of paneling from the nearby Sally Hart House (1740) in Newington, New Hampshire.[57] Arranged in an artistic rather than historic fashion, the panels lent the structure a playful and romantic quality—a cottage that one contemporary described as "a little house fit for a Hans Anderson story."[58] Elise Tyson Vaughan would remark in the 1940s that "in these days of more careful correctness in detail, especially in early American affairs, it probably would have been planned differently."[59] Yet for Sleeper, the Tysons' alchemy of history and fantasy opened a world of new possibilities.

Given Sleeper's early and extensive use of architectural salvage at Beauport, historians often point to this Cogswell-Hamilton-House thunderbolt as the first major development in his home's design. And yet if we look past his fascination with historic fabric, his reaction suggests a variety of other, equally important factors that would shape his design philosophy. First, it bears noting how quickly and effectively Sleeper adopted another's novel idea—the Tysons were pioneers of the architecturally salvaged interior— and, in making it his own, improved upon it. Second, in his attraction to the Doll's House, a diminutive structure that eclipsed for him even the Hamilton mansion, we see his early fascination with the garden folly as a type. In this, too, he would prove to be a visionary, for it is one thing to create a folly in its traditional garden setting and quite another to imagine an entire home using the garden folly as a matrix.

Last, it is important to understand the critical connection Sleeper made between the people he loved and the spaces he created. It is no accident that he adopted the Tysons' approach while also befriending them. At Beauport he honored this bond as much as he did their use of architectural salvage—a gesture Vaughan responded to, in kind, by bringing him a tiny steeple model once displayed in the Doll's House.[60] Rather unsurprisingly, Sleeper also credited Andrew as a generative force on this trip. "It was going to [the Tysons'], you remember, that you discovered the possibilities of the Cogswell House," Sleeper wrote him in 1908, adding that Andrew's mere photograph of the Essex house, taken on a subsequent visit, "makes Beauport twice as interesting to everyone as it would otherwise be."[61]

4.9
Dabsville visits the Cogswell House in Essex, MA (September 12, 1907). L to R: Isabella Stewart Gardner, Joanna Davidge, and Henry Davis Sleeper. Red Roof Archive, courtesy Historic New England.

The men undertook this second trip to Essex on September 12, 1907, five weeks after their first visit and a month after Sleeper purchased his Eastern Point property. Bringing Davidge and Gardner along this time—this was the date of Gardner's first visit to "Fogland"— the jolly outing constituted a kind of Dabsvillian blessing on Sleeper's salvage project. By purchasing the Cogswell House paneling and reconstituting it at Beauport, Sleeper surrounded himself with the memory of that happy day, and its company, perhaps even more so than with the panels' historical associations.

Sleeper laid Beauport's cornerstone on October 12, 1907, a month to the day after this second Essex trip. The home's initial historical source derived from a catalogue of sorts. Serendipitously for him, in the winter of 1906–1907 the period's premier design magazine, *The Studio*, produced a special issue devoted to "Old English Cottages."[62] Surveying nearly a hundred different homes, most dating to the medieval period, the issue's editor Charles Holme introduced the volume with one guiding criterion: "Would it look well in a painting?" The issue answered his question with copious illustrations of ivy-covered homes in quaint, rural settings.[63]

Among these Sleeper was particularly drawn to a sixteenth-century Hampshire cottage today known as "Restalls" (identified in *The Studio* only by its village name, Steep), a home British architect William Unsworth had purchased and recently restored. The cottage's diminutive proportions, vast sloping roof, clipped gables, and prominent chimneys all recommended it to Sleeper's project—as did, whether he knew it or not, Unsworth's fanciful manipulations of the historic structure. (Declared by the British Listed Buildings to be the very "epitome of the romantic English cottage," Restalls is in fact an amalgamation of three different historic structures.) The only home accompanied by two color plates in *The Studio*, a pair of atmospheric watercolors by Walter Tyndale, Restalls indeed looked well—even dreamy—in a painting.

When completed in the spring of 1908, Little Beauport not only epitomized the Arts and Crafts Movement's romanticization of the English medieval past but it also represented a specifically *masculine* domestic style. As the fictional character Bachelor Bluff declared in 1881, men were properly drawn to the "pointed gables and chimneys after the old, quaint Tudor fashion" as opposed to fussy French styles or an exotic

4.10
Walter Tyndale, *Steep, Hampshire* [Restalls] (1906). Reproduced in Charles Holme, ed., *Old English Houses: Special Winter Number of the Studio* (1906). Collection of the author.

4.11
Halfdan "Dick"
Hanson (1884–1952)
in 1912. Courtesy
Historic New England.

"ornamental chalet."[64] For her part, Emily Post—whose father Bruce Price was a celebrated architect in the Arts and Crafts mode—declared that sixteenth-century English architecture "cannot be other than masculine, no matter how it is completed."[65]

The home's interior was another story. If Bachelor Bluff warned that a "jumble of ill-contrived rooms" constituted an unmanly approach to interior design, then Sleeper's home surely would have courted his disapproval.[66] Even before later additions to the house created its more labyrinthine effect, the twenty-six rooms of the original 1908 house constituted an asymmetrical hive without any logical pathway from one space to the next. (It is worth noting that the home's large, unifying Stair Hall was among the very last additions to the house, created in the late 1920s.) Few images of Beauport's interiors survive from this first period, but one 1909 profile declared the house "filled with treasures . . . and quaint chintzes," a curatorial method that itself belied the apparent stolidity of the home's Tudor-inspired exterior.[67] This divided approach points not to Restalls (*The Studio* included no interior images) but to Shingle Blessedness, whose "elegant . . . interior appointments were in strange contrast," the *Boston Globe* noted, "with the outward simplicity of the cottage and the wilderness effect of its surroundings."[68]

To understand Little Beauport's unusual plan we must consider the man Sleeper entrusted with its construction: Halfdan "Dick" Hanson, a Norwegian-born artisan raised in Gloucester and introduced to Sleeper in 1907.[69] Trained as a woodcarver and carpenter, the twenty-three-year-old Hanson had by this date completed only a correspondence course in architecture. However ironically, it appears to have been his very *lack* of building experience, combined with his mastery of wood craftsmanship, that made him such a perfect impresario for Sleeper's vision. An older, more experienced architect—or one less focused on the beauty of a well-executed, intimate detail—might have steered Sleeper toward a more conventional design.

The novel character of the completed 1908 home reflected not just the men's relative inexperience but also their shared delight in diminutive spaces. From its start Beauport resembled nothing so much as an overgrown dollhouse, a type to which both men were attracted. (Toys and miniature furniture were among the first objects Hanson made as a carpenter, whereas the elaborate dollhouse he later created for his daughter received its own press coverage.)[70] Critically important to Beauport's aesthetic, too, was the men's mutual admiration, a friendship and design partnership that would span the next twenty-six years. As with the Tysons, Andrew, and others, their emotional bond was essential to Sleeper's creative process. As Paul Hollister has written of the men's collaboration: "For Sleeper's domineering but erratic genius the catalyst was Hanson's craftsmanship, his sense of honor, duty, and adventure. . . . It was Sleeper's imaginative appeal and Hanson's good-natured receptivity to it that made Beauport possible."[71]

However drawn Sleeper may have been to Red Roof, at this early stage his home bore only a passing resemblance to Andrew's. Both houses displayed features commonly found in the Arts and Crafts period bungalow—sweeping roofs, prominent chimneys, stucco walls, exposed beams—but Red Roof initially featured a far more straightforward plan, rawer use of materials, and an emphasis on outdoor living that differed from the more insular and finely detailed Beauport. Only in later years, and largely due to Sleeper's influence, did Red Roof start to resemble Beauport in its proportions, collections, and complex plan. For if Andrew constituted Dabsville's emotional center, then Sleeper claimed the group's aesthetic leadership almost from the start. Speaking of their neighbor's home, a beaming Sleeper wrote Andrew in 1908: "I had a dear letter from Miss Sinkler last night . . . [who] said she heard that 'Beauport' had a subtle charm which quite slobbed 'Wrong Roof.'"[72] Even Gardner—who had commissioned a number of grand homes in her own right—confessed to Andrew that year, "I have *of course* taken people to see Little Beauport. That seems to be my mission in life."[73]

The eccentricity of Beauport's plan was matched by the imaginative character of its themed rooms. The home's entryway, dubbed the Cogswell Room, showcased the panels Sleeper had removed from Essex (these also lined the room's mirrored twin, the Green Dining Room). Much in the spirit of the Doll's House, these rooms distilled the grander proportions of their original context to present the visitor with a pocket-sized version of the eighteenth century. The diminutive scale of these rooms intentionally contrasted with their neighboring space, the Hall, a cavernous room that ran the full width of the house and rose to its second story. Modeled and furnished in the style of a medieval English hall, the room "gives one the impression of an old castle . . . of the past ages," marveled

4.12
The Hall (built 1908) in 1910. Photograph by Thomas E. Marr and Son. Courtesy Historic New England.

The *Gloucester Daily Times*, "you can almost see the iron girded knights strutting around, so striking is the scene and the memory it evokes."[74] (Delighted by the Hall, Gardner—who rightly perceived in it a tribute to her own Fenway Court—wrote in anticipation of a 1908 Thanksgiving meal there, "dinner . . . will be as mediaeval [*sic*] as we can make it!")[75] On the second floor of Little Beauport Sleeper introduced similarly romantic English themes. His mother's bedroom suite, the Strawberry Hill Room, honored Horace Walpole's eighteenth-century home; the Blue Willow Room recalled the English Aesthetic Movement's favored china pattern; and a pair of adjoining, jewel-like bedrooms honored Lord Byron and Admiral Horatio Nelson.

Featuring eight bedrooms in all, Little Beauport was less a summer hideaway than a home built for entertaining—and for Dabsvillians, no event held more significance than a housewarming. When Andrew opened Red Roof in September 1902 he hosted overnight guests Beaux, Davidge, Davidge's mother, and illustrator Henry McCarter.[76] By contrast, Little Beauport's inaugural dinner, held May 12, 1908, was a smaller affair. As a bemused Andrew recorded in his diary that night, "I went over to Sleeper's house-warming dinner. Just two of us."[77]

At precisely the moment Sleeper should have felt triumphant—hosting an intimate dinner for two in the very house Andrew inspired—he faced his greatest rival yet. James Fiske "Jack" Mabbett first appeared at Red Roof six months before, over the weekend of November 9–10, 1907. Then midway through his senior year at Harvard, the dashing and athletic Salem native was, at twenty-four, a few years older than the classmates who introduced him to "Doc." Though Andrew was known for the sudden intensity of his affairs, his relationship with Mabbett represented something of a new order—both for the swiftness with which it began (not a full day after they'd met, Andrew invited Mabbett for a

4.13
James Fiske ("Jack") Mabbett aboard Piatt Andrew's boat, the *Eisor* (May 1, 1908). Red Roof Archive, courtesy Historic New England.

nude jog along Brace's Cove) and for the candor with which he documented its unfolding.[78]

Andrew's frequent diary remark "____ spent the night with me," a likely bedpost-notch notation following a young man's visit, became in Mabbett's case "slept with me," and in one case, "spent day in my bed."[79] It is worth noting, as well, how many late nights Andrew spent in the company of others—including Sleeper—only to join Mabbett for an overnight upon his return. Uncharacteristically, Andrew also appeared eager to introduce Mabbett to Dabsville. The day after their first meeting, and just hours before the men stripped down for their run, Andrew invited Beaux to lunch with Mabbett. The following month he introduced him to Gardner, a first for one of his beaux and an encounter that appears to have been mysteriously intense. Writing Gardner the next day, Mabbett thanked her for "the happiest and the saddest night I remember ever having experienced."[80]

Between December 1907 and early January 1908, Andrew saw Mabbett almost daily in Boston or at Red Roof, even staying with him during the younger man's brief hospitalization for an unknown cause.[81] By Christmastime an increasingly desperate Sleeper began to write, telephone, or telegraph Andrew sometimes several times a day. When Andrew gave him a Napoleonic medal for Christmas that year, an ecstatic Sleeper wrote to tell him: "I haven't had it off for an hour since I put it on," adding, "every night it goes into the pocket of my pajamas!"[82] Showering Andrew with Christmas presents by mail—the professor was visiting his parents in Indiana for the holiday—Sleeper wrote on New Year's Eve to tell him he had thought of him "a hundred times" in the few days he'd been gone.[83] On New Year's Day he confided to Andrew that Gardner, aware of the frequency of their communication—and likely sympathetic to his lovelorn state—had asked him to relay a few messages on her behalf. "She flattered me delightfully," he added, telling him, "she had yet to see me slip up on anything I had attempted to do."[84] For the following eight months Andrew saved not one of Sleeper's letters.

As Andrew's guest books indicate, that winter and spring found Mabbett at Red Roof for increasingly long stretches of time, and in the rare absence of other houseguests. (Significantly, Mabbett's name would not appear in Beauport's guest book for two more years.) By April the Harvard senior had more or less taken up permanent residence at the house, including a marathon two-week run leading up to Little Beauport's inaugural dinner. When Andrew traveled to New York and Washington that spring, Jack kept house at Red Roof; upon his return to Gloucester, Andrew noted in his diary, the pair "developed nude photos" in the home's dark room.[85]

Mabbett's final weeks at Red Roof that summer, from late May to early July 1908, were a period of comedy and high drama. When he arrived with a pet crow for Andrew on May 30, Sleeper responded on June 4 by presenting his neighbor with a pair of black bear cubs, "caged odiferously on the porch," as Andrew noted.[86] (Three days later Mabbett appeared alongside Andrew in a remarkable photograph that likely references the cubs. The men crouch and grin while a beaming Beaux leads them across the rocks on a dual leash.) On June 25 their summer idyll came to an abrupt end. As Andrew tersely noted, "Jack summoned home by irate father."[87] Though briefly reunited with Andrew for a farewell meal in Salem the following day, Mabbett left for an extended trip to Utah on July 6, suggesting a compulsory "West Cure" of his own. Two weeks later his crow was dead. Andrew honored the bird with a funeral at Red Roof, accompanied by the strains of Jules Massenet's "Elégie."[88]

4.14
Scenes from July 1908.
LEFT: Jack Mabbett
and Piatt Andrew with
crow at Red Roof.
RIGHT: Cecilia Beaux,
Mabbett, and Andrew
on Gloucester Harbor.
Red Roof Archive,
courtesy Historic New
England.

Within weeks of the showdown with Mabbett's father, Andrew resigned from Harvard to join the recently formed National Monetary Commission, led by Senator Nelson Aldrich of Rhode Island. Serving as the group's special assistant, Andrew committed to spending the rest of that summer and fall traveling with the commission in Europe. Dabsville tempered its grief over his departure with a grand costume party in his honor ("fancy a lot of enchanting people missing one man," Gardner wrote).[89] Describing the July 30 event, held at Beaux's studio, Andrew wrote his parents:

> Miss Beaux . . . and Sleeper had done nothing for a week but plan for that party . . . I was made to wear the robe of a Roman emperor, with a jeweled fillet on my forehead, and I sat on a kind of throne of red velvet with R.R. in gold. Mrs. Gardner sat opposite me on a less imposing throne of purple emblazoned with a large Y . . . the air of the studio was heavy with incense and tube roses, the tables were gorgeous with old rose damask and fruit. I shall never forget the picture.[90]

Signing their names that evening above the other guests', Andrew styled himself "Piatt R.I" ("Romanus Imperator") while Gardner embellished her "Ysabella – R" ("Regina") with a hand-drawn crown. For a brief shining moment, Fogland was Camelot—complete with its own Merlin. Sleeper wore a conical wizard's hat for the occasion.

Writing his parents on the eve of his departure Andrew confided it had been difficult to shake Sleeper, who followed him as far as New Haven before Andrew insisted on continuing to New York alone.[91] In his subsequent letter to Andrew, Sleeper exhorted him to "think of me sometimes," adding, "how eager I am to show you all the happiness which the last two years have brought . . . my best hours, now, will be looking after Red Roof."[92] Gardner and the bear cubs were Red Roof's sole residents that August, yet as Sleeper explained to Andrew, he spent "nearly half of every day" at his neighbor's home "I should have yielded to depression many times," he confided, without "the stillness of

4.15
Posing before
Andrew's farewell
party at Cecilia Beaux's
home, Green Alley
(July 30, 1908).
L to R: Natale
Gavagnin (Green
Alley's major domo),
Beaux, Andrew, and
unidentified reclining
woman. (Note
Andrew's Red Roof
"throne" at rear). Red
Roof Archive, courtesy
Historic New England.

Red Roof, and the sight of the little familiar things."[93] In another letter he noted: "When I went to Red Roof this evening as I always do, I stayed a while and played one or two familiar things—and then the [Massenet] Eligee [*sic*]."[94]

Sleeper was not simply pining away in these rooms. In Andrew's absence he added to the home's collections ("I've been to Boston [and] saw some pretty amusing and attractive dinner plates. They are now at Red Roof"); he forwarded, and in some cases opened and answered, Andrew's mail; and he even took charge of his neighbor's wardrobe, brushing his trousers, sending items out for cleaning, and shining his shoes (he reassured Andrew "the lock is . . . on your bedroom door—and the key is in my pocket").[95] The temporarily ownerless Red Roof, it seems, offered Sleeper the greatest intimacy he had ever known with Andrew.

When he wasn't acting as Red Roof's custodian, Sleeper contented himself with gazing at the house from Beauport. It is no accident that he built his bedroom suite, the South Gallery, to face Andrew's property—indeed, the small writing nook that extended from his bedroom (see figure 4.19, p. 148) served as a kind of lookout post. ("I am now looking at Red Roof," Sleeper began one letter to Andrew.)[96] Rather than imposing a barrier between the men's homes, Sinkler's property constituted for Sleeper a kind of decorative transitional space. In 1915 he would hire an English designer to reimagine Sinkler's gardens, assuring Andrew the result would be "a glorious mass of color for Red Roof."[97] Once describing the "moon [that] steals over our arc [between Red Roof and Beauport]," he made Sinkler's home vanish altogether.[98]

Sleeper's voyeuristic confessions must occasionally have been unnerving to his neighbor. Writing not long after Andrew's departure for Europe, he recalled "one afternoon last June, when there were two white figures on the rocks [at Red Roof]; you—lying in the sun—and Jack, standing, with his arm raised high, holding the crow with its wings spread to fly."[99] (Seven years later Sleeper returned to the same theme: "Do you sometimes think of spring mornings at Red Roof with the sky and sea turquoise blue . . . ? I think of you such days—and of you and Jack lying in the sun.")[100] On the eve of Andrew's return in the fall of 1908, Sleeper found himself "wishing you were lying in the sun on the rocks by Red Roof," later confessing, "I went down to your beach—& lay, for an hour, breathing the sea. You always seem so near when it is still there."[101]

Writing Andrew that September, Sleeper reported, "I know you'll be glad to hear a nice thing that just happened to me":

> Arthur Little has just written me a very laudatory letter—offering me the services of his draughtsmen, superintendents, contractors, etc. if I should want to build a house for anyone else! (you remember one or two people asked me to), & that if it turns out as well as this house has in every detail, he should be only too glad to have his office affiliated with the making of it. It was flattering—& I haven't mentioned it to anyone (even mother, yet). The only reason I speak of it now is because I've been thinking I should never have taken the pains I did—nor would Beauport have existed—but for you.[102]

It is unsurprising that, in response to the first professional encouragement Sleeper received, his immediate impulse was to deflect the complement onto Andrew: had he never been invited to Red Roof ("but for you"), Sleeper's home would never have materialized. Yet his confession may also be read in another way. Beauport, he tells Andrew here for the first time, also exists "*for* you," its every pain taken on his behalf. As the house continued to expand, Sleeper's primary motivation remained unaltered.[103]

A "SURPRISINGLY DOMESTIC" BACHELOR

In the spring of 1930 the Chase and Sanborn Coffee Company issued an advertisement proclaiming its product was "served in the homes of these surprisingly domestic *well-known bachelors*."[104] The group included five men: urbane *New Yorker* theater critic Alexander Woollcott; former actor turned interior designer William "Billy" Haines; bohemian adventurer and travel writer Richard Halliburton; screen idol Gary Cooper; and Sleeper—whose decorating career had, by this date, elevated him to something of a household name. The advertisement constituted a less-than-subtle wink to readers. Featuring only men whose homosexuality or bisexuality was suspected—or in Haines's case, openly confirmed—Chase and Sanborn appealed to the stereotype of the preciously discerning gay man. Sleeper, identified here as a "collector and connoisseur," provided the endorsement: "I like using things that have proven themselves by long trial." And yet the surprising nature of Sleeper's domesticity owed, in the end, nothing to staid tradition. Rather, from the opening of Little Beauport until the flowering of Sleeper's professional decorating career in the 1920s, his environments projected an affective and deeply mannerist character.

Beauport underwent its first substantial enlargement between 1911 and 1912, yet in the period immediately following Andrew's return from the National Monetary

Commission it was Red Roof that witnessed the most significant change. To house Andrew's growing collection of economics books, Sleeper asked Hanson in spring 1909 to build an unusual addition at his neighbor's home. A combination library/office/loft bedroom, the new wing's entrance was artfully concealed within the original house—a form of secrecy that reflected Andrew's wish for privacy when he worked. (Later, with the advent of Prohibition, the room would also serve as a hidden bar.)[105] To enter this space required removing the back panel of a built-in settee in Red Roof's living room. Passing through this narrow opening and moving through a short hallway, visitors entered a vaulted space that, although no larger than the living room, felt both grander and more intimate (a combination that, more than anything else in the room, betrays Sleeper's hand).

Andrew's description of the library's inaugural dinner, held at Easter 1909, conjures an event more Roman bacchanalia than Christian celebration—with Sleeper directing its decoration. On the evening of April 17 seven guests assembled on the library's floor, seated around a low table whose centerpiece featured two live baby rabbits and eighteen chicks. As Andrew recorded:

> The walls and ceiling of the room were hung with Turkey red made up like a tent, in the top of which hung two flaming Roman lamps. On the sides of the tent were tiger and bear and leopard skins, which Harry had rented for the occasion and other skins and skulls lay about on the stone floor. It was a dreamlike scene for us all, but especially for those who saw it for the first time.[106]

4.16
Piatt Andrew's hidden library (1909) at Red Roof. Courtesy Andrew L. Gray.

The "dreamlike" nature of the room points to Sleeper's interventions as much as to Andrew's Olympian hosting skills. The skins he rented for the party eventually became part of the library's permanent décor and the stuff of Red Roof legend—appearing draped across Andrew's guests or wrapped around their host. (Indeed, the earliest memory of Andrew's great-nephew, Andrew Gray, involved "Uncle Doc" chasing the four-year-old around the house in a leopard skin.)[107] Though he would never have attempted such a cartoonishly masculine touch at Beauport, it must have struck Sleeper as eminently appropriate for Andrew.

Among those who encountered Red Roof for the first time that Easter was the nineteen-year-old heiress Dorothy Payne Whitney, chaperoned by Gardner. Sharing the news of their mutual friend George Proctor's engagement, Gardner had asked Andrew, "When does your turn come?"—a question she hoped to answer by bringing the eligible Whitney to Gloucester.[108] Two years before, Whitney had inherited fifteen million dollars on the death of her father; beautiful and well connected, she struck Gardner as Andrew's perfect mate. And yet for all his descriptions of the library's décor that evening, he failed even to mention Whitney's presence—a lapse explained in part by the appearance of his old flame, Edgar Rust. (Eight weeks later Rust would marry, with Andrew standing as best man.)[109]

Mabbett, too, had returned to Andrew's life. Having endured five months of paternal exile ("Jack writes gloomy letters from Utah," Andrew confessed to Gardner, adding, "how much happier life would be if we could live close"), the two reunited for a whirlwind ten days starting in late December 1906.[110] Spending December 21–23 together in Chicago, they rejoined the day after Christmas to hunker down at Red Roof; "arose late," Andrew noted the morning after their arrival, inscribing a cryptic "x2" next to Mabbett's name in his guest book. The men then traveled to New York—cue the montage scene—to attend the opera, visit galleries, shop for suits, and celebrate New Year's Eve at the Plaza Hotel. Over the next two years Andrew continued to see Mabbett off and on—and also, occasionally, Whitney. Persistent in her matchmaking, Gardner at last brought Andrew to a half-hearted marriage proposal in April 1911 (a decision perhaps spurred by Joanna Davidge's surprise marriage, the month before, to a man thirteen years her junior). Rebuffed by Whitney, Andrew wrote a follow-up letter that began well—"I long for the chance to be with you . . . to live for you and love you always"—but included the likely unwelcome observation that he was "with S [Sleeper] at my elbow as I write."[111] Whitney married Willard Straight that fall.

Beyond serving as Andrew's amanuensis, Sleeper was busy in these years with a flurry of projects at Beauport—a collection of new rooms that demonstrated his increasing confidence and creativity as a designer, if also his financial recklessness. (Despite his love for a nationally recognized finance expert—Andrew was in 1910 appointed Assistant Secretary of the Treasury—Sleeper never seemed to pay much attention to Beauport's construction costs.) Between 1911 and 1912, Sleeper extended the house's eastern footprint to create a new dining space, the Linebrook Parish Room, alongside an enlarged bedroom first known as the Paul Revere Room and eventually called the Chapel Chamber. Above the Linebrook Parish Room he created the steeply gabled Belfry Chamber bedroom, reached by a secret staircase. Recalling the concealed entrance to Red Roof's library, the stairs to the Belfry Chamber are disguised on the first floor by false paneling; in this case, however, the design signaled less Sleeper's desire for privacy than his love of surprise.

(Reportedly, he enjoyed magically appearing from the woodwork when his guests were assembled in the new dining room.)

The most dramatic addition Sleeper made to the house in this period, to the east of his bedroom suite, was the two-story Book Tower. Connecting the library to the South Gallery by a one-story transitional space he named the Pineapple Room, he added above this another second-floor bedroom, the Shelley Room (a fitting extension of the English heroes theme on this floor). Not counting the three servants' bedrooms he also added in this expansion, Beauport now included ten bedrooms in all—a number hardly required by the overnight guests Sleeper typically entertained. To finance this complex and costly expansion (the Book Tower alone came to nearly $6,000), in 1911 he took out an $18,000 second mortgage on a house originally built for just $16,000.[112] (In Gardner's guest book that summer, Sleeper underlined the Shakespearian quote, "I am poor as Job but not as patient.")[113] It was the first of six mortgages to come, a series of financial maneuvers that constituted their own kind of sorcery.

Two factors appear to have driven this manic building phase. First, as Sleeper now well understood, it was the *novelty* of his home that held Andrew's attention. As fickle about design as he was about young men, Andrew's passions burned strong but were never of long duration (even his intense connection with Mabbett began to fade in these years). His enduring love for Red Roof appears to be the exception, but even Andrew's relationship with his architectural "wife" required continual renewal to maintain his interest—and nowhere did he find a better model for this dynamic than the house two doors down. The second and related reason for Beauport's growth in these years was the expansion of Sleeper's collection. No evidence survives to confirm precisely when or

4.17
Belfry Tower (built 1911–1912) at center. The second-story bay window marks the Belfry Chamber. Photograph by Thomas E. Marr and Son. Courtesy Historic New England.

where he acquired the home's contents, but given the depth of his holdings in folk art and colonial Americana—two novel areas that, like the practice of architectural salvage, he adopted and made his own—it was likely an influx of objects that required new rooms, rather than the reverse. Indeed, in several instances in later years a single object or type was all Sleeper needed to conjure a new room into existence. He created Beauport as much for his collection, then, as for Andrew—and in some cases there was little distinction between these impulses.

Beauport's 1911–1912 expansion blended familiar and entirely new visual strategies. For the Linebrook Parish Room Sleeper once again relied upon historic paneling, in this case from a seventeenth-century house in Linebrook, Massachusetts. Although the room echoes the medieval character of the Hall—Andrew called this new space Sleeper's "Elizabethan Room"—its far more intimate scale suggests its miniaturized twin (in 1929 *Country Life* declared this the "coziest" room at Beauport).[114] Entered from the Linebrook Parish Room, the vaulted Paul Revere/Chapel Chamber bedroom features a historic wallpaper discovered in 1906 at Revere's home in Boston, its pattern characterized by a repeated steeple design; initially the room also housed Sleeper's valuable collection of Revere silver (an early example of the ways his collection shaped the home). Several years later the room showcased the designer's manipulation of "borrowed" scenery. In 1917 Sleeper added a dovecote in the shape of a small Gothic chapel along the roofline facing this bedroom's windows, a miniature folly intended to be spotted precisely from this vantage point.

In the Belfry Chamber upstairs Sleeper used another historic wallpaper pattern, Zuber's 1832 "Décor Chinois," to create the effect of a treehouse. Climbing the room's sharply pitched alcoves (the Belfry Chamber has been described as "The House of the Seven Gables turned inside out"), the floral paper encloses the room in a bower; Sleeper even went so far as to cut out additional birds from the sheets, pasting them onto the walls in strategic locations.[115] The dominant color in this garden-themed room is green—from the brilliant foliage of its wallpaper to its apple-green woodwork and the glowing jade of its translucent, oversized vase—yet in a contrasting touch, the designer washed the room's eastern gable with the rosy glow of a garnet-glassed railway signal lantern. Sleeper's surprising use of this fixture—in contemporary terms, a bit like installing a traffic light indoors—became a recurring motif in Beauport's subsequent rooms.

The Book Tower likely owes its inspiration to Andrew's library project, completed eighteen months before. The tower effectively stands free of the main house, like Andrew's room, even if its diminutive scale and steep, cylindrical shape set it apart from any traditional library type (as the designer Thomas Jayne has said of this space, "Who builds a round room for *books*?").[116] Sleeper often used books for visual impact, but by concentrating this collection in a dedicated room he declared his affinity with his neighbor's bookishness—a trait he did not exactly share—and enshrined the form that Andrew's gifts most frequently took. Writing him the year he built the Book Tower, and thanking him for a memoir he'd recently given him, Sleeper insisted: "I have no intention of letting *any* one borrow it—or read it out of my sight! Ditto with *all the books* you gave me—I shall love them for their own qualities of interest—& for other good reasons—more than any of the other books in the round-room at Beauport."[117] Indeed, as if to manifest a Book Tower in his own person, he suggestively adds: "I lay reading in bed, with all of them around me, last night." Sleeper's finishing touch to the Book Tower may say more about the room's private intent than it does about his aims as a collector of colonial

4.18
Belfry Chamber,
built 1911–1912.
Photograph by David
Bohl. Courtesy
Historic New England.

Americana. Installed along the room's mezzanine balcony, a revolutionary-era battle flag declares "WE APPEAL TO HEAVEN."

For Christmas 1911 Andrew gave Sleeper a book he particularly prized: the 1842 auction catalogue for Strawberry Hill House, the home Horace Walpole built outside London in the mid-eighteenth century. Writing Helen Patch the next day Sleeper

4.19
Beauport's southern
(Red-Roof-facing)
façade after the
1911–1912 expansion.
At foreground right
stands the new
Book Tower; the
peaked, ground-level
extension at left is
Sleeper's writing
nook. Photograph by
Thomas E. Marr and
Son. Courtesy Historic
New England.

marveled: "think of Piatt finding me a catalogue of 'Strawberry Hill'—the house which inspired so many details at Beauport."[118] Sleeper's prior knowledge of Strawberry Hill had undoubtedly come through secondary sources like this one, for there is no record of his having visited the house by this date. Yet by 1916 the designer was telling journalists that the lacquered wallpaper in his Strawberry Hill bedroom had been removed from Walpole's house itself—a fabrication that magazines and guidebooks repeated long after Sleeper's death (the wallpaper is today identified as a London product from 1907).[119] However fantastic his story, the connection between Beauport and Strawberry Hill is worth examining more closely. For if Sleeper removed no artifacts from Walpole's home, then he certainly channeled many of his ideas—and rather uncannily mirrored, in his own life, the sexual and social milieu from which Walpole's design philosophy emerged.

Credited with the invention of the Gothic novel, Walpole was also the leader of the eighteenth-century Gothic (or "Gothick") Revival in domestic design. His home in Twickenham, a romantic confection of Gothic elements—including a rounded tower that likely inspired Sleeper's—served as a theatrical setting for his vast collection of medieval and medieval-inspired works. Yet to comprehend Walpole's aesthetics is also to understand their origin within his intimate, all-male circle. Calling themselves "The Committee of Taste," this group was like an eighteenth-century prototype of Dabsville. Clubbish, unmarried, and childless, the men were either likely, or confirmed to be, homosexual; and like the Eastern Point crowd, too, the men continually expanded their homes in response to one another, a dynamic that reflected their personal relationships as much as their taste.[120] (When Walpole's friend James Wyatt built his own "Strawberry Room" Walpole called the space his "Gothic child.")[121]

The committee was passionate about Gothic and Chinese aesthetics, two "exotic" traditions they viewed as complementary, and ones that ran strictly counter to the prevailing English taste for Palladian classicism. Even more subversive was the group's attraction to the trappings of the Roman Catholic Church. However suspicious this affinity might have appeared to their Protestant English contemporaries, the committee's embrace of Catholic forms—pseudo-chapels, collections gathered into altar-like settings—were all the more suspect for their theatrical, quasi-blasphemous quality. The combination of the group's unorthodox tastes produced what might today be labeled a Queer aesthetic, but which Walpole's peers labeled a "fribblish" one. (The term "fribble" in this period described an effete, dandyish man; as a contemporary critic said of Walpole's friend Dickie Bateman, his library was "as fribblish as the man himself.")[122]

What particularly worried the men's contemporaries was the committee's mannerist and fantasy-driven attitude toward the past. Walpole, who coined the very term "serendipity," celebrated surprising juxtapositions (for example, light-filled rooms leading to darkened ones); abrupt changes in scale (small doors leading to grand spaces and vice-versa); intentionally baffling floorplans; and allusional spaces that miniaturized historic models (picture the majesty of King's College Chapel reduced to the size of a hallway). If one critic damned Strawberry Hill as a "raree show"—a cheap, pocket-sized peep show—then Walpole went him one better, celebrating his home as "a baby-house [dollhouse] full of playthings."[123] The demonstrable admiration Walpole's circle attracted, regardless of the conservative criticism they endured, may be explained in the ways they harnessed—and even propelled—the rise of romanticism. Their interiors targeted the emotions rather than the intellect, conjuring visual "moods" with little regard for historical authenticity or even the intrinsic value of individual objects. These were Sleeper's people.

Given the widespread criticism Walpole and his circle faced in their day, and the precipitous decline of his reputation in the nineteenth century, one might well ask: How did Sleeper manage to resurrect Walpole's mannerisms with such impunity? The 1842 auction of Strawberry Hill's contents demonstrated that, for all the public interest it generated—the four-week sale attracted eighteen thousand curiosity seekers in its first two weeks alone—the nearly half-century since his death had not been kind to him. In its coverage of the auction, the *London Times* declared Strawberry Hill a "dusthole of the debris of semi-barbarism and bad taste."[124] As late as 1890 the American critic Philip Wharton agreed, declaring, "we now despise the poor, over-ornate, miniature Gothic style of Strawberry Hill," in large part because the home was "too closely connected with the annals of [Walpole's] life."[125]

Describing Strawberry Hill's creator as "the generalissimo of all bachelors," Wharton decries the "scandal, trifles, and littleness of mind" attached to this "society wit" (condemnations that would echo, five years later, at the trial of Oscar Wilde). The spotlessness of Sleeper's reputation, by contrast—both in his day and ours—may be explained in part by his application of Walpole's mannerisms to colonial American fabric. If Walpole's exotic, anticlassical approach rubbed against the grain of conservative British aesthetics, then Sleeper's apparently patriotic tastes shielded him from all criticism. At Beauport, the figure of George Washington stands like a chaperone in nearly every room.

The house once known as "The American Strawberry Hill," Indian Hill Farm in West Newbury, Massachusetts, formed another important model for Sleeper. (Though he likely visited the house more than once his only recorded trip there, and likely his first, is the one Andrew led in the summer of 1912.)[126] Benjamin Poore built the site's original home in 1830, but it reached its fullest expression between 1860 and 1888 under his son, Ben: Perley Poore (the colon in his name, like so much at Indian Hill, was his own esoteric addition). This eccentric house incorporated many elements that would later reappear at Beauport: reassembled architectural salvage, a maze-like assemblage of rooms ("chambers full of suggestion," as one 1887 newspaper noted), and what Elizabeth Stillinger has called "a majestic disregard for consistency."[127] In his ever-multiplying rooms Poore indiscriminately mixed the nineteenth with earlier centuries—hooked rugs, Native American basketry, transfer-printed china, old pewter, and the occasional suit of armor

4.20

Interior (n.d.) of Ben: Perley Poore's Indian Hill Farm, West Newbury, MA. The home's hooked rugs, historic prints, symmetrical compositions, and use of architectural salvage foretold Beauport's interiors. Courtesy Historic New England.

lined the walls—even if his balanced, symmetrical groupings wove the objects into visually coherent compositions.

William Sumner Appleton, though generally insistent upon historical consistency, eventually acquired Poore's home and Beauport for SPNEA as an instructive pairing (in 1939 and 1942 respectively). Perceiving a direct link between the houses, he wrote a colleague in 1940: "if you will only go through Indian Hill you will be astonished to find how it suggests the Gloucester house in one detail after another."[128] Citing "Mr. Sleeper's determination to do something of the kind, only better," Appleton points to Sleeper's strengths as an early adopter—or perhaps in this instance, a kind of decorative usurper. By elevating the charming jumble of Indian Hill's rooms Beauport surpassed its closest American model, eventually obviating the need for SPNEA to keep both properties. In 1948, citing diminishing numbers of visitors at Indian Hill (Beauport was then, as now, one of the organization's most frequently visited sites), SPNEA deaccessioned the West Newbury property. In August 1959 the house was destroyed by fire.

Given the fertile trips Andrew conducted to Cogswell House, Hamilton House, and Indian Hill in these years—and considering, too, the connection he confirmed between Strawberry Hill and Beauport—we are left to wonder: Did Sleeper draw upon these sources *because* they appealed to Andrew, or was Andrew simply so finely attuned to his friend's aesthetic that he became, in effect, Beauport's greatest talent scout? The possibilities are not mutually exclusive, but in the end we must acknowledge—as Sleeper did himself— that Andrew's fingerprints are all over Beauport's sources, starting with Red Roof. The extraordinary ways Sleeper combined, manipulated, and surpassed his models is a measure of his genius, yet the base note to this creative synthesis was his neighbor's approval. Andrew's interest in a house rendered it, *a priori*, more attractive to Sleeper; to translate these sources into a new expression constituted the only union he and Andrew were ever likely to consummate.

Sleeper's methods famously defy categorization, but to understand Beauport in all its mannerist glory—and to comprehend Andrew's refracted role in its creation—requires indexing the house's magical whole into its constituent parts. Broadly defined, these overlapping elements include Sleeper's subjective manipulations of history, his reliance upon artifice and theatricality, and (slipperiest of all to pin down) his evocation of mood. If Edith Wharton and Ogden Codman Jr.'s *The Decoration of Houses* (1897) sought to codify the eternal principles of interior design, then Sleeper's methods turned these all on their head, with two exceptions. First, like Wharton and Codman, he believed that privacy—intimacy, really—was essential to any design. (When Wharton writes that "every room should be a small world unto itself," she could be describing Beauport.)[129] Second, however strictly Wharton and Codman insisted upon structure, hierarchy, and tradition in their treatise, they also invoked *pleasure* as a guiding (even an overriding) design principle. For Sleeper, visual enjoyment represented an article of faith. He, too, insisted that the eye must be delighted, stimulated, or allowed to rest—yet he took this approach one step further. At Beauport he not only created an atmosphere that gratifies our senses, but one that proclaims his very delight in pleasing us—and Andrew, above all.

It is a fitting irony that Sleeper's home achieved National Historic Landmark status for thumbing its nose at history. The house's "playful interpretations of historical themes," as lauded by the National Park Service, are reflected most clearly in its themed rooms and the many spaces Sleeper created using architectural salvage. Each of these rooms is a romantic reimagining of a man or place, as projected through the lens of a totalizing decorative scheme. Color, line, scale, and humor always trump factual chronology in these spaces. And while he clearly admired works that bore the patina of age, he was uninterested in antiquity for its own sake. In one letter Sleeper exhorted a client to find objects that were "old, with a little originality and style," "really old and right," "old and very good," or "very archaic and attractive."[130]

In forming his own collection of colonial American works, Sleeper clearly applied the same criteria. In 1934 the American Institute of Architects proclaimed him a "protector of the culture of early America," but the designer's interest in this period was always more emotional, associative, and formal than historical or preservationist-minded. Even his fascination with George Washington, whose image appears throughout the house like so many Easter eggs, recalls less the man's historical figure or character than it does a collector's delight in the variation of an object type. (It is tempting, too, to consider the emotional dimension of Sleeper's attraction to this, the ultimate historical Alpha Male.)

"Mightn't it be fun," the designer is reported to have said, "to have a house in which each room could recapture some of the spirit of a particular mood or phase or 'period' of our American life?"[131] Critics frequently cite this observation to confirm Sleeper's devotion to historic preservation, while entirely missing his stated aim: he wants to have *fun*. At Beauport, "fun" is inextricably tied to notions of theater, artifice, and surprise—and nowhere are these on fuller display than in its funhouse manipulations of scale. From its earliest incarnation *Little* Beauport celebrated the miniature, its intimate rooms and Lilliputian constellations of objects suggesting a doll-like environment. These diminutive spaces, in turn, exaggerate the scale of the home's larger rooms; when passing from one room to the next, visitors may feel their own bodies growing or shrinking. In some instances Sleeper exploited the scale of a single feature to giddily disorient—as on Beauport's southern roof, where in 1912 he absurdly (and wonderfully) paired the Shelley Room's commanding, 138-paned window alongside a gabled dormer tiny enough to encircle with two hands (see figure 4.19, p. 148).

Beyond these dramatic juxtapositions of scale, Sleeper also theatrically combined valuable and valueless objects: a pickle jar next to a rare piece of glassware, or a colonial portrait flanked by a railway lantern. Indeed, there is little in the house that rises to the level of a museum-quality object. (As one designer has said of Beauport, "There are moments when you're completely unsure if anything is *good*. But does it matter?")[132] As Sleeper well knew, the artistry of these pairings elevated the perceived value of both objects—a mannerism Susan Sontag has identified as one of the very signatures of camp, which "finds beauty in the elevation of the everyday to the extraordinary."[133]

Sleeper's high-low juxtapositions represent just one dimension of his sly sense of humor (Andrew once asked Caroline Sinkler, "Is Harry as ribald and shocking as ever?").[134] Consider the collection of glass balls that line his Red Roof–facing window—as much a joke about Andrew's virility as they are an homage to nineteenth-century craft—or the military epaulette he placed in the Nelson Room, converted into a lady's pincushion. As for the half life-scale statue of Washington at the center stage of the Stair Hall—a room "dedicated to the Father of this Country," as Beauport's 1965 guidebook solemnly declares—the work is nothing more than a cast-iron stove. "It's wonderful to sit here and see him get hot," Sleeper is reported to have said of this piece; "he is slow to anger, but so comforting."[135]

Even his collection of nineteenth-century prints, seemingly a poor source for comedy, suggest Sleeper sometimes regarded these images with a gimlet eye; the designer once advised a client to collect "old railroad pictures" for his home, citing their "quaintness and humor."[136] One striking example of this found humor appears in a Victorian mourning picture Sleeper hung in his writing nook (a room wallpapered, it should be noted, with the French humor journal *Le Rire*). The scene's weeping willow, a traditional emblem of bereavement, encloses two grief-stricken men apparently locked in a passionate embrace. Homoeroticism was hardly the artist's original intent, but under Sleeper's eye the work—like every other artifact in the house—was cast anew.

The designer's wish to delight and surprise was connected to a larger project. As Hollister wrote in the 1950s, Sleeper's strategy was "to establish the 'mood' of a room, [and] give you a little time to conjure it"; once that connection was made, he adds, "you give up, you'll go anywhere now—submissively."[137] He enacted these emotional states most powerfully through color. Decorator Nancy McClelland credits Sleeper with inventing no fewer than seven colors—among them "golden brown," "pumpkin yellow," and "sage green—yet his inventiveness involved more than simply conjuring new hues.[138] Rather, it is his color *harmonies* that make his rooms sing. Dramatic, single-color schemes in spaces like the Souvenir de France Room allowed him to seamlessly link objects as disparate as a scientific instrument, a stuffed bird, and a leather knifebox; the works' variety disappears under the heat of their pulsing reds. And by alternating cool and warm colors, or juxtaposing complementary colors (red and green was a favorite combination), he quickened the eye, creating a kind of visual jazz riff.

Nowhere was Sleeper's palette more inventive than in his use of colored glass, perhaps the Aesthetic Movement's most favored medium. (As the *Boston Herald* floridly claimed in 1882, "the great aesthetic wave, which has carried taste and beauty into the adornment

4.21
LEFT: Mourning scene (1825–1835). Felt, silk, watercolor, printed paper, and hairwork (6 ¼" x 7 ¼" x ¾"). Gift of Constance McCann Betts, Helena Woolworth Guest, and Frasier W. McCann, 1942.2686.
RIGHT (Detail). Given the work's diminutive size, the embracing men are virtually invisible to the casual observer. Courtesy Historic New England.

4.22
Sleeper's amber glass
window in the Stair
Hall (built 1929).
Photograph by David
Bohl. Courtesy
Historic New England.

of the modern home, has borne colored glass upon its crest.")[139] Whereas Aesthetic
Movement artists looked to medieval stained glass windows as models, however, Sleeper
creatively reinvented this tradition. Using the existing windows of his home, or sometimes
inserting historic architectural framing, he curated dense collections of antique glass in
single-color combinations. Exploiting natural and electric light, hidden light sources and
mirrors, he turned the projected colors of his glassware collection into a physical presence
in his rooms—an effect as dazzling as it is disorienting. One Beauport legend has it that a
1940s visitor to the Stair Hall, upon encountering the room's spectacular 130-piece display
of amber glass, fainted on the spot—was revived—and fainted a second time.[140] The story
feels apocryphal, but its endurance underscores the power ascribed to these installations.
Often tucked into interstitial spaces within the house, Sleeper's monochromatic glass
compositions create a quasi-religious atmosphere—an effect Walpole and his circle would
have applauded.

The final ingredient in Sleeper's atmospheric strategy is another Walpolean trick: the
"Gothic" sensibility he lent his rooms. Not strictly related to medieval style—although in
some rooms it is—this approach depends upon the baffling nature of the house's plan,
which summons the hidden chambers of a Gothic novel. (As Beauport's 1990 guidebook
suggests, the home's "shape has always suggested secrets, and mysteries cling to the

house like the vines that once shrouded its walls.")[141] The house's famously confusing arrangement of rooms—what a mid-century visitor called a "charming maze" and *Country Life* labeled a "demonically muddled plan"—was not an accidental byproduct of Beauport's expansion.[142] Always in control of his rooms' final arrangement, Sleeper aimed to evoke the kind of romantic interior Charles Dickens describes in his novel *Bleak House* (1853):

> It was one of those delightfully irregular houses where you go up and down steps out of one room into another, and where you come upon more rooms when you think you have seen all there are, and where there is a beautiful provision of little halls and passages, and where you find still older cottage-rooms in unexpected places, with lattice windows and green growth pressing through them.[143]

In his 1981 descriptions of the "queer cubbyholes" and "quaint closets" of Beauport *and* Red Roof, Joseph Garland went so far as to suggest the houses' puzzling nature reflected the men's perversity (an assertion that says more about the 1980s than it does about Andrew or Sleeper).[144] Far from an indication of shameful secrecy, the labyrinths and hidden rooms in these homes suggest instead Sleeper's childlike joy in benign manipulation—and also, perhaps, an intimate code shared between the men (for in the end only they could confidently navigate one another's houses).

It is often claimed that Beauport's variety served Sleeper as a kind of professional showcase for his decorating clients. There are two problems with this premise, however. First, the majority of Beauport's rooms predate the period when his career officially began. (As late as 1920, Sleeper listed his occupation as "none" on the United States census; he would not open his Boston decorating office until the following year.) Second, although the eccentricity of these rooms might have delighted visitors, they would more than likely have sent a potential client running for the hills. Sleeper himself complained that his clients routinely failed to understand his aesthetic. Writing Henry Francis du Pont—a client initially sympathetic to his approach—he confided, "I have so constantly to do things that I do not like much and would not do in my own house."[145] It makes sense, then, that his first and most loyal clientele, beginning in the 1910s, were those within his own circle—Andrew, Sinkler, and Gardner—or Gloucester clients on the periphery of Dabsville. Yet as talented as he was, he never managed to translate the spirit of Beauport to another setting; even the deadening tone of his advertising ("Norman and English Country Houses / 17th and 18th c. American interiors") fails to summon the magic of his own spaces.

Sleeper's work for du Pont in the 1920s provides a useful model to understand both the successes and limitations of his professional career. His wealthy client is today best known for founding Winterthur, a museum that grew from his family's Delaware mansion to include a staggering 175 American period rooms. Long before he conceived Winterthur, du Pont considered himself a Sleeper acolyte. As he later told the story, in October 1923 he had a pair of epiphanies; after visiting the home of collector Electra Havemeyer Webb in Shelburne, Vermont, du Pont proceeded to Beauport—where he claimed his eyes suddenly opened, not only to the attraction of American antiques but also to the possibilities of recreating historical interiors.[146] When he hired Sleeper that fall to decorate Chestertown House, his new summer home in Southampton, New York, the designer could hardly believe his good luck. Not only had he found a client with virtually unlimited resources but one who also appeared to understand his eclectic approach. Closing one of his letters to du Pont, Sleeper confided: "Between ourselves, I think that you are about as capable as I am."[147]

At Chestertown House as at Beauport, the designer believed historical authenticity should never compromise the home's overall mood. He advised du Pont to create nested spaces within his Long Island home, explaining "unless you insist upon the seeming eccentricities, I think the room might look too Georgian and ordinary"; at one point he even advocated mixing reproduction and genuine furniture, an approach that would later horrify his client ("you would not feel the difference," Sleeper insisted).[148] Du Pont recognized that his own installations fell short of Beauport's charm. Bemoaning how "perfectly conventional" his lighting appeared in comparison to Sleeper's "delightfully arranged" examples, he exhorted him to "show me anything that you want me to have or do or copy at Southampton."[149] Providing his client a glimpse of his own criteria for selecting objects, he once offered du Pont a carved eagle whose charm lay in that "it is a little different . . . than the ordinary eagle"; yet "if it gives you no emotion," he added, du Pont should reject it.[150]

By the time Chestertown House was completed in 1926, the two men's design philosophies had significantly diverged. In 1928 du Pont hired Sleeper to advise him on the redecoration of Winterthur, then still a private home but already imagined as a future museum. In 1930 he wrote to Sleeper, "I am doing the house archaeologically and correctly, and I am paying the greatest attention even to the fringes"—a declaration that doubtless bored Sleeper to tears.[151] Beset with health problems and increasingly distracted by design work on the west coast, Sleeper lost all interest in the Winterthur project; du Pont's "unending chain of perfection," as an admiring critic dubbed his eventual museum, represented the very antithesis of Beauport's colorful eccentricity.[152] In February 1931, du Pont fired Sleeper, who failed to respond until July. Losing the most promising, and initially the most sympathetic client he would ever have, Sleeper likely realized his "surprisingly domestic" approach would never get him much further than Eastern Point Boulevard.

MY FUNNY VALENTINE

Du Pont's first visit to Beauport had occurred thirteen years before his 1923 epiphany. Though it's possible the future collector was then simply blind to the home's attractions, it bears noting that the Beauport of 1910 was a very different place from the house du Pont saw in 1923. The home's original suite of rooms provided no hint of the dramatic changes that would take place between 1911 and 1912, and again between 1917 and 1923. Faced in this latter period with a string of personal losses, and navigating a rapidly changing social milieu on Eastern Point, Sleeper turned to Beauport more than ever as a form of consolation, control, and escape. Despite, or more likely because of, Andrew's long absences from Eastern Point in these years—first due to his military service in World War I and subsequently in his new role as a Massachusetts congressman—Sleeper continued to elaborate his home while keeping Red Roof's owner uppermost in his mind. In 1921 he created the room now widely acknowledged as Beauport's centerpiece; known as the Souvenir de France or Octagon Room, it is the greatest love letter he ever wrote Andrew.

By the 1910s Sleeper's once tightly bound community on Eastern Point began to unravel. Since her 1911 marriage Davidge was living abroad for long periods, while Beaux and Sinkler now spent more of the year in Philadelphia. Even Gardner, now in her seventies and slowing down, was visiting Gloucester less frequently. Still in the prime of his career, Andrew resigned as Assistant Secretary of the Treasury in 1912 to work on the Federal Reserve Act—his eyes set on a larger role in Washington. It was around this time a distance appears to have grown between the men.

In May 1912, Sleeper wrote Andrew a heartbreaking letter. Sending him the receipt for a pair of cigarette holders Andrew had bought for Mabbett, he begs not to be relieved of the many duties he had undertaken for his neighbor over the years. It is worth quoting at length:

> For a good many years now, I have given a service which, whatever its value, most obviously have [*sic*] been sincere—by its voluntary—and insistent—character—and I can truly say that I have never had—and have not now—any wish "to be relieved," in the least degree of welcome labor your friendship involves. You have never asked very much of me—but as I have always been fonder of you than any friend I've had, such few things as you have accepted from me have been a very potent factor in my happiness. In a world in which each man is really so solitary . . . it would compensate for my many disappointments if I knew you believed in my stability. I have no less admiration now, for your fineness, than I have ever had—and am eager now as I have ever been for your approval and affection . . . so please keep what is yours by virtue of long possession & believe me, as always, faithfully, H.D.S.[153]

4.23

Henry Sleeper and Piatt Andrew at Red Roof (November 3, 1914). Red Roof Archive, courtesy Historic New England.

To a certain degree, Andrew's exasperation with Sleeper was understandable. Not only did he likely find his constant attention exhausting (as early as 1909 he confided to his parents, "I still get clippings every day from H.D.S. and several letters every week") but he was also in a fragile emotional state himself that May.[154] Just weeks before he received Sleeper's letter he'd lost a close friend, Archibald Butt, in the sinking of the *Titanic* (he attended Butt's memorial service the day Sleeper wrote him).[155] And as Andrew struggled to maintain his long-distance relationship with Mabbett that spring, Sleeper's continual presence at the couple's infrequent Red Roof dinners could not have been entirely welcome.[156]

In the following year three of Dabsville's principals mustered, perhaps for a last time, the spirited sense of play that characterized their early years. On February 4, 1913, Andrew, Beaux, and Sleeper attended Louis Comfort Tiffany's "Egyptian Fête" in New York City—a costume ball "of such brilliancy," as *Vogue* reported, "it is doubtful it has ever been equaled."[157] Posing for their group portrait that evening the friends presented a telling tableau. Under "the spell of some magic known to Mr. Louis Tiffany" Andrew reprised his role as an Imperial Roman, bearing an enormous spear and baring his much admired legs. Sleeper, on the other hand—a Babylonian vizier for the night—appeared nearly mummified in a heavy beard, fringed tablecloth, and leopard skin from Red Roof. Separating the two men stands Beaux, a regal Egyptian princess. Further complicating the image's emotional dynamics is the presence of Beaux's ex-lover, Dorothy Gilder, who kneels at her feet. Three years later Gilder would marry the man at right, Dallas McGrew (Harvard '03)—a longtime Red Roof habitué and former beau of Andrew's. Even the two most dazzling figures in Dabsville, it appears, were now ceding their places to a younger set.

If the first years of the 1910s were relatively quiet for Eastern Point, then the events of 1914 upended this community of friends. In February the forty-one-year-old Andrew—whose years-long relationship with Mabbett had finally drawn to a close—embarked on an intense affair with twenty-five-year-old John Hays Hammond Jr. Wealthy, attractive, and worldly for a man so young—he had grown up in Cape Town and London, held a Yale degree, and was already a promising radio engineer—Jack Hammond moved to Gloucester as a seventeen-year-old when his father, a South African diamond mining magnate, built a sprawling estate on the western side of Gloucester Harbor. After Yale and a brief stint in the US Patent office in Washington, Jack returned in the early 1910s to

4.24
Louis Comfort Tiffany's "Egyptian Fête" in New York City (February 4, 1913). Standing, L to R: Piatt Andrew, Cecilia Beaux, Henry Sleeper, Kate Trubee Davison, and Dallas McGrew. Kneeling, L to R: Dorothea and Rosamond Gilder. Courtesy Helen Patch Gray.

found the Hammond Radio Research Laboratory on his father's estate. By the winter of 1914 he was as busy at Red Roof as he was in his laboratory.

In another surprising pivot, Andrew decided that summer to run for the North Shore's congressional seat. It was a bold move not only given the popularity of his opponent, incumbent Republican Augustus Peabody Gardner, but also because the congressman was Isabella's nephew. Andrew's campaign, which naturally placed "Y" in an awkward position, led to his humiliating defeat in September's primary—and a subsequent, reactive decision that changed his life's trajectory. Not to be outdone, at the start of November Sleeper scrambled the group's dynamics himself by introducing the dashing British actor Leslie Buswell to Eastern Point. (The two had recently met in Boston, introduced by Gardner.) Like others before him, Buswell fell under Gloucester's spell from the start; as he wrote Sleeper a year later, "there is around me the net that started to unfold on November 7, 1914."[158]

Buswell's impact on Eastern Point was immediate. Sleeper, clearly smitten with the handsome Englishman, brought him to Gloucester just ten days after their November 7 meeting—whereupon the actor developed an instant and mutual attraction to Hammond, then still seeing Andrew. Within weeks Buswell had himself fallen for Red Roof's owner. Once more at the heart of an adoring, clubbish clique—now an all-male Dabsville styled with the new acronym, BASH (Buswell/Andrew/Sleeper/Hammond)—Andrew was doubtless gratified but also restless and bruised on the heels of his congressional defeat. His next move rocked the small Eastern Point community. Writing his parents in early December he confided he had "just about decided that I must go over to France for a few months" to volunteer as an ambulance driver in the months-old First World War.[159] On December 18, Buswell recorded one of the last entries in Red Roof's guest books for many years to come, his signature joined by a dramatic (even apparently tear-stained) "Finis." The following day Andrew sailed for France, where he remained nearly half a decade.

He left a lovelorn crowd in his wake. Writing Andrew two days after his departure, Sleeper confided he had walked New York's streets with Beaux in a daze after the ship sailed. "Your going was a very big thing for both of us," he confessed, adding, "from where you stood and waved to me as the *Touraine* slipped away I could see you long after all the other people were lost in shadow."[160] That winter and spring found the remaining members of BASH frequently at Red Roof, comparing letters from its absent owner. "We will all go over to Red Roof and think of you," Sleeper wrote Andrew in March 1915; "[Buswell] is 'awful pleased' to get a letter you wrote him—care of Jack," he teased.[161] ("To tell you the truth," he continued, "I think he has a secret longing to be with you" despite the fact that "he is very fond of Jack . . . intensely and wholly spellbound by him.") The following month Sleeper wrote, "I am writing in your library while 'Buzzy' plays the organ . . . reading your letters makes him restless & irritable (with Jack!) & the latter is conscious & jealous of yr. lure—and *fears* it!"[162]

As Buswell and Hammond were now learning, the very atmosphere of Red Roof fed their love for its absent owner—but for Sleeper this had always been the case. Writing Andrew in the spring of 1915, he declared that in his long visits to his neighbor's home,

the remembrance of each room there holds as much happiness as that of any other friendship I have known—& more of confidence and contentment. . . .
To you—in the midst of vast and vital things it may seem a far cry from the

ties that make home—but they matter to you, I know—so please remember sometimes, that I look forward with constant and eager longing to your coming. My love to you ever.[163]

In this remarkable passage he not only collapsed Andrew and his home—Sleeper's love for its rooms was always a reflected passion—but he also inserts himself into these spaces. By insisting "they matter to you," what he really means is: "*I* matter to you."

By this date the ceaselessly energetic Andrew had risen to Inspector General for ambulances at the American Hospital in Paris; within the year he would form the independent American Ambulance Field Service, later simply the American Field Service (AFS). In May Buswell joined him in Paris. "It is a great happiness to have you speak so warmly of yr. hours with Buzzie," Sleeper wrote Andrew after his friend's arrival.[164] Speaking as if by emotional proxy, he continued: "His unconscious *demand* on your affection and attention make him . . . about the most engaging person I have ever encountered. He is *your* loyal and appreciative friend as much as mine—for whenever your name was spoken, this past winter . . . he was instantly on fire to acclaim your virtues." When he received photographs of the two men in their uniforms, Sleeper exclaimed that he "loved them—but C.B. [Beaux] had such a look of longing in her eye when I showed them to her that I gave her one—on impulse."[165] However much he wished to join Andrew himself, he remained home; "if it were not for mother," he wrote, "I should go over."[166] Instead Sleeper became one of the AFS's most ardent stateside recruiters, sending Andrew scores of drivers and raising funds for new vehicles. (Gardner sponsored an ambulance that Andrew painted with an enormous "Y.")

In July 1917, nearly two and a half years after Andrew's departure, Gardner wrote him: "It is years since I have heard from you—And the war goes on & the horrors &

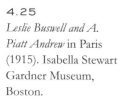

4.25

Leslie Buswell and A. Piatt Andrew in Paris (1915). Isabella Stewart Gardner Museum, Boston.

terrors increase. . . . Just now it is all so sad for poor Harry Sleeper. His mother died yesterday & the world seems quite different to him."[167] However unassuming a figure Maria Sleeper cast at Beauport, her son felt her loss keenly. Writing Helen Patch on the first anniversary of her death he explained: "So many of the things I care most for in my house are the fruits of hours with my mother. . . . Scarcely a day passes that I do not wish she were here to share with me each new treasure."[168] The connection between his mother and collecting had always been a strong one, and so it is unsurprising that he consoled himself with a new room at Beauport to honor her. The Pembroke Room, also known as the Pine Kitchen, would become one of the his most influential designs—spawning myriad imitations, including half a dozen versions he produced for clients—but its importance for Beauport lies in its role as an architectural portrait.

Completed in the winter of 1917–1918, the Pembroke Room called upon Sleeper's decade-long practice of repurposing architectural salvage. The difference here was that he installed material from a historic home connected to his mother's family: the Barker House of Pembroke, Massachusetts. Built in 1628 by Robert Barker—Sleeper's maternal grandmother had been the last of the Barkers—the structure was believed to be the oldest surviving home in the United States at the time of its 1885 dismantling.

4.26
The Pembroke Room, also known as the Pine Kitchen (built 1917). Photograph by David Bohl. Courtesy Historic New England.

(Purchasing the Barker panels, doors, ceiling beams, and even its chimney bricks from a dealer, Sleeper acquired the room's flooring from another historic source, the Dillaway House in Boston's North End.)[169] Unprecedented, too, was the room's extraordinary size. Replacing the East Loggia Sleeper added to the house in 1909 and expanding well beyond the porch's footprint, the Pembroke Room was larger than the Hall and South Gallery combined.

This new L-shaped space included a colonial "kitchen"—a fireplace filled with antique cooking utensils—alongside a dining room lined with colonial redware and a "tap room" that served as a bar.[170] Beyond the dining room Sleeper created a pendant space, the Franklin Game Room, with a central memorial to Maria Sleeper: her portrait hangs here above the fireplace, flanked by dried floral arrangements. As Kevin Murphy has said of these new spaces, Sleeper had by this stage become "a family man in reverse"—a bachelor tending only to absent relations.[171]

The following years were eventful ones for Sleeper and Beauport. With this memorial to his mother complete, he found himself free to join Andrew in Paris. Sailing

4.27
Final configuration of Beauport's first floor. Courtesy Historic New England.

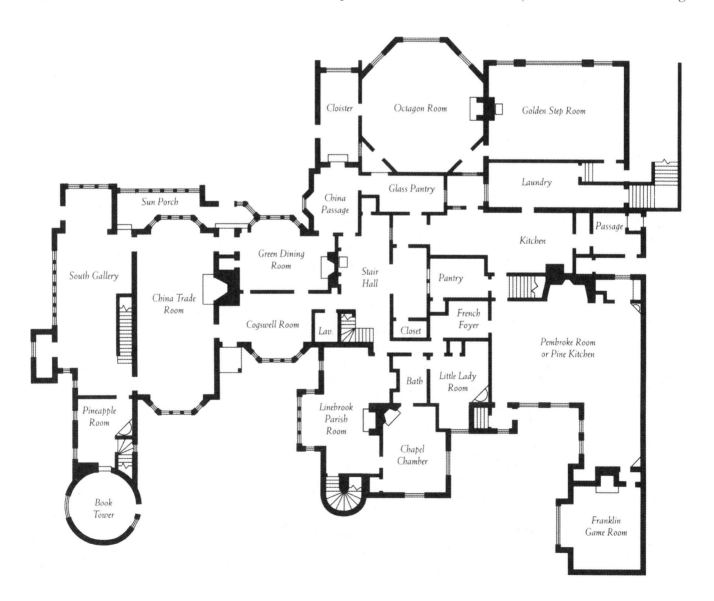

for France in the summer of 1918 he established himself at 21 Rue Raynouard, a five-acre private estate lent to the AFS for its Paris headquarters. Despite his continued poor health, including a recurrent flu and variety of gastrointestinal problems, Sleeper worked tirelessly behind the scenes as an administrative fixer for Andrew. (When he sailed back to the United States in September 1919 he did so as *Chevalier* Sleeper, a member of the French Legion of Honor.) Following his return Sleeper endured another a year of ill health and, as he later confided to Hanson, a "seemingly endless" period of depression.[172] As ever, he turned to Beauport for relief. In spring 1920 he embarked on another major expansion of the house, fueled in part by an unexpected windfall from his great-aunt's estate.[173] This infusion quickly vanished with the construction of two new rooms in 1920–1921, the Golden Step and Souvenir de France Rooms (the latter also known as the Octagon Room). Today these spaces are so closely associated with Beauport's identity it is impossible to imagine the house without them.

The harbor-facing Golden Step Room represented a number of departures for Sleeper. One of the only spaces at Beauport to take its cue from Red Roof (the line of inspiration generally ran in the opposite direction), it resembles the harbor-side dining room Andrew completed in 1913. Whereas Red Roof's model was lined with blue-and-white Delft tiles, however, Sleeper used stark white walls for this space—wholly uncharacteristic for him—in order to highlight the room's unusual furnishings. Most striking was its colossal ship model (a vessel named the *Golden Step*) that recalled, at dramatically larger scale, a similar model at Red Roof. Around verdigris-colored tables he placed a collection of Windsor chairs whose varying vintages and silhouettes magically disappear beneath a unifying layer of robin's egg blue paint. (Exemplifying their owner's insistence on tonal consistency over historical authenticity, the choice would have been an unforgivable act for any other antiquarian.) To complement the furniture's sea-inspired

4.28
The Golden Step
Room (built 1921).
Photograph by David
Bohl. Courtesy Historic
New England.

palette, Sleeper lined the room's northern wall with bright green Wedgwood plates and created table centerpieces using sky-blue fishermen's floats suspended in clear glass urns. Most ingenious of all, he designed the room's water-facing window to fully retract into the floor, seamlessly combining room and harbor when lowered. As if to slyly reinforce the impression of floating underwater, he installed two carved mermen on the room's northern wall.

Moving from the ethereal Golden Step Room into the lacquered cave of the Souvenir de France Room, created in the same period, provides the greatest room-to-room contrast found at Beauport. As he explained to Gardner in March 1920, he created this theatrical octagonal space—the fifth and last dining room in the house—to display the red tin toleware he had collected during his time in France ("I have all the details visualized," Sleeper wrote her well before the room was begun, "and am enjoying it accordingly").[174] Using this collection as his starting point he created a constellation of brooding reds set against dark aubergine walls. Scarlet Morocco-bound books, oxblood ceramics, ruby Bohemian glass, rose-colored hooked rugs, a red lacquer screen, and even a hot pink stuffed ibis surround the room's central portrait of a crimson-jacketed Marquis de Lafayette. In Sleeper's day arrangements of bright red maple leaves emerged from the toleware pots while "turkey-red calico" awnings, once installed outside the room's windows, cast a salmon pink glow across the room's white ceiling.

From the moment of its creation this room has been hailed as one of the great jewels in Beauport's studded crown. "One could sit for hours in this room absorbing its beauty and color," *Country Life* declared in 1929; half a century later, the same magazine pronounced it "surely one of the great American rooms of its day, and [Sleeper's] finest work."[175] Yet however much critics agree on the room's powerful mood—a romantic, erotically charged atmosphere that "seems to crackle" with colors "red as embers"—none have identified its rather obvious object: the master of Red Roof.[176] Not since his 1906 Wallace Bryant portrait, painted in the first flushes of his passion for Andrew, had Sleeper so insistently celebrated his neighbor's signature color.

Deep reds suggested a range of associations with Andrew, beginning but not ending with his home's name. Whether impersonating a Roman centurion or a Pope, Andrew's costumes invariably included his "gorgeous . . . robe of turkey red"; occasionally, too, he swathed his house itself in scarlet fabric, hanging bolts from the ceiling of his new library or draping them along a terrace to salute a passing schooner.[177] So closely associated with the color was Andrew—whose birthday fell two days shy of Valentine's Day—that its reference became a kind of running joke with his friends. Writing Andrew on the eve of his return home in 1908, Sleeper found "heavy blood-red" paper to welcome him back; not to be outdone, Gardner used her own plain stationery to assure Andrew she would be "blood-red glad" to see him.[178] Sleeper's scarlet metaphors extended even to the passage of time without Red Roof's owner. Writing Andrew about the awful "*langsamkeit*" (slowness) of his absence in 1908, Sleeper consoled himself that the "years that shade . . . harden the ruby in a million years."[179] Last, it must also be noted that the emblem Andrew chose to represent the AFS was a blazing red torch (Sleeper installed a carved pair of these in the adjacent South Gallery). Not only did the device recall the men's shared wartime work, but it also served as a fitting icon for Beauport itself. From its multiple garnet railway signal lanterns to its new crimson dining room, the house emblematized the very torch Sleeper held for Andrew.

Nearly as telling as the room's insistent color references was the associative power of its name. By christening this space the Souvenir de France Room, Sleeper did not intend (as the house's first guidebook suggested) to honor the history of Franco-American relations.[180] Rather, the room enshrines the memory of his Parisian idyll with Andrew at 21 Rue Raynouard. Souvenirs are by their nature consolatory, memorializing a time to which we can never return—and in 1921 the men's close proximity was drawing to a painful close. At last elected to Congress the year of the room's completion, Andrew would soon be living in Washington for much of each year. The Souvenir de France Room served, then, both as a parting gift to him—a regal reminder of his importance to Sleeper—and also a way to relieve the pain of his loss.

The designer appears to have enshrined their bond even in the room's unusual shape. When he designed Red Roof's Pewter Room in the 1910s, a space that recalled Beauport more than any other in Andrew's home, Sleeper installed an octagonal "Sailor's Valentine," a framed shellwork composition arranged in floral patterns. Matching a similar piece in his own collection, the object served, like Sleeper's new dining room, as a token of affection. Indeed, the characteristic silhouette of this "valentine" recalls the octagon's long history as a devotional shape. Associated with Gothic chapels, baptisteries, and chapter

4.29
The Souvenir de France Room, also known as the Octagon Room (built 1921). Photograph by David Bohl. Courtesy Historic New England.

houses, octagons traditionally symbolized the mystic joining of the earthly (square) and heavenly (round) realms. In the dining room's very profile, then—insistently repeated throughout the room, from its central table to its doorknobs—the designer pointed to a kind of celestial union.

Clearly aware of the shape's medieval associations Sleeper included a variety of Gothic touches in this room, from the ogival arches of its lolling chairs to the chapel-like spaces along the octagon's eastern periphery (see Beauport's first-floor plan, figure 4.27, on p. 162). The more dramatic of these two rooms, whose very shape evokes Andrew's capital "A," is the Amethyst Passage. With its moody installation of purple glass, curated within an ogee-arched window, this pocket-sized chamber serves like a traditional "Lady Chapel"—a transitional space preparing the eye for the fantasia of reds to come. In its palette and position the room also obliquely honors the "Lavender Lady" next door, Caroline Sinkler, whose property formed its own prelude to Red Roof. Exiting through the dining room's second triangular space, named the Ruby Passage, visitors experience its crimson theme like a retreating echo.

Nor was the power of the Souvenir de France Room contained to the first floor. Its construction allowed Sleeper to create a large bedroom above, where he translated the dining room's palette into a floor-to-ceiling environment. The expansive Red Indian Room nominally embraces a Native American theme, but its real leitmotif is the room's unpainted red pine walls, floor, and ceiling—a color one can actually smell in the summer's heat. If the Amethyst and Ruby Passages formed chaplets to the Octagon Room's nave, then this bedroom serves as its *forêt*—the arched timbers found beneath a cathedral's roof. According to Hanson, Sleeper once planned to build a chapel on the southern edge of his property, facing Red Roof.[181] This assemblage of rooms rendered such a project unnecessary.

After the Golden Step and Souvenir de France Rooms, the most spectacular transformation at Beauport in this period was Sleeper's conversion of the Hall—the home's 1908 centerpiece—into the China Trade Room. The reason for the change was, to use Walpole's word, serendipitous. In 1923 Sleeper purchased a large cache of hand-painted eighteenth-century Chinese wallpaper scrolls, originally ordered by Philadelphia banker Robert Morris in 1784 and discovered in their original shipping crate at Marblehead's Elbridge Gerry House.[182] Removing the Hall's medieval objects and paneling, Sleeper papered its walls with nineteen scrolls illustrating the production of tea and porcelain. Above, he recast the room's ceiling into a tented pagoda shape. ("When the magician lifted the curtain" on this new room, as Hollister writes, "the Puritan chapel had vanished.")[183] As sharp a turn as these changes appear to represent, it must be remembered that, for Sleeper's Walpolean forebears, Chinese and Gothic design represented two sides of the same exotic coin—traditions that, in their perceived emotive fantasy, challenged the more cerebral nature of prevailing classicism. Sleeper also thought pagodas were great fun.

Nowhere at Beauport was Sleeper's screwball sense of fantasy more apparent than in the full-size pagoda he built into the room's southern wall. Mimicking a traditional garden folly, this indoor structure extended from the China Trade Room into the adjoining South Gallery; by intersecting the walls' architectural scenes, it therefore allowed visitors to "enter" the space of the wallpaper. To encounter the room from this vantage point would have been a rich sensory experience. Incense was an important part of its *mise-en-scène*, as were the juxtapositions of scale that surrounded the pagoda. Dwarfed by the

4.30
William Ellis Ranken, *China Trade Room* (1928). Watercolor on paper (35 5/8" x 24 ½" x 7/8"). Gift of O.D. Garland, 1976.169. One of a series of Beauport interiors Ranken painted for *Country Life*. At right, the half-pagoda that once extended into the South Gallery. Courtesy Historic New England.

room's tented ceiling, the structure towered, in turn, over the room's collection of temple models—works that created a kind of miniature skyline in the room. Baffled by this Orientalist mirage at the center of his home, critics have attempted to shoehorn the China Trade Room into a story about colonial American trade. In the end, however, the room is more escapist fantasy than history lesson. As the philosopher Gaston Bachelard has written, the primary role of a home—as crystallized by this space, and above all by its built-in pagoda—is to "shelter daydreaming . . . [and] allow one to dream in peace."[184]

The extraordinary, nested follies of the China Trade Room epitomize Beauport's frequent blurring of playfulness and madness. A folly's role is to punctuate a natural environment with artificial points of fantasy (the structure's very name conjures joyful foolishness), yet at Beauport there is no mitigating "landscape" in the form of conventional rooms or even a hallway to throw his rooms—follies, all—into relief. Uninterrupted, these spaces raise the offstage specter of lunacy, like the threat of a cloistered madman in a Gothic novel. By this date Sleeper even had one of these upstairs. Declared legally insane in 1920, his brother Jacob spent the next ten years periodically confined to Beauport's Shelley and Blue Willow Rooms, like a living avatar of his brother's decorating mania.[185]

In the final years of his life Beauport's creator never surpassed the creativity, fantasy, and longing of these 1920s transformations. With Andrew living primarily in Washington, Hanson hospitalized in a Denver tuberculosis sanitarium, and Gardner in Mount Auburn Cemetery (the doyenne of Fenway Court died the year after Sleeper completed the China Trade Room), Beauport's audience had left the building. Ironically enough, Sleeper was never busier than in these years—designing for others. From the mid-1920s to the early 1930s he boasted an impressive roster of clients from the Vanderbilt family to Joan Crawford, but the work never lent him the same satisfaction as designing for himself. And certainly, these commissions did not come close to covering the bills for Beauport's final expansion. (Together the Golden Step, Souvenir de France, and China Trade Rooms represent a third of the cost to build Beauport in its entirety.)[186]

In the last rooms Sleeper completed at Beauport, between 1925 and 1929, the house appears to be feeding upon itself. For the pine-paneled Master Mariner's Room on the second floor—built in 1925 from his mother's former outdoor loggia—the designer used historic paneling from his own home, recycling parts of the deconstructed Hall. The room's comically oversized door leads to a passageway created at the same time, the North Gallery, whose compressed space pushes the very limits of Beauport's boundaries. (From the North Gallery's exterior balcony, one can touch the house next door.) Four years later Sleeper built the central Stair Hall (1929), a room theoretically intended to impose a sense of order on the house's circulation, but one that

4.31
Henry Sleeper in the early 1930s. Courtesy Historic New England.

stands instead like a distillation of Beauport's confounding eccentricities. Bristling with no less than seven functional doors, the Stair Hall's grand, primary door leads nowhere. It is here that Sleeper curated his faint-inducing amber glass composition (see figure 4.22, p. 154), a virtuoso installation that, like the Amethyst Passage writ large, transforms the hall into a sacred space. Just as a sculpted saint might face his own image in a rose window, the hall's George-Washington-as-stove gazes at the crowning motif of the amber window: a bitters bottle in the shape of the first president.

In their correspondence from the 1920s Sleeper and Hanson often adopted a nostalgic tone about the house. Writing his employer/collaborator in 1921, Hanson reminisced:

> It makes quite an interesting affair when you look at the whole and look back over the various circumstances associated with each particular addition and renovation as they in turn took place from year to year[,] and it all seems such a short while too. It does not seem possible to duplicate again anywhere, Little Beauport, because into it has been placed your very life, and it breathes in every nook and corner of the whole place . . . as I look back over those years, it moves me very much.[187]

Hanson's understanding of the home's emotional core explains, in large part, the success of their partnership. The one man Sleeper had hoped to move all these years had never expressed Beauport's meaning so eloquently.

When Sleeper died on September 22, 1934, following a long battle with leukemia, the house's fate appeared uncertain. Bequeathed to his brother Stephen but heavily mortgaged, Beauport could not enter SPNEA's portfolio—as Appleton very much hoped it would—without an endowment. Unsuccessful in persuading Andrew or Hammond to purchase the house and endow it for SPNEA, Appleton could only look on as Stephen sold the home to Woolworth heiress Helena McCann in October 1935.

At some point during this transfer several trunks full of Sleeper's personal papers, listed in his estate inventory, vanished. However incalculable the loss, and whatever the reason for the documents' disappearance—Andrew's great-nephew suspected Stephen might have destroyed his papers, fearful of his brother's "homosexual streak"—this loss has thrown a veil of mystery over the home's contents that has, itself, become an important part of its mystique.[188] With its prior history utterly erased, his collection now exists exclusively in its Beauport context: the house is its own Found Object. A far greater loss for Beauport, from Sleeper's perspective, was the sudden death of its muse in June 1936. After a brief bout with influenza, the sixty-three-year-old Andrew died in Red Roof's Garden Room. His ashes were later scattered over the house by plane.

The immediate fates of Red Roof and Beauport appeared to represent a reversal of their owner's personalities. The gregarious host of Red Roof was so profoundly mourned by his sister Helen that she effectively shuttered the house, "roping it off like a stage set," in the words of her great-granddaughter Corinna Fisk. (It was not until the 1950s that Fisk's father, Andrew Gray, convinced his grandmother to reopen the house—fittingly enough, for a sleepover with his Harvard classmates.)[189] As for Beauport, the *Boston Evening Transcript* reported that in the period immediately after Sleeper's death his brother Stephen "opened [the house] to a beauty-loving public" who poured into its rooms.[190] And yet, however contrary this arrangement might seem to Sleeper's retiring personality, Beauport had functioned like a quasi-public museum even in his own lifetime. As early as the 1910s the designer reported encountering strangers touring the house, and by 1929 *Country Life* noted that Beauport received as many as forty visitors a day in the summer months.[191] (Even after McCann was in residence, the *Boston Globe* continued to call "the old Sleeper estate" an "extraordinary museum.")[192]

Soon after McCann purchased Beauport she received some valuable advice from du Pont, who cautioned her to preserve the house intact. "Naturally," he wrote McCann, "the minute you take things out of the house, or change them about, the value of the collection does not exist, as really the arrangement is ninety-percent."[193] Tragically, he gave Beauport's new owner license to alter one space. "I have no feeling whatsoever about the Chinese room," he declared, "as I think it is distinctly bad." And so, in 1937 McCann auctioned off the entirety of the China Trade Room's contents. Leaving the eighteenth-century wallpaper in place, she introduced her collection of Chippendale furniture, added china display cabinets, hung a massive Waterford chandelier from the room's "tented" ceiling, and dismantled the walk-in pagoda. In just a few gestures her New York decorators, French & Company, demonstrated how easily the spell of a Beauport room may be broken. One of the house's primary showstoppers had become a yawn of Patrician Good Taste.

And yet McCann would ultimately save Beauport as a whole. Upon her death in 1938 the house and its contents transferred to SPNEA, along with a sizable endowment. Opening to the public in 1943, the site quickly became one of the organization's most popular destinations—a position it maintains to this day. Over the decades Beauport's interpretation has changed in significant ways, perhaps inevitably so given the *tabula rasa* that its documentary vacuum presents. During the 1980s, for example—at the height of Ronald Reagan's "Morning in America"—its guides were encouraged to emphasize the house's contributions to "America's early heritage" and convey that the home was "not the work of an eccentric individual."[194] In our own time site managers like Pilar Garro and Martha Van Koevering have reclaimed Sleeper's identity as a gay man, telling more nuanced stories about his life and deepening visitors' experience of the house. As Hollister wrote a SPNEA administrator in 1981: "the whole phenomenon of Beauport is much more complicated and fascinating than the oohers and aahers over the decades ever dreamed."[195]

Sleeper, of course, had had but one visitor in mind. Writing Andrew from his deathbed in 1934, he declared his love one last time—as ever, through the rooms of Red Roof—and conferred upon him the blessing Beauport had already bestowed. "My very dear Piatt," he begins:

> I was deeply touched by the thought and perfume your letter brought— Memories of so many consecrated and happy days, for nothing was ever more dear to me than Red Roof. I hope we will meet again. . . . Meanwhile bless you always.[196]

CODA

What lasts, in the end?

These four houses—most of their contents—some of their views—and to greater or lesser degrees, the integrity of their interior arrangements. But what becomes of the profound joys and wicked disappointments, the thrill of ambition and rage of loss, the triumphant pride and haunting shame that once roiled inside their walls? What happens to the homesickness, the madness, the yearning—for beauty, status, love, or all three—that once set these rooms ablaze? Where does it all go? We might ask the same question of our own mortal bodies. But if I believe in anything, it's that the material object—whether a shoe worn to a ball or a forty-six-room love poem—contains resurrective powers. I hold as an article of faith that our houses, if not our lives, hold the key to a kind of eternity.

When I finished this book I made a pilgrimage to see Sleeper's pagoda. Once the magical centerpiece of his China Trade Room, it survived the 1937 McCann redecoration only through the intervention of Andrew's former chauffeur (a sign that Beauport's muse, however obliquely, continued to exercise his power from the grave). Today the pagoda lies in fragments at Historic New England's collections facility in Haverhill, Massachusetts. As I planned the HNE exhibition that would accompany this book, I became single-mindedly focused on reassembling this fantasy structure as the centerpiece of my show. In the end the idea proved logistically impossible, so I requested instead to pay my respects to its remains.

When I saw the elements laid out before me I was charmed, even moved, by the work's disassembled parts. On closer inspection, the undulating ornaments that once decorated the pagoda's roof (see figure 4.30, p. 167) turned out to be scaly snakes terminating in *rooster heads*, each bird holding a delicate turned bell in its beak. (Like the eagle Sleeper once selected for du Pont, these were "a little different . . . than the ordinary" chicken.) As for the structure's elaborate fretwork railings, they struck me as no more substantial than theatrical props. Of course. On the drive home I wondered how this inert, dismantled set piece had developed into such an obsession for me. And I've come to realize it's because Sleeper—or perhaps, Sleeper in the person of Beauport—had become to me precisely what Andrew once was to him: the bachelor whose attention I craved above all others. By reconstructing his crowning folly, I could earn his love. And so the longing lives on.

The men in this book longed, themselves, for things beyond their grasp. Few found what they were after—How many of us do?—but they earned other, more interesting prizes. Pendleton sought to disappear behind a fictive character, only to inspire contemporary artists who love nothing more than prodding his manufactured image. Every few years another Russian oligarch pays a few hundred million Euros for La Léopolda, while the obsessive genealogist's family home has become one of New England's most popular venues for weddings (celebrations that now include, of course, the unions of many same-sex couples. One can only imagine Codman and Little's response to the paired grooms.) Gibson, who craved literary fame and eternal youth, has become the historical toast of Boston Gay Pride—but it's now his home that takes the star turn, providing a pitch-perfect Victorian setting for magazine spreads, television, and movies (most recently Greta Gerwig's 2019 film, *Little Women*). Sleeper hoped to charm a single neighbor—and today, Beauport seduces everyone who walks through its front door.

Each of these men imagined his home as a static monument, yet here, too, they achieved a different—and, I would argue, more valuable—goal. By powerfully combining what Lisa Cohen has called "the texture of daily life and the vertigo of history," these houses offer a space where we can be truly *at home* with their owners despite their absence.[1] The stories of Pendleton, Codman, Gibson, and Sleeper do not end in these spaces, but rather—to paraphrase Susan Pulsifer's 1953 letter to Gibson—they extend through time to meet us.

SELECTED BIBLIOGRAPHY

The following acronyms in these entries represent frequently cited collections or institutions:

[GHM] Gibson House Museum Archives (Boston, MA)

[HNE] Historic New England Library and Archives (Boston, MA)

[ISGM] Isabella Stewart Gardner Museum Archives (Boston, MA)

[RIHS] Rhode Island Historical Society (Providence, RI)

[RISDA] Rhode Island School of Design Archives (Providence, RI)

[RISDR] Rhode Island School of Design Museum, Registrar (Providence, RI)

[YMA] Yale University Library, Manuscripts and Archives (New Haven, CT)

Alswang, Hope, and Judith Tannenbaum, eds. "After You're Gone: An Installation by Beth Lipman." Providence: Museum of Art, Rhode Island School of Design. *Exhibition Notes*, no. 33 (Fall 2008).

The American Architect and Building News. XCI, no. 1624 (February 9, 1907).

Amory, Cleveland. *The Proper Bostonians.* New York: E. F. Dutton and Co., 1947.

———. *Who Killed Society?* New York: Harper and Brothers, 1960.

"Art and Artists." *New York Sun,* May 25, 1902.

Ayer, Hannah Palfrey, ed. *A Legacy of New England: Letters of the Palfrey Family,* Vol. I. Boston: Privately printed, 1950.

Bachelard, Gaston. *The Poetics of Space.* Boston: Beacon Press, 1969.

Ball, Tom, and Catherine Ball. *Paradox: Puritans and Epicures in the Codman Family, 1637–1960.* Privately published, 2021.

Barrett, Dawn, and Andrew Martinez, eds. *"Infinite Radius": Founding Rhode Island School of Design.* Providence: Rhode Island School of Design, 2008.

Bear, Mark Roberts Wilson. "Charles Leonard Pendleton, Antique Collecting, and the American Period Room." Unpublished master of arts thesis, Brown University, 1989.

Beach, Laura. "Pendleton House in Providence." *Antiques and the Arts Weekly,* May 29, 2001.

Beebe, Lucius. *Boston and the Boston Legend.* New York: D. Appleton-Century Co., Inc., 1936.

Betsky, Aaron. *Queer Space: Architecture and Same-Sex Desire.* New York: William Morrow and Co., 1997.

Bizardel, Yvon. *Deux Yankees et Trois Demeures Parisiennes.* Paris: Librairie Historique Clavreuil, 1980.

Blanchard, Mary. "The Soldier and the Aesthete: Homosexuality and Popular Culture in Gilded-Age America." *Journal of American Studies* 30, no. 1 (April 1996).

Blanford, William B., and Elizabeth Clay Blanford. *Beauport Impressions: An Introduction to Its Collections.* Boston: Society for the Preservation of New England Antiquities, 1965.

Blythe, Sarah Ganz, and Andrew Martinez. *Why Art Museums? The Unfinished Work of Alexander Dorner.* Cambridge: MIT Press, 2016.

Brayton, Linda L., and Jannifer A. Holmgren. "Halfdan M. Hanson: The Making of an Architect." *Historic New England* 15, no. 2 (Fall 2104).

Brown, Nell Porter. "Beauport's Lovely Creative Spirit." *Harvard Magazine* (May–June 2018).

———. "Preserving Heirs and Airs: Boston's History Glimpsed Through One Eccentric's Home." *Harvard Magazine* (January–February 2015).

Bunce, Oliver Bell. *Bachelor Bluff: His Opinions, Sentiments, and Disputations.* New York: D. Appleton and Co., 1881.

Bunting, Bainbridge. *Houses of Boston's Back Bay: An Architectural History, 1840–1917.* Cambridge, MA: Belknap Press of Harvard University, 1967.

Burke, Doreen Bolger, et al. eds. *In Pursuit of Beauty: Americans and the Aesthetic Movement.* New York: The Metropolitan Museum of Art, 1986.

Camille, Michael, and Adrian Rifkin, eds. *Other Objects of Desire: Collectors and Collecting Queerly.* Oxford: Blackwell Publishers, 2001.

Carlisle, Nancy. *Cherished Possessions: A New England Legacy.* Boston: Society for the Preservation of New England Antiquities, 2003.

Carryl, Guy Wetmore. *Far from the Maddening Girls.* New York: McClure, Phillips & Co., 1904.

Carter, Alice A. *Cecilia Beaux: A Modern Painter in the Gilded Age.* New York: Rizzoli, 2005.

Catalogue of an Extraordinary Collection of Antique Furniture, the Property of C. L. Pendleton. F. J. Shelton, auctioneer (December 8–9, 1897). Providence, 1897 [RIHS].

Catalogue of the Pendleton Collection of Colonial Furniture. RISD Museum, 1932 [RISDR].

Chaffee, Frank, *Bachelor Buttons.* New York: George M. Allen Co., 1892.

———. "Bachelor Bits." *The Home-Maker,* February 1889.

"Charles L. Pendleton." *Providence Journal,* June 27, 1904 [RISDA].

"Charles Leonard Pendleton." *Proceedings of the Rhode Island Historical Society, 1904–1905,* Vol. V. Providence, 1905 [RISDA].

"A Charming Gloucester Home" [no author indicated]. *The Gloucester Daily Times,* December 11, 1909 [HNE].

Chauncey, George. *Gay New York: Gender, Urban Culture, and the Making of a Gay Male World.* New York: HarperCollins, 1994.

Chomet, Seweryn. *Count de Mauny: Friend of Royalty.* New York: Begell House Inc., 2002.

Chudacoff, Howard P. *The Age of the Bachelor: Creating an American Subculture.* Princeton: Princeton University Press, 1999.

Clouston, Kate Warren. *The Chippendale Period in English Furniture.* London: Debenham and Freebody and Edward Arnold, 1897.

Codman, Ogden Jr. *La Léopolda: A Description.* Privately printed, 1939 [HNE].

Codman, Richard. *Reminiscences of Richard Codman.* Boston: North Bennet Street Industrial School, 1923 [HNE].

Cohen, Lisa. *All We Know: Three Lives.* New York: Farrar, Straus, and Giroux, 2012.

Colby, Kate. *Beauport.* Brooklyn: Litmus Press, 2010.

Coleman, Debra, Elizabeth Danze, and Carol Henderson, eds. *Architecture and Feminism.* New York: Princeton Architectural Press, 1996.

Cook, Clarence. *The House Beautiful.* New York: Scribner, Armstrong and Company, 1877.

Cornforth, John. "Beauport, Gloucester, Massachusetts." *Country Life* (October 28, 1982) [HNE].

Copp, Edward Amasa. "The Married Men." *Report of the Triennial Meeting and Biographical Record of the Class of 1869.* New Haven: Tuttlemore, Morehouse and Taylor, 1873 [YMA].

Crouzet, François. "Opportunity and Risk in Atlantic Trade During the French Revolution." In *Interactions in the World Economy: Perspectives from International Economic History*, edited by Carl-Ludwig Holfrerich. New York: Harvester Wheatsheaf, 1990.

Cummings, Abbott Lowell, ed. *Old-Time New England*, LXI, no. 258 (1981).

Curley, James Michael. *I'd Do It Again! A Record of All My Uproarious Years*. Englewood Cliffs, NJ: Prentice-Hall, Inc., 1957.

Curtis, Nancy, and Richard Nylander. *Beauport*. Boston: Society for the Preservation of New England Antiquities, 1990.

Dame, Lawrence. "A Minstrel and Horticulturalist Looks Back on an Independent Life." *Boston Herald*, October 8, 1950.

Davidson, Grace. "About People." *Boston Post*, 1953 [HNE].

De Mauny Talvande, Maurice. *The Gardens of Taprobane*. London: Williams and Norgate, Ltd., 1937.

De Wolfe, Elsie. *The House in Good Taste*. New York: The Century Co., 1913.

Denison, Frederick. *Westerly and Its Witnesses, 1626–1876*. Providence: J. A. and R. A. Reid, 1878.

Donnelly, Max. "British Furniture at the Philadelphia Centennial Exhibition, 1876." *Furniture History* 37 (2001).

Doyle, David D., Jr. "'A Very Proper Bostonian': Rediscovering Ogden Codman and His Late Nineteenth-Century Queer World." *Journal of the History of Sexuality* 13, no. 4 (October 2004).

Elsner, John, and Roger Cardinal, eds. *The Cultures of Collecting*. London: Reaktion Books, Ltd., 1994.

Fellows, Will. *A Passion to Preserve: Gay Men as Keepers of Culture*. Madison: University of Wisconsin Press, 2004.

Ford, James L. "Luxurious Bachelordom." *Munsey's Magazine* 20 (March 1899).

Frary, Ihna Thayer. "A Bachelor's Retreat." *The House Beautiful*, September 1909.

Garland, Joseph E. *Boston's Gold Coast: The Northern Shore, 1890–1929*. Boston: Little, Brown and Co., 1981.

———. *Eastern Point: A Nauttical, Rustical and More or Less Sociable Chronicle of Gloucester's Outer Shield and Inner Sanctum, 1606–1990*. Beverly: Commonwealth Editions, 1999.

———. *The North Shore: A Social History of Summers Among the Noteworthy, Fashionable, Rich, Eccentric, and Ordinary on Boston's Gold Coast, 1823–1929*. Beverley: Commonwealth Editions, 1998.

Gay, Eben Howard. *A Chippendale Romance*.

New York: Longmans, Green and Co., 1915.

Gere, Charlotte, and Marina Vaizey. *Great Women Collectors*. New York: Harry N. Abrams, 1999.

Gibson, Charles Hammond, Jr. *Little Pilgrimages Among French Inns*. New York: L. C. Pages and Co., 1905.

———. *The Spirit of Love and Other Poems*. Cambridge: Riverside Press, 1906.

———. *Two Gentlemen in Touraine*. New York: Fox Duffield and Co., 1906; originally published 1899.

———. *The Wounded Eros: Sonnets*. Riverside Press, 1908.

Gibson, Rosamond Warren. *Recollections of My Life*. Boston: Privately published by the Meadow Press, 1939 [GHM].

Gross, Steve, and Susan Daley with text by Henry Wienceck. *Old Houses*. New York: Stewart, Tabori & Chang, 1991.

Harvard College Class of 1861 Sixth Report (1892–1902). Cambridge: University Press/John Wilson and Son, 1902.

Hayden, E. Parker, and Andrew L. Gray, eds. *Beauport Chronicle: The Letters of Henry Davis Sleeper to Abram Piatt Andrew, Jr., 1906–1915*. Boston: Historic New England, 1991.

———. *Diary of Abram Piatt Andrew 1902–1914*. Princeton: Privately printed, November 1986 [ISGM].

Hayden, Philip A. "Inspiring Beauport: The Design Source for Henry Davis Sleeper's Summer Cottage." *Historic New England* 15, no. 2 (Fall 2014).

Hofer, Matthew, and Gary Scharnhast, eds. *Oscar Wilde in America: The Interviews*. Chicago: University of Illinois Press, 2010.

Hollister, Pail. *Beauport at Gloucester: The Most FASCINATING House in America*. New York: Hastings House, 1951.

———. "The Building of Beauport, 1907–1924." *The American Art Journal* 13, no. 1 (Winter 1981).

Holme, Charles, ed. "Old English Country Cottages." *The Studio*, Special Winter Number (1906–1907).

Holmes, Oliver Wendell. "The Professor's Story." *Atlantic Monthly* 5, no. 27 (1860).

Hosmer, Charles B., Jr. *Preservation Comes of Age: From Williamsburg to the National Trust, 1926–1949, Volume I*. Charlottesville: University Press of Virginia, 1981.

Howells, William Dean. *The Rise of Silas Lapham*. New York: Penguin, 1983.

James, Henry. *The Portrait of a Lady*. Boston: Houghton Mifflin, 1881.

———. *The Spoils of Poynton*. New York: Oxford, 2001; originally published 1897.

Kent, Henry Watson, and Florence N. Levy, eds. *Catalogue of an Exhibition of American Paintings, Furniture, Silver, and Other Objects of Art*. New York: Metropolitan Museum of Art.

Kingsbury, Felicia Doughty. "First Impressions of Some Society Houses." *Old-Time New England* XL, no. 1 (July 1949).

Lambourne, Lionel. *The Aesthetic Movement*. London: Phaidon, 1996.

Landman, Hedy. "The Pendleton House at the Museum of Art, R.I.S. of D." *The Magazine Antiques*, May 1975.

Li-Marcus, Moying. *Beacon Hill: The Life and Times of a Neighborhood*. Boston: Northeastern University Press, 2002.

Lockwood, Luke Vincent. *The Pendleton Collection*. Providence: The Rhode Island School of Design, 1904.

Lopez, Russ. *The Hub of the Gay Universe: An LGBTQ History of Boston, Provincetown, and Beyond*. Boston: Shawmut Peninsula Press, 2019.

Lovell, Margaretta M. *Art in a Season of Revolution: Painters, Artisans, and Patrons in Early America*. Philadelphia: University of Pennsylvania Press, 2003.

Marsh, Richard. *Curios: Some Strange Adventures of Two Bachelors*. London: John Long, 1898.

Martin, Marrgaret Mutchler. *The Chambers-Russell-Codman House and Its Family in Lincoln, Massachusetts*. Lincoln: Lincoln Historical Society, 1996.

Marquand, John P. *The Late George Apley*. New York: Modern Library, 1937.

"Marquand's Boston: A Trip with America's Forcmost Satirist." *Life* 10, no. 12 (March 24, 1941).

McClelland, Nancy. *The Practical Book of Decorative Wall-Treatments*. Philadelphia: J. B. Lippincott Company, 1926.

McQuaid, Cate. "Family Portraits, With a Twist." *Boston Globe*, May 9, 2010.

Metcalf, Pauline, *Ogden Codman and the Decoration of Houses*. Boston: David R. Godine/The Boston Athenaeum, 1988.

Monkhouse, Christopher P., and Thomas S. Michie. *American Furniture in Pendleton House*. Providence: Museum of Art, Rhode Island School of Design, 1986.

Moran-Bates, Holly. "Love and Letters: An Edition of the Letters of Charles Hammond Gibson." Unpublished manuscript, 2002 [GHM].

Murphy, Kevin D. "Secure from all Intrusion: Heterotopia, Queer Space, and the Turn-of-the-Century Resort." *Winterthur Portfolio* 43, no. 2/3 (Summer/Autumn 2009).

Nichols, Beverley. *Crazy Pavements*. London: Jonathan Cape, 1927.

Nylander, Jane C., and Diane L. Viera. *Windows on the Past: Four Centuries of New England Homes*. Boston: Little, Brown and Co., 2000.

Nylander, Richard C., Elizabeth Redmond, and Penny J. Sandler, *Wallpaper in New England*. Boston: Society for the Preservation of New England Antiquities, 1986.

Ohanesian, Liz. "Beth Katleman's Ornate Sculptures Delve into Themes of Opulence and Over-Consumption." *Hi-Fructose* 49 (October 1, 2018).

Orlando, Emily J. "The 'Queer Shadow' of Ogden Codman in Edith Wharton's *Summer*." *Studies in American Naturalism* 12, no. 2 (Winter 2017).

Patch, Isaac IV. *Closing the Circle (A Buckalino Journey Around Our Time)*. Wellesley: Wellesley College Printing Series, 1996.

———. *Growing up in Gloucester*. Gloucester: The Curious Traveler Press, 2004.

Pendleton, Charles Leonard. *Inventory of the Antique Furniture, Paintings, and Other Objects of Art Constituting "The Charles L. Pendelton Collection," So Called, and Included in the Deed of Gift From Charles L. Pendleton to the Rhode Island School of Design 1904.* [RISDR].

Pendleton, Everett Hall. *Brian Pendleton and His Descendants, 1599–1910*. Privately published, 1910 [RIHS].

———. *Early New England Pendletons*. South Orange, NJ: Privately printed, 1956 [RIHS].

"Pendleton Memorial Is Opened to the Public," *Providence Journal*, October 23, 1906 [RISDR].

Perrett, Antoinette. "A Notable Collection of Tole." *The House Beautiful*, February 1924 [RISDR].

Poland, William Carey. "Tributes to C. L. Pendleton." *Providence Journal*, June 29, 1904 [RISDA].

Post, Emily. *Etiquette in Society, in Business, in Politics, and at Home*. New York: Funk and Wagnalls, 1922.

———. *The Personality of a House*. New York: Funk and Wagnalls, 1930.

Potvin, John. *Bachelors of a Different Sort: Queer Aesthetics, Material Culture, and the Modern Interior in Britain*. Manchester: Manchester University Press, 2014.

Raid the Icebox I with Andy Warhol. Providence: Museum of Art, Rhode Island School of Design, 1969.

Rainey, Ada Rainey. "A Colonial Reincarnation." *The House Beautiful* XXXVIII, no. 5 (October 1915) [RISDR].

Rathbone, Penny. "Rediscovery: Copley's Corkscrew." *Art in America*, no. 3 (June 1965).

Reeve, Matthew M. "Dickie Bateman and the Gothicization of Old-Windsor: Gothic Architecture and Sexuality in the World of Horace Walpole." *Architectural History* 56 (2013).

———. "Gothic Architecture, Sexuality, and License at Horace Walpole's Strawberry Hill." *The Art Bulletin* XCV, no. 3 (September 2013).

Rhode Island School of Design. *Catalogue: The Pendleton Collection*. Providence: Rhode Island School of Design, 1909 [RISDR].

"A Royal Gift." *Providence Journal*, June 9, 1904 [RISDR].

Rutherford, Emma. *Silhouette: The Art of the Shadow*. New York: Rizzoli, 2009.

"Sale of Antiques." *Providence Journal*, December 10, 1897 [RIHS].

Saunders, Richard Henry. *American Decorative Arts Collecting in New England, 1840–1920*. Unpublished master's thesis, University of Delaware, May 1973.

Seiberling, Catherine L. *A Study Report of the Gibson House Museum*. Boston: Gibson Society, Inc., 1991.

Shand-Tucci, Douglass. *Boston Bohemia: 1881–1900*. Amherst: University of Massachusetts Press, 1995.

———. *The Crimson Letter: Harvard, Homosexuality, and the Shaping of American Culture*. New York: St. Martin's Press, 2003.

Sixth Biographical Record of the [Yale] Class of 'Sixty-Nine, 1884–1889. New Haven: Tuttle, Morehouse and Taylor, 1895 [YMA].

Slocum, Grace. "The Pendleton House—A Study in Georgian Decoration and Furnishings." *The International Studio* 31, nos. 121–24 (March–June 1907) [RISDR].

Snodin, Michael, ed. *Horace Walpole's Strawberry Hill*. New Haven: Yale University Press, 2009.

Stegner, Wallace. *Angle of Repose*. New York: Penguin Books, 1971.

Stillinger, Elizabeth. *The Antiquers*. New York: Alfred A. Knopf, 1980.

———. *A Kind of Archaeology: Collecting Folk Art, 1876–1976*. Boston: University of Massachusetts Press, 2001.

Talbot, J. Richmond. *Turf, Cards and Temperance, or Reminiscences in a Checkered Life: Containing the Most Important Events in the Life of J. R. Talbot*. Bristol: Eastern Publishing Company, 1882.

Townsend, Reginald T. "An Adventure in Americana." *Country Life*, February 1929 [HNE].

Tremaine, Julie. "A Uniquely Providence Home: Inside the Edward Dexter House." *The East Side Monthly*, January 25, 2017.

Van Vechten, Carl. *The Blind Bow-Boy*. New York: Alfred A. Knopf, 1923.

Wells, H. G. *The Future in America: A Search After Realities*. New York: Harper and Brothers, 1906.

Westerly Vital Statistics, 1854–1875. Westerly [Rhode Island] Historical Society.

Wharton, Edith, and Ogden Codman Jr. *The Decoration of Houses*. New York: Scribner's, 1897.

Wharton, Grace, and Philip Wharton. *The Wits and Beaux of Society in Two Volumes*. Philadelphia: Porter and Coates, 1890.

Wheeler, George. "The Pendleton Collection," *Official Souvenir and Program, Rhode Island Old Home Week*. Providence: Remington Printing Company, July 28– August 3, 1907 [RISDR].

Wilde, Oscar. *The Picture of Dorian Gray*. New York: Oxford University Press, 2006.

Wills, Matthew. "Go West, You Nervous Men." *JSTOR Daily*, May 1, 2019.

Wilson, Richard Guy. *The Colonial Revival House*. New York: Harry N. Abrams, 2004.

Wineapple, Brenda. *Sister Brother: Gertrude and Leo Stein*. New York: G. P. Putnam, 1996.

Woolf, Virginia. *The London Scene: Six Essays on London Life*. New York: Ecco, 1975.

Wolcott, Cora Codman. *The Codmans of Charlestown and Boston 1637–1929*. Boston: Thomas Todd and Co., 1930.

Yale Class of 1869 Sexennial; Report of the Sexennial Meeting and Biographical Record of the Class of 'Sixty Nine. New Haven: Tuttle, Morehouse, Taylor, 1875 [YMA].

Yale Faculty Records, 1862–1883 [YMA].

The Yale Pot-Pourri, 1865–66. New Haven: Tuttle, Morehouse, and Taylor, 1866 [YMA].

Young, Linda. *Historic House Museums in the United States and United Kingdom: A History*. New York: Rowman and Littlefield, 2017.

NOTES

INTRODUCTION
BEAUTY AND THE BACHELOR

1   Oscar Wilde, *The Picture of Dorian Gray* (New York: Oxford University Press, 2006; originally published 1891), 151.
2   Cited in Matthew Hofer and Gary Scharnhast, eds., *Oscar Wilde in America: The Interviews* (Chicago: University of Illinois Press, 2010), 22; and Lionel Lambourne, *The Aesthetic Movement* (London: Phaidon, 1996), 141.
3   Howard P. Chudacoff, *The Age of the Bachelor: Creating an American Subculture* (Princeton: Princeton University Press, 1999), 51.
4   James L. Ford, "Luxurious Bachelordom," *Munsey's Magazine* 20 (March 1899), 584.
5   Oliver Bell Bunce, *Bachelor Bluff: His Opinions, Sentiments, and Disputations* (New York: D. Appleton and Co., 1881), 26; italics original.
6   Guy Wetmore Carryl, *Far from the Maddening Girls* (New York: McClure, Phillips and Co., 1904), 19.
7   For a full account of this episode, see Douglass Shand-Tucci, *The Crimson Letter: Harvard, Homosexuality, and the Shaping of American Culture* (New York: St. Martin's Press, 2003), 67.
8   Frank Chaffee, *Bachelor Buttons* (New York: George M. Allen Co., 1892), 5, 11, and 10.
9   Oscar Wilde, *An Ideal Husband* (New York: Mockingbird Classics, 2015; originally published 1895), 70.
10   Kevin D. Murphy, "Secure from All Intrusion: Heterotopia, Queer Space, and the Turn-of-the-Twentieth-Century Resort," *Winterthur Portfolio* 43, no. 2/3 (Summer/Autumn 2009), 39.
11   Emily Post, *Etiquette in Society, in Business, in Politics, and at Home* (New York: Funk and Wagnalls, 1922), 297.

ONE
PENDLETON'S GHOST

The following acronyms in these notes represent frequently cited collections or institutions:
[RISDA] Rhode Island School of Design: Archives
[RISDR] Rhode Island School of Design: Registrar
[YMA] Yale University Library, Manuscripts and Archives

1   Lewis Carroll, *Through the Looking-Glass and What Alice Found There* (New York: Random House, 1946), 10 and 11.
2   [No author cited], "Charles L. Pendleton," *Providence Journal*, June 27, 1904 [RISDA].
3   "Charles Leonard Pendleton," *Proceedings of the Rhode Island Historical Society, 1904–1905*, Vol. V (Providence, 1905), 61 [RISDA].
4   Sarah Ganz Blythe and Andrew Martinez, *Why Art Museums? The Unfinished Work of Alexander Dorner* (Cambridge: MIT Press, 2016), 108.
5   Author interview with Aaron Pexa, August 16, 2021.
6   Email to the author from a senior RISD Museum official who wishes to remain anonymous, September 19, 2019.
7   Everett Hall Pendleton, *Brian Pendleton and His Descendants, 1599–1910* (privately published, 1910), 161 [RIHS].
8   Pendleton, *Brian Pendleton*, 56.
9   Pendleton, *Brian Pendleton*, 292; and Frederick Denison, *Westerly and Its Witnesses, 1626–1876* (Providence: J. A. and R. A. Reid, 1878), 242 [Westerly Historical Society].
10   *Charles Leonard Pendleton Chronology* [undated typescript], 1 [RISDA].
11   Charles Leonard Pendleton, *Account Book of C.L.P./P.A. 1863–1865*; stamp sale entered March 17, 1864.
12   Pendleton, *Account Book, 1863–1865* (August 20, 1864, and January 5, 1865) [RISDR].
13   *Phillips Academy Andover Classbook, July 1865*; hand inscriptions by Richard Theodore Greener and Edward Jonathan Burrell [RISDR].
14   In Pendleton's *Classbook*, Julius Sanderson Phillipston shared his wish "that you may be as successful at Yale, and be as shrewd in handling that 'Hadley's Greek Grammar' as you have been at Phillips"; *Phillips Academy Andover Classbook* (July 1865).
15   Cited in Christopher P. Monkhouse and Thomas S. Michie, *American Furniture in Pendleton House* (Providence: RISD Museum, 1986), 13.
16   *Yale Faculty Records, 1862–1883* (September 1865–January 1866), 58–93 [YMA].
17   *Yale Faculty Records*, 72 (March 21, 1866).
18   *Yale Faculty Records*, 76 (June 6, 1866).
19   *Yale Class of 1869 Sexennial; Report of the Sexennial Meeting and Biographical Record of the Class of 'Sixty Nine* (New Haven: Tuttle, Morehouse, Taylor, 1875), 152 [YMA].
20   *Sixth Biographical Record of the [Yale] Class of 'Sixty-Nine, 1884–1889* (New Haven: Tuttle, Morehouse and Taylor, 1895), 174 [YMA].
21   Edward Amasa Copp, "The Married Men," *Report of the Triennial Meeting and Biographical Record of the Class of 1869* (New Haven: Tuttlemore, Morehouse and Taylor, 1873), 37 [YMA].
22   Monkhouse and Michie, 15.
23   *Sixth Biographical Record of the Class of 'Sixty-Nine, 1884–1889*, 168 [YMA].
24   John Potvin, *Bachelors of a Different Sort: Queer Aesthetics, Material Culture and the Modern Interior in Britain* (Manchester: Manchester University Press, 2014), 4.
25   *Report of the Triennial Meeting and Biographical Record of the Class of 1869*, 82 [YMA]. Pendleton's clerkship is noted in Denison, 242.
26   Rhode Island Governor Ambrose Burnside appointed Pendleton Justice of the Peace on June 6, 1867. See Denison, 242.
27   *Charles Leonard Pendleton Chronology* [undated typescript], 1 [RISDA]; and Denison, 242.
28   Denison, 242.
29   *Westerly Vital Statistics, 1854–1875*, 22 [Westerly Historical Society].
30   For the terms of John Pendleton's will, see the photostat copy of his handwritten will at RISDA.
31   *Providence City Directories: 1874–77* [RIHS].
32   *Catalogue of an Extraordinary Collection of Antique Furniture, the Property of C. L. Pendleton*, F. J. Shelton, auctioneer (December 8–9, 1897), Providence, 1897, Lot 131.
33   Cited in Max Donnelly, "British Furniture at the Philadelphia Centennial Exhibition, 1876," *Furniture History* 37 (2001): 91.
34   "The Nation's Jubilee," *National Republican* (May 18, 1876), in United States Centennial Commission, Vol. 31.
35   RISD Museum, Museum Committee Minutes (see October 6, 1913, and June 28, 1921) [RISDR].

36   *Pendleton Chronology*, 1.

37   Providence City Directories indicate that Pendleton lived at 288 High Street from 1882 to 1895 (Durfee's shop was at 295 High Street) insurance maps from this period indicate the house was a relatively small, wood frame structure [RIHS].

38   Luke Vincent Lockwood, *The Pendleton Collection* (Providence: The Rhode Island School of Design, 1904), 2.

39   *Charles Leonard Pendleton Chronology*, 1 [RISDA].

40   Monkhouse and Michie, 65.

41   [No author indicated], "This Should Be in Grand Rapids," *Grand Rapids Press*, July 26, 1918, 12 [RISDR]; for Pendleton's New York connections, see Monkhouse and Michie, 17.

42   J. Richmond Talbot, *Turf, Cards and Temperance, or Reminiscences in a Checkered Life: Containing the Most Important Events in the Life of J. R. Talbot* (Bristol: Eastern Publishing Company, 1882), 30.

43   Hedy Landman, "The Pendleton House of the Museum of Art, R.I.S. of D.," *The Magazine Antiques*, May 1975, 925.

44   "Sale of Antiques," *Providence Journal*, December 10, 1897, 10 [RISDR].

45   "Sale of Antiques," 10.

46   Talbot, 88.

47   Ward McAllister, "The Only Four Hundred," *New York Times*, February 16, 1892.

48   Julie Tremaine, "A Uniquely Providence Home: Inside the Edward Dexter House," *The East Side Monthly*, January 25, 2017.

49   Henry James, *The Spoils of Poynton* (New York: Oxford, 2001; orig. published 1897), 33.

50   Donnelly, 93.

51   Margaretta M. Lovell, *Art in a Season of Revolution: Painters, Artisans, and Patrons in Early America* (Philadelphia: University of Pennsylvania Press, 2003), 250.

52   Kate Warren Clouston, *The Chippendale Period in English Furniture* (London: Debenham and Freebody and Edward Arnold, 1897), 3.

53   Emma Rutherford, *Silhouette: The Art of the Shadow* (New York: Rizzoli, 2009), 11.

54   James, 20.

55   Eben Howard Gay, *A Chippendale Romance* (New York: Longmans, Green and Co., 1915), 53.

56   Gay, 63–64.

57   Ihna Thayer Frary, "A Bachelor's Retreat," *The House Beautiful*, September 1909, 82.

58   Author interview with Patricia E. Kane, Friends of American Arts Curator of American Decorative Arts at the Yale University Art Gallery, November 16, 2018.

59   Richard Marsh, *Curios: Some Strange Adventures of Two Bachelors* (London: John Long, 1898), 7–8.

60   Gay, 50.

61   Charles Pendleton, *Inventory of the Antique Furniture, Paintings, and Other Objects of Art Constituting "The Charles L. Pendleton Collection," So-called, and Included in the Deed of Gift from Charles L. Pendleton to the Rhodes Island School of Design, 1904*, 15 [RISDR].

62   Gay, 187.

63   Pendleton, *Deed of Gift*, 2–4, 10, 13, and 24 [RISDR].

64   Cited in Will Fellows, *A Passion to Preserve: Gay Men as Keepers of Culture* (Madison: University of Wisconsin Press, 2004), 40.

65   Ada Rainey, "A Colonial Reincarnation," *The House Beautiful* XXXVIII, no. 5 (October 1915): 132.

66   James L. Ford, "Luxurious Bachelordom," *Munsey's Magazine* 20 (March 1899), 593.

67   Pendleton, *Inventory*, 4–15.

68   Gay, 159.

69   Quoted in Fellows, 13.

70   Marsh, 17 and 106.

71   Laura Beach, "Pendleton House in Providence," *Antiques and the Arts Weekly*, May 29, 2001, 1.

72   Monkhouse and Michie, 29.

73   Pendleton, *Inventory*, 3.

74   Monkhouse and Michie, 24.

75   Monkhouse and Michie, 25.

76   The descriptors "genuine," "authentic," and "worthy" in regard to Pendleton's collection appear in more sources than may be listed here. The assertion that "no imperfect nor doubtful piece is to be found in the house" appears in "A Royal Gift," *Providence Journal*, June 9, 1904, 12.

77   Rainey, 132.

78   Elsie de Wolfe, *The House in Good Taste* (New York: The Century Company, 1913), 14.

79   Monkhouse and Michie, 31.

80   "Charles L. Pendleton," *Providence Journal*, June 27, 1904, and *Charles Leonard Pendleton Chronology*, 1 [RISDA].

81   Lovell, 266.

82   John Frazier, "History of the R.I.S.D.," an address delivered at the Rhode Island Historical Society (November 13, 1960); transcript in Dawn Barrett and Andrew Martinez, eds., *"Infinite Radius": Founding Rhode Island School of Design* (Providence: Rhode Island School of Design, 2008), 90.

83   "A Royal Gift," 12.

84   "A Royal Gift," 12.

85   *Proceedings of the Rhode Island Historical Society*, 61, notes the museum wing was "modeled after Mr. Pendleton's own home on Waterman Street." In 1907 George Wheeler claimed the design of Pendleton House was based on "the Pendleton and Governor Arnold Homes"; see Wheeler, "The Pendleton Collection," in *Official Souvenir and Program, Rhode Island Old Home Week* (Providence: Remington Printing Company, July 28–August 3, 1907), 40.

86   Landman, 924.

87   [No author indicated], "Art and Artists," *New York Sun*, May 25, 1902, 4.

88   William Carey Poland, "Tributes to C. L. Pendleton," *Providence Journal*, June 29, 1904 [RISDA].

89   *Indenture Between Charles Leonard Pendleton and the Rhode Island School of Design*, May 25, 1904, 1 [RISDA].

90   Charles Pendleton to Eliza Metcalf Radeke, April 25, 1904 [RISDA].

91   The liabilities on Pendleton's estate included $19,300 owed to Canfield and $2,500 for a "note-loan." *Charles Leonard Pendleton Copybook*, 150–51 [RISDR].

92   On June 30, 1896, Pendleton's executor, Walter Durfee, noted that the collector's estate remained "insufficient to pay debts"; most of these fell to Metcalf. See *Charles Leonard Pendleton Chronology*, 1 [RISDA].

93   Fred Stewart Greene to RISD Museum Secretary Howard M. Rice, November 18, 1904 [RISDR].

94   The earliest versions of this phrase appears in the *Providence Journal*'s coverage of Pendleton's gift, starting in June 1904.

95   *Indenture*, 1 [RISDA].

96   Pendleton, *Early New England Pendletons*, viii [RIHS].

97   Luke Vincent Lockwood to Walter Durfee, June 27, 1904, as quoted in Monkhouse and Michie, 32.

98   The Museum of Fine Arts, Boston,

stipulation appears in Pendleton's *Indenture*, 3.

99   Wheeler, 40.

100   Frederick C. Bursch, ed., *The Literary Collector: A Monthly Magazine of Book Lore and Bibliography* IX, no. 1 (November–December 1904): 30.

101   The downstairs hall at 72 Waterman and Pendleton House are, respectively, 9'3" versus 11'10" wide; their stairs are 43" versus 50" wide; interior doorways are 32" versus 37" wide; and their first floor ceilings are 10'2" versus 10'9" high. Ironically, the front door to 72 Waterman is slightly wider than its counterpart at Pendleton House (45" wide versus 41" wide). All measurements taken by the author.

102   A *Providence Journal* article from October 23, 1906 ("Pendleton Memorial Is Opened to the Public") explains: "The house is located on Benefit Street, with the main entrance on that thoroughfare." In 1906 the collection was on view for a period of "calling hours" every day from 2:00 to 4:00 p.m. (the rest of the museum was open 10:00 to 5:00). See Bronson, 69.

103   Lockwood, dedication page and 2.

104   Lockwood, 1.

105   Lockwood, 56.

106   Lockwood, 128.

107   The earliest known reference to Pendleton House as "Colonial House" appears in the 1904–1905 *Annual Report of the Museum Committee* at RISD: "The building of the Colonial House to be erected by Mr. Stephen O. Metcalf . . . has been begun." *Annual Report of the Museum Committee (June 1904–June 1905)*, 1 [RISDA]. From this date until the 1930s, "Colonial House" (and sometimes the variant "Colonial Building") appears to have been the preferred name for the wing.

108   *Catalogue of the Pendleton Collection of Colonial Furniture* (RISD Museum, 1932) [RISDA]; italics mine.

109   RISD Curator Thomas S. Michie references this passage in a July 28, 1993, letter to Mr. Merrill Budlong [RISDA].

110   Flagler proposed this "tablet," as he called it, in the fall of 1914, and it appears to have been installed in spring 1915; see Flagler's letter to RISD Museum Director L. Earle Rowe, October 10, 1914, and Rowe's response to Flagler, February 20, 1915 [RISDA]. Though Metcalf's plaque is undated, it almost surely dates to the completion of Pendleton House in 1906.

111   Lockwood, 7–8.

112   Henry Watson Kent and Florence N. Levy, eds., *Catalogue of an Exhibition of Amer-ican Paintings, Furniture, Silver, and Other Objects of Art* (New York: Metropolitan Museum of Art), 29. Reflecting how little was known about American furniture, the catalogue's bibliography contains just two volumes devoted to the topic.

113   Edith Wharton and Ogden Codman Jr., *The Decoration of Houses* (New York: Scribner's, 1897), 82.

114   Linda Young, *Historic House Museums in the United States and United Kingdom: A History* (New York: Rowman and Littlefield, 2017), 2.

115   Dominique de Menil, "Foreword," in *Raid the Icebox I with Andy Warhol* (Providence: Museum of Art, Rhode Island School of Design, 1969), 5.

116   Daniel Robbins, "Confessions of a Museum Director," *Raid the Icebox I with Andy Warhol*, 15.

117   Robbins, 15.

118   Al Ridenour, "The Automated Andy Warhol Is Reprogrammed," *Los Angeles Times*, May 16, 2002.

119   Andy Warhol and Pat Hackett, *Andy Warhol's Party Book* (New York: Crown Publishers, 1988), 49; italics original.

120   Hope Alswang and Judith Tannenbaum, eds., "After You're Gone: An Installation by Beth Lipman," Providence: Museum of Art, Rhode Island School of Design, *Exhibition Notes*, no. 33 (Fall 2008): 4.

121   Alswang and Tannenbaum, 4.

122   Or even, if coincidentally, the artist's identical twin daughters—conceived at the same time she created the settee; author interview with Beth Lipman, August 18, 2021.

123   Author interview with Lipman, August 18, 2021.

124   Artdaily.com [undated press release], "The RISD Museum of Art Presents *After You're Gone*, an Installation by Beth Lipman."

125   Author interview with Lipman, August 18, 2021.

126   Author interview with Aaron Pexa, August 16, 2021.

127   Author interview with Pexa, August 16, 2021.

128   This quote derives from Pexa's RISD thesis, sent to the author by email, August 18, 2021; Pexa's original design for the righthand window might have baited viewers even more pointedly: a neon sign flashing ROOMS / ROOMS / ROOMS in the manner of the strip club come-on, GIRLS / GIRLS / GIRLS (author interview with Pexa, August 16, 2021).

129   Bronstein artist statement, *Historical Rhode Island Décor*, RISD Museum ("Raid the Icebox Now").

130   As explained by RISD curator Jan Howard, in her "Exhibition Overview" presentation at the RISD Museum, October 3, 2019.

131   Author interview with Pablo Bronstein, February 24, 2020.

132   Morlock and Bayer copied this headboard for Pendleton directly from Plate 42 in Chippendale's 1754 *Director*; see Monkhouse and Michie, 27.

133   Jan Howard, "Exhibition Overview," October 3, 2019.

134   CFGNY podcast (n.d.) hosted by *Triple Canopy*, 2019.

135   Email to the author from Alexander Provan, March 15, 2020.

136   CFGNY podcast (n.d.) hosted by *Triple Canopy*, 2019.

137   Gallery label, *Can I Leave You?* RISD Museum, 2019.

138   CFGNY podcast (n.d.) hosted by *Triple Canopy*, 2019.

139   Email to the author from Provan, March 15, 2020.

140   Author interview with Beth Katleman, February 20, 2020.

141   Delivered by Bassanio in *The Merchant of Venice* (Act III, Scene Two).

142   Liz Ohanesian, "Beth Katleman's Ornate Sculptures Delve into Themes of Opulence and Over-Consumption," *Hi-Fructose* 49 (October 1, 2018).

143   Designed to look like a woefully outdated 1990s site, complete with a counter in the lower lefthand corner, this website included the prompt "Click to enlarge" under a postage stamp shot of the *Games of Chance* room, purportedly taken during Pendleton's lifetime. When you clicked on the image, it became smaller. Author interview with Katleman, February 20, 2020.

144   Author interview with Katleman, February 20, 2020.

145   Jean Baudrillard, "The System of Collecting" (Paris, 1968), as quoted in John Elsner and Roger Cardinal, eds., *The Cultures of Collecting* (London: Reaktion Books, Ltd., 1994), 16.

146   "The Pleasures of Ownership" was written by Katleman and directed by Carolyn Gennari. Katleman made this remark about the film during the program, "Ferrin Contemporary: A Conversation with Paul Scott, Beth Katleman, and Curator Elizabeth A. Williams" (Zoom virtual presentation, June 8, 2021).

147   *Games of Chance* opened November 8,

2019, and was meant to remain in Pendleton House until August 16, 2020. It would in fact remain at the museum until July 4, 2021—but for fifteen of these months (March 13, 2020–June 13, 2021) the RISD Museum was closed to the public due to the COVID-19 pandemic.

148 In a 2018 communication to the author, RISD Museum Deputy Director Sarah Ganz Blythe wrote: "I have been asking around about the mystery of the 'MYTH' on the sidewalk and apparently it has been there for possibly 5 to 7 years, probably installed by a rather ingenious student" (December 13, 2018). Today its whereabouts are unknown.

TWO
DOUBLE VISION AT THE CODMAN ESTATE

The following acronyms in these notes represent frequently cited collections or institutions:
[CFMC] Codman Family Manuscript Collection
[HNE] Historic New England Library and Archives

Given the frequency of their appearance, the following names have been abbreviated following their first appearance:
[OC] Ogden Codman Jr.
[SBC] Sarah Bradlee Codman
[TNC] Thomas Newbold Codman
[AL] Arthur Little

1   Henry James, *The Portrait of a Lady* (Boston: Houghton Mifflin, 1881), 175.
2   Sasami Ashworth, "Portrait" [theme song for the podcast "Articles of Interest"], Radiotopia, 2018.
3   This and subsequent citations from Adams's account derive from Tomas Boylston Adams, "Lincoln and the Codmans," in Abbott Lowell Cummings, ed., *Old-Time New England*, LXI, no. 258 (1981): 1–4.
4   Ogden Codman Jr. to Charles F. Adams, September 7, 1904, CFMC Folder 1699 [HNE], 1.
5   My thanks to Jeff Shore for pointing out—over a memorable dinner party at Candy's (November 11, 2023)—that the White Album is only a colloquial name for *The Beatles* (1968). Where would we be without Candy?
6   OC to Fiske Kimball, March 3, 1935); Ogden Codman Jr. Collection, Letters to Fiske Kimball (I.A., Vol. 24), The Boston Athenaeum.

7   Tom and Catherine Ball, *Paradox: Puritans and Epicures in the Codman Family, 1637–1960* (Privately published, 2021), 4.
8   As cited in Pauline Metcalf, *Ogden Codman and the Decoration of Houses* (Boston: David R. Godine/The Boston Athenaeum, 1988), 34.
9   Margaret Mutchler Martin, *The Chambers-Russell-Codman House and Its Family in Lincoln, Massachusetts* (Lincoln: Lincoln Historical Society, 1996), 19.
10   Cited in Martin, 64, 53, and 52.
11   Cited in Martin, 87.
12   Cited in Martin, 58.
13   Mary Wheelwright Russell to Dudley Wheelwright, April 10, 1752, CFMC Box 118/Folder 1923 [HNE].
14   Martin, 98.
15   Martin, 98.
16   Martin, 102.
17   For the complete story of this work, see Penny Rathbone, "Rediscovery: Copley's Corkscrew," *Art in America*, no. 3 (June 1965): 49–51.
18   This story appears in many sources, but Martin provides its fullest account in the work's caption following p. 132.
19   Cora Codman Wolcott, *The Codmans of Charlestown and Boston 1637–1929* (Boston: Thomas Todd and Co., 1930), 14.
20   From Robert Codman's *History of Martha's Vineyard* [transcribed by Ogden Codman Jr. in 1919], CFMC Box 118/Folder 1 [HNE].
21   Martin, 32.
22   Ball and Ball, 17.
23   Papers of John Codman III (1755–1803), "Description" [HNE].
24   Ball and Ball, 34.
25   John Codman III to Samuel Dexter Jr., December 8, 1797), Codman House Documentation Binder, Volume I [HNE].
26   John Codman III to Catherine Amory Codman, January 14, 1796, CFMC Box 118, Bound Volume II [HNE].
27   John Codman III to Catherine Amory Codman, December 30, 1800, CFMC Box 118, Bound Volume II [HNE].
28   Cited in Martin, 139.
29   John Codman III to Catherine Amory Codman, August 24, 1800, Codman House Documentation Binder, Volume I [HNE].
30   Ball and Ball, 33.
31   John Codman III to Mary Russell, March 9, 1802, Codman House Documentation Binder, Volume I [HNE].
32   Nancy Carlisle, *Cherished Possessions: A New England Legacy* (Boston: Society for the

Preservation of New England Antiquities, 2003), 39–40.
33   Cited in Martin, 142.
34   Richard Codman to John Codman III, January 31, 1794, CFMC Box 115/Folder 1894 [HNE].
35   The fullest account of Richard Codman's real estate dealings in these years appears in Yvon Bizardel, *Deux Yankees et Trois Demeures Parisiennes* (Paris: Librairie Historique Clavreuil, 1980).
36   François Crouzet, "Opportunity and Risk in Atlantic Trade During the French Revolution," in *Interactions in the World Economy: Perspectives from International Economic History*, ed. Carl-Ludwig Holfrerich (New York: Harvester Wheatsheaf, 1990), 130.
37   Bizardel, 50; Richard Codman to John Codman III, September 16, 1795, and December 23, 1795, CFMC Box 115/Folder 1894 [HNE].
38   Richard Codman to John Codman III, December 23, 1795, CFMC Box 115/Folder 1894 [HNE].
39   Crouzet, 133.
40   "Truly respectable . . ." is excerpted from a memorial tribute by Codman's brother-in-law, Judge Lowell, as cited in Martin, 142. The second observation, by an anonymous writer, formed part of an obituary pasted into the Codman family Bible and included in a typescript in CFMC Box 118, Bound Volume II [HNE].
41   Cited in Crouzet, 133.
42   John Codman III to Catherine Amory Codman, July 20, 1800, CFMC Box 118, Bound Volume II [HNE].
43   John Codman III to Catherine Amory Codman, July 21 and September 4, 1800), CFMC Box 118, Bound Volume II [HNE].
44   John Codman III to Catherine Amory Codman, October 24, 1800, CFMC Box 118, Bound Volume II [HNE].
45   John Codman III to Catherine Amory Codman, December 30, 1800, CFMC Box 118, Bound Volume II [HNE]; and Bizardel, 82.
46   Richard Codman, *Reminiscences of Richard Codman* (Boston: North Bennet Street Industrial School, 1923), 20 [HNE].
47   John Codman III to Catherine Amory Codman, April 25, 1800, CFMC Box 118, Bound Volume II [HNE].
48   Bizardel, 84.
49   John Codman III to Charles Russell Codman, June 4, 1800, CFMC Box 118, Bound Volume II [HNE].
50   Charles Russell Codman to John Cod-

man IV, October 31, 1807, CFMC Box 20/ Folder 308 [HNE].

51 Cited in Codman, *Reminiscences*, 31.

52 Cited in Wolcott, 32.

53 John Codman III to Catherine Amory Codman, September 4, 1800, CFMC Box 118, Bound Volume II [HNE].

54 Cleveland Amory, *The Proper Bostonians* (New York: E. F. Dutton, 1947), 23.

55 Charles Russell Codman Jr. to Ogden Codman Sr., October 9, 1854, CFMC Box 35/Folder 805 [HNE].

56 James McMaster Codman to Ogden Codman Sr., March 11, 1854, CFMC Box 35/ Folder 808 [HNE].

57 Ogden Codman Sr. Account Book (1855); CFMC Box 36/Folder 834; letters from "Flora" and "Hattie," CFMC Box 35/ Folder 798; and from the Allens, CFMC Box 35/Folder 798 [HNE].

58 Charles Russell Codman Jr. to Ogden Codman Sr., October 16, 1855, CFMC Box 35/Folder 805 [HNE].

59 S. A. A. Allen (Mrs. T. Prentiss Allen) to Ogden Codman Sr., October 18, 1857, CFMC Box 35/Folder 798 [HNE].

60 Ogden Codman Sr. to James Bowdoin Bradlee, June 1, 1858), CFMC Box 22/Folder 345 [HNE].

61 Charles Russell Codman Jr. to Ogden Codman Sr., February 22, 1859, CFMC Box 35 / Folder 805 [HNE]; italics original.

62 *Harvard College Class of 1861 Sixth Report (1892–1902)* (Cambridge: University Press/ John Wilson and Son, 1902), 63.

63 Carlisle, 273; and Ellie Reichlin, "'Reading' Family Photographs: A Contextual Analysis of the Codman Photographic Collection," in Abbott Lowell Cummings, ed., *Old-Time New England* LXI, no. 258 (1981): 147.

64 CFMC Box 45/Folder 1062 [HNE].

65 Adams, 4.

66 Christine Fernandez, "The Codman House: Extra-Familial Owners, 1807–1862. Summary and Selected Documents; Society for the Preservation of New England Antiquities, 1979," Codman House Documentation Binder, Volume I [HNE].

67 Ogden Codman Jr. Collection; I.D. Vol. 41 ("Ancestral Tablets"), The Boston Athenaeum.

68 OC to Thomas Newbold Codman, October 19, 1925, CFMC Box 87, Bound Volume (1923–1925) [HNE].

69 Floyd, 55.

70 Clarence Cook, *The House Beautiful* (New York: Scribner, Armstrong and Company,

1877), 320.

71 In 1867, a typical year for Codman's earnings at this time, he reported income of $11,619 from rents, $5,600 from bonds, and $3,000 from dividends; CFMC Box 43/ Folder 1022 [HNE].

72 *Harvard College Class of 1861 Sixth Report*, 63.

73 James Bowdoin Bradlee's net worth just three years before was $522,000. Codman Papers, Biographical Essays [HNE].

74 Moying Li-Marcus, *Beacon Hill: The Life and Times of a Neighborhood* (Boston: Northeastern University Press, 2002), 50.

75 Martin, 160.

76 OC to TNC, September 7, 1934, CFMC Box 142, Bound Volume (1933–1936) [HNE].

77 OC to SBC, July 9, 1883, and September 30, 1895, CFMC Box 49/Folders 1148 and 1161 [HNE].

78 Reichlin, 137.

79 OC to Sarah Bradlee Codman, April 7, 1883, CFMC Box 49/Folder 1147 [HNE].

80 Reichlin, 137.

81 OC to SBC, June 2, 1880, CFMC Box 48/Folder 1141 [HNE].

82 OC to SBC, July 9, 1883, CFMC Box 49/Folder 1148 [HNE].

83 OC to SBC, September 29, 1894, CFMC Box 49/Folder 1155; and March 13, 1896, CFMC Box 49/Folder 1163 [HNE].

84 OC to SBC, April 15, 1896, CFMC Box 49/Folder 1164 [HNE].

85 OC to Arthur Little, January 15, 1892, CFMC Box 87/Folder 1701 [HNE].

86 OC to SBC, January 28, 1884, CFMC Box 49/Folder 1150 [HNE].

87 OC to TNC, August 14, 1938, CFMC Box 143/Bound Volume (1937–1940) [HNE].

88 OC to SBC, May 1880, CFMC Box 48/ Folder 1140 [HNE].

89 John Hubbard Sturgis to Ogden Codman Sr., November 20, 1880, CFMC Box 35/Folder 801 [HNE].

90 OC to SBC, "Sunday" 1992—likely February, CFMC Box 49/Folder 1144 [HNE]; italics original.

91 OC to SBC, July 13, 1882, CFMC Box 48/Folder 1142 [HNE].

92 OC to SBC, July 18, 1883, CFMC Box 49/Folder 1148; and December 6, 1883, CFMC Box 49/Folder 1149 [HNE].

93 Charles Russell Codman Jr. to Ogden Codman Sr., February 4, 1883, CFMC Box 35/Folder 806 [HNE].

94 Charles Russell Codman Jr. to Ogden

Codman Sr., March 26, 1883, CFMC Box 35/Folder 806 [HNE].

95 OC to SBC, March 19, 1883, CFMC Box 49/Folder 1146 [HNE].

96 OC to SBC, February 1, 1884, CFMC Box 49/Folder 1150 [HNE].

97 Cited in Metcalf, *Ogden Codman*, 5.

98 OC to SBC, March 24, 1884, CFMC Box 49/Folder 1150 [HNE].

99 OC to SBC, November 8, 1881, CFMC Box 49/Folder 1144 [HNE].

100 OC to SBC, December 10, 1882, CFMC Box 48/Folder 1143 [HNE].

101 OC to SBC, April 7, 1883, CFMC Box 49/Folder 1147 [HNE]; and Pauline Metcalf, "Ogden Codman, Jr. and 'The Grange,'" in Abbott Lowell Cummings, ed., *Old-Time New England* LXI, no. 258 (1981): 70.

102 OC to SBC, January 29, 1884, CFMC Box 49/Folder 1150 [HNE].

103 OC to SBC, April 7, 1883, CFMC Box 49/Folder 1147 [HNE].

104 Adams, 3.

105 OC to SBC, June 14, 1883, CFMC Box 49/Folder 1147 [HNE].

106 OC to SBC, December 13, 1883, CFMC Box 49/Folder 1149 [HNE].

107 OC to SBC, November 6, 1883, CFMC Box 49/Folder 1148 [HNE].

108 Codman, *Reminiscences*, 36.

109 OC to SBC, July 18, 1883, CFMC Box 49/Folder 1148; and November 22, 1883, CFMC Box 49/Folder 1149 [HNE].

110 OC to SBC, March 13, 1896, CFMC Box 49/Folder 1163 [HNE].

111 Metcalf, *Ogden Codman*, 7.

112 John Codman Ropes to Ogden Codman Jr., November 12, 1887, CFMC Box 71/ Folder 1507 [HNE].

113 Robert D. Andrews to OC (September 16, 1889), CFMC Box 72 / Folder 1509 [HNE].

114 OC to AL, November 1893, CFMC Box 87/Folder 1701 [HNE].

115 OC to SBC, December 13, 1893, CFMC Box 49/Folder 1154 [HNE].

116 Richard Morris Hunt to OC, January 15, 1895, CFMC Box 99/Folder 1840 [HNE].

117 OC to SBC, July 20, 1895, CFMC Box 49/Folder 1161 [HNE].

118 Cited in Metcalf, *Ogden Codman*, 149.

119 OC to SBC, January 25, 1897, CFMC Box 49/Folder 1167 [HNE].

120 OC to SBC, December 30, 1894, CFMC Box 49/Folder 1158 [HNE].

121 OC to SBC, April 15, 1896, CFMC Box 49/Folder 1164 [HNE].

122 Cited in Emily J. Orlando, "The 'Queer Shadow' of Ogden Codman in Edith Wharton's *Summer*," *Studies in American Naturalism* 12, no. 2 (Winter 2017): 223.

123 OC to SBC, May 1 and 14, 1896, CFMC Box 49/Folder 1164 [HNE].

124 David D. Doyle Jr., "'A Very Proper Bostonian': Rediscovering Ogden Codman and His Late Nineteenth-Century Queer World," *Journal of the History of Sexuality* 13, no. 4 (October 2004): 446–76.

125 OC to TNC, February 25, 1935, CFMC Box 142, Bound Volume (1933–1936) [HNE].

126 AL to OC, May 20, 1892, CFMC Box 83/Folder 1661 [HNE].

127 OC to AL, February 1, 1894, CFMC Box 87/Folder 1701 [HNE].

128 AL to OC, April 26, 1892, CFMC Box 83/Folder 1661 [HNE].

129 OC to AL, February 1, 1894, CFMC Box 87/Folder 1701; and AL to OC, April 29, 1892, CFMC Box 83/Folder 1661 [HNE].

130 AL to OC, May 14, 1892, CFMC Box 83/Folder 1661 [HNE].

131 George Chauncey, *Gay New York: Gender, Urban Culture, and the Making of a Gay Male World* (New York: HarperCollins, 1994), 38; and OC to AL, November 27, 1891, CFMC Box 87/Folder 1701 [HNE].

132 AL to OC, December 13, 1891, CFMC Box 83/Folder 1661 [HNE].

133 OC to AL, November 21, 1891, CFMC Box 87/Folder 1701 [HNE].

134 OC to AL, November 22, 1891, CFMC Box 87/Folder 1701 [HNE].

135 OC to AL, January 19, 1892, and November 1893, CFMC Box 87/Folder 1701 [HNE].

136 The Codman "erotica" collection at HNE (MS001, Folders 1–11) is still officially "attributed to the possession of Thomas N. Codman." Folder 10 contains the envelope addressed to "O. Codman" [HNE].

137 These studios include Guglielmo Pluschow and Vicenzo Galdi of Rome; J. Chiurazzi of Naples; and Wilhelm Von Gloeden of Sicily. CFMC MS001 [HNE].

138 AL to OC, March 3, 1892, CFMC Box 83/Folder 1661 [HNE].

139 AL to OC, February 16, 1894, CFMC Box 83/Folder 1661 [HNE].

140 AL to OC, May 14, 1892, CFMC Box 83/Folder 1661 [HNE].

141 OC to SBC, December 25, 1896, CFMC Box 49/Folder 1166; and January 5, 1897, CFMC Box 49/Folder 1167 [HNE].

142 Edith Wharton to OC, "Thursday," 1897, CFMC Box 83/Folder 1670 [HNE]. Though undated, the letter is likely to have been written in late May as Wharton mentions Macmillan's cancellation of their contract that month.

143 Edith Wharton and Ogden Codman Jr., *The Decoration of Houses* (New York: Charles Scribner's Sons, 1897), xxi.

144 Edith Wharton to OC, February 20, 1897, CFMC Box 83/Folder 1670 [HNE]; "sanity . . ." appears in Wharton and Codman, 33.

145 Wharton and Codman 14 and 22.

146 Wharton and Codman, 44, 126, and 176.

147 "*The Decoration of Houses* [review]," *The Nation*, December 21, 1897, CFMC Box 70/Folder 1455 [HNE].

148 Wharton and Codman, 39.

149 OC to SBC, January 5, 1897, CFMC Box 49/Folder 1167 [HNE].

150 *The Decoration of Houses* (1897 draft, Vol. I); CFMC Box 115/Folder 1889, 18 [HNE].

151 OC to SBC, September 13, 1895, CFMC Box 49/Folder 1161 [HNE].

152 Alice Newbold Codman to Ogden Codman Sr., "Tuesday 2nd," 1903, CFMC Box 131/Folder 2107 [HNE].

153 OC to SBC, May 24, 1897, CFMC Box 49/Folder 1167 [HNE].

154 OC to Dorothy Codman, June 16, 1927, CFMC Box 142; and OC to TNC, August 9, 1927, CFMC Box 142, Bound Volume (1923–1932) [HNE].

155 Metcalf, *Old-Time New England*, 73

156 Alan Emmet, "The Codman Estate—'The Grange': A Landscape Chronicle," in Abbott Lowell Cummings, ed., *Old-Time New England* LXI, no. 258 (1981): 17.

157 Codman Family Photograph Collection, COD 3 (Ogden Codman Jr.) [HNE]; italics my own.

158 OC to SBC, September 7, 1883, CFMC Box 49/Folder 1148 [HNE].

159 OC to SBC, July 4, 1895, CMFC Box 49/Folder 1161 [HNE].

160 Reichlin, 144.

161 Papers of Ogden Codman Jr. (1863–1951), "Historical/Biographical" section [HNE].

162 Cited in Metcalf, *Ogden Codman*, 15.

163 *Architectural Record* (1905) cited in Vanessa Chase, "Edith Wharton, *The Decoration of House*s, and Gender in Turn-of-the-Century America," in *Architecture and Feminism*, ed. Debra Coleman, Elizabeth Danze, and Carol Henderson (New York: Princeton Architectural Press, 1996), 134; Henry James cited in Metcalf, *Ogden Codman*, 21.

164 OC to SBC, December 7, 1896, CFMC Box 49/Folder 1166 [HNE].

165 OC to AL, April 10, 1894, CFMC Box 87/Folder 1701 [HNE].

166 As cited in Metcalf, *Ogden Codman*, 68.

167 Martin, 213n27.

168 Martin, 165–66.

169 OC to SBC, March 1897, CFMC Box 49/Folder 1167 [HNE].

170 *New York Press*, "Mrs. H.W. Webb Will Wed Again Saturday," October 6, 1904; and *New York Herald*, "Mrs. Water Webb to Marry Again," October 6, 1904 [HNE].

171 "Mrs. H. W. Webb Will Wed Again on Saturday," *New York Press*, October 6, 1904 [HNE].

172 OC to TNC, November 21, 1904, CFMC Box 50/Folder 1175 [HNE].

173 OC to SBC, October 26, 1904, CFMC Box 50/Folder 1775 [HNE].

174 OC to SBC, August 9, 1908, CFMC Box 50/Folder 1179 [HNE].

175 OC to TNC, January 19 and February 5, 1910, CFMC Box 152/Folder 2180 [HNE].

176 OC to TNC, January 19 and 5 February 5, 1910, CFMC Box 152/Folder 2180 [HNE].

177 OC to TNC, June 14, 1910, CFMC Box 50/Folder 1181 [HNE].

178 OC to TNC, February 5, 1910, CFMC Box 152/Folder 2180 [HNE].

179 OC to SBC, July 24 and September 27, 1910, CFMC Box 51/Folder 1182 [HNE].

180 Dorothy Codman to SBC, January 1921, CFMC Box 52/Folder 1260 [HNE].

181 Emmet, *Old-Time New England*, 20.

182 OC to TNC, February 28, 1935, CFMC Box 142, Bound Volume (1933–1936) [HNE].

183 OC to TNC, March 24, 1924, CFMC Box 87, Box 87, Bound Volume (1923–1925); and OC to TNC, March 15, 1934, CFMC Box 142, Bound Volume (1933–1936) [HNE].

184 OC to TNC, March 15, 1934, CFMC Box 142, Bound Volume (1933–1936) [HNE].

185 OC to TNC, April 9, 1924), CFMC, Box 87, Bound Volume (1923–1925) [HNE].

186 Eichlin, 118.

187 OC to Dorothy Codman, January 3, 1925, CFMC Box 87, Bound Volume (1923–1925) [HNE].

188 OC to TNC, July 9, 1934, CFMC Box 142, Bound Volume (1933–1936); and

August 24, 1924, Box 87, Bound Volume (1923–1925) [HNE].

189 Martin, 178.

190 Emmet, 17.

191 OC to Martha Codman Karolik, June 15, 1937, CFMC Box 142, Bound Volume (1937–1940) [HNE].

192 OC to TNC, June 12, 1924, CFMC Box 87/Folder 1702 [HNE].

193 OC to TNC, June 26, 1925, CFMC Box 87, Bound Volume (1923–1925) [HNE].

194 On November 24, 1918, Codman sent his Uncle Dick a "final payment" of $1,000 for the Copley. Receipt filed in CFMC Box 96/Folder 1804 [HNE]. Codman Estate guide Prentice Crosier placed the total sum for this transaction at $4,000 ("Portraits Tour at Codman Estate," October 27, 2018). Codman's story about Dick's inheritance of the work appears in OC to Ahla Codman, April 16, 1923, CFMC Box 131/Folder 2102 [HNE].

195 OC to Dorothy Codman, January 8, 1919, CFMC Box 185/Folder 2792 [HNE].

196 Holmes made this observation in *Autocrat of the Breakfast-Table* (1858). Cited in Cleveland Amory, *Who Killed Society?* (New York: Harper and Brothers, 1960), 250.

197 OC to SBC, August 23, 1908, CFMC Box 50/Folder 1179 [HNE].

198 OC to TNC, June 21, 1923, CFMC Box 87, Bound Volume (1923–1925) [HNE].

199 OC to SBC, July 17, 1906, CFMC Box 50/Folder 1177 [HNE].

200 OC to TNC, April 27, 1925, and June 20, 1931), CFMC Box 142, Bound Volume (1923–1932) [HNE].

201 Codman included this story in his 1948 rental prospectus for Grégy; see CFMC Box 116/Folder 1903 [HNE].

202 OC to TNC, May 23, 1926, CFMC Box 142, Bound Volume (1926–1932) [HNE].

203 Wharton and Codman, 141.

204 James Russell to Sarah Russell, November 21, 1816, CFMC Box 118 [HNE]; cited in Reichlin, 124.

205 OC to TNC, August 18, 1927, CFMC Box 142, Bound Volume (1926–1932) [HNE].

206 "Not 100 kilometers," cited in Elizabeth Redmond, "The Codman Collection of Pictures," in Abbott Lowell Cummings, ed., *Old-Time New England*, LXI, no. 258 (1981): 110; "no associations" appears in OC to TNC, April 4, 1934, CFMC Box 142, Bound Volume (1933–1936) [HNE].

207 Pauline C. Metcalf, "Ogden Codman Builds His Dream House: The Story of La Leopolda," *Historic New England* 13, no. 3 (Winter/Spring 2013): 16.

208 Ogden Codman Jr., *La Léopolda: A Description* (privately printed, 1939), CFMC Box 116/Folder 1901 [HNE].

209 Cited in Metcalf, *Ogden Codman*, 33.

210 Wharton and Codman, 135.

211 OC to TNC, February 9, 1929, CFMC Box 142, Bound Volume (1926–1932) [HNE]; cited in Metcalf, *Ogden Codman*, 105.

212 Cited in Metcalf, *Ogden Codman*, 102

213 OC to TNC, November 10, 1929, CFMC Box 142, Bound Volume (1923–1932) [HNE].

214 OC to Edith Wharton, December 26, 1934; Ogden Codman Jr. Collection (I.A. Vol. 27), The Boston Athenaeum.

215 OC to TNC, CFMC, May 15, 1930, CFMC Box 142, Bound Volume (1926–1932) [HNE].

216 TNC to OC, April 7, 1930, CFMC Box 142, Bound Volume (1923–1932) [HNE].

217 OC to TNC, May 15, 1930, CFMC Box 142, Bound Volume (1923–1932) [HNE].

218 OC to TNC, December 17, 1931, CFMC Box 142, Bound Volume (1926–1932) [HNE].

219 OC to Edith Wharton, December 26, 1934; Ogden Codman Jr. Collection (I.A. Vol. 27), The Boston Athenaeum.

220 Wharton and Codman, 101.

221 Lorna Condon, "Unusual Source," *Historic New England* 13, no. 3 (Winter/Spring 2013): 13.

222 OC to TNC, September 7, 1934, CFMC Box 142, Bound Volume (1933–1936) [HNE].

223 Martin, 180.

224 TNC to Dorothy Codman, August 30, 1947, CFMC Box 187/Folder 2825 [HNE].

225 TNC to Dorothy Codman, August 2, 1946, CFMC Box 187/Folder 2825 [HNE].

226 Codman's French death certificate, issued by the American Foreign Service, January 19, 1951, is filed in CFMC Box 87/Folder 1707 [HNE].

227 Dorothy Codman "Biography" document [n.d.], CFMC Box 221/Folder 3405 [HNE].

228 Author interview with Richard Nylander, who was in 1969 a curatorial assistant at SPNEA, October 15, 2014.

229 OC to TNC, June 20, 1937, CFMC Box 143, Bound Volume (1937–1940) [HNE].

THREE
THE BARD OF BEACON STREET

The following acronyms in these notes represent frequently cited collections or institutions:
[CFMC] *Codman Family Manuscript Collection*
[GHM] *Gibson House Museum Archives*
[HNE] *Historic New England Library and Archives*

Given the frequency of their appearance, the following names have been abbreviated following their first appearance:
[AL] *Arthur Little*
[CHG] *Charles Hammond Gibson Jr.*
[OC] *Ogden Codman Jr.*

1 Cleveland Amory, *The Proper Bostonians* (New York: E. F. Dutton and Co., 1947), 12.

2 Helen N. Rowland, *A Guide to Men: Being Encore Reflections of a Bachelor Girl* (New York: Dodge Publishing Co., 1922), 15.

3 Charles Hammond Gibson Jr. to Nel. K. Mercier, October 6, 1945, Manuscript Collection [GHM]; Elizabeth Clarke Babbitt to CHG, April 21 and March 31, 1936, Personal Papers Box [GHM].

4 Carl Van Vechten, *The Blind Bow-Boy* (New York: Alfred A. Knopf, 1923), 131.

5 Samuel Stone to CHG, March 23, 1936, Personal Papers [GHM].

6 These two shows aired on Station WXYZ in Coral Gables, Florida, February 4, 1936, Personal Papers [GHM].

7 Shared by the radio announcer for Station WXYZ, noted above. Personal Papers [GHM].

8 As quoted in Catherine L. Seiberling, *A Study Report of the Gibson House Museum: Book I* (Boston: Gibson Society, Inc., 1991), Vol. I: frontispiece.

9 Hannah Palfrey Ayer, ed., *A Legacy of New England: Letters of the Palfrey Family*, Vol. I (Boston: privately printed, 1950), 108.

10 William Dean Howells, *The Rise of Silas Lapham* (New York: Penguin, 1983; originally published 1885), 126.

11 Howells, 40 and 159.

12 Joseph E. Garland, *Boston's Gold Coast: The Northern Shore, 1890–1929* (Boston: Little, Brown and Co., 1981), 7.

13 Joseph E. Garland, *The North Shore: A Social History of Summers Among the Noteworthy, Fashionable, Rich, Eccentric, and Ordinary on Boston's Gold Coast, 1823–1929* (Beverley: Commonwealth Editions, 1998), 8–9.

14 Sieberling, Vol. I: 17.

15   Rosamond Warren Gibson, *Recollections of My Life* (Boston: Meadow Press, 1939), 17 [GHM].

16   H. G. Wells, *The Future in America: A Search After Realities* (New York: Harper and Brothers, 1906), 230.

17   Cited in Bainbridge Bunting, *Houses of Boston's Back Bay: An Architectural History, 1840–1917* (Cambridge: Belknap Press of Harvard University, 1967), 18.

18   Rosamond Gibson, 64; and Annie Warren to Ogden Codman Jr., August 28, 1889, CFMC Box 72/Folder 1509 [HNE].

19   CHG to Rosamond Gibson, November 1881 [GHM].

20   Madeline and Richard Merrill, *Dolls and Toys of the Essex Institute* (Salem: Essex Institute, 1976), 8.

21   Rosamond Gibson, 65.

22   Rosamond Gibson, 69.

23   Wallace Stegner, *Angle of Repose* (New York: Penguin Books, 1971), 302.

24   Bunting, 15–16.

25   Charles Hammond Gibson Sr. to OC, October 2, 1891, CFMC Box 72/Folder 1511 [HNE].

26   OC to Arthur Little, July 14, 1891, CFMC Box 87/Folder 1701 [HNE].

27   AL to OC, January 7, 1892, CFMC Box 83/Folder 1661 [HNE].

28   Oliver Wendell Holmes Sr., "The Professor's Story," *Atlantic Monthly* 5, no. 27 (1860): 98.

29   CHG, "Satire: On Myself," 1899, Manuscript Papers [GHM].

30   Oscar Wilde, *An Ideal Husband* (New York: Mockingbird Classics, 2015; first published 1895), 67.

31   AL to OC, December 4, 1891, CFMC Box 83/Folder 1661 [HNE]; italics original.

32   AL to OC, April 29, 1892, CFMC Box 83/Folder 1661 [HNE].

33   AL to OC, February 16, 1894, CFMC Box 86/Folder 1662 [HNE].

34   OC to AL, January 24, 1892, CFMC Box 87/Folder 1701 [HNE].

35   AL to OC, February 17, 1892, CFMC Box 83/Folder 1661 [HNE].

36   Lucius Beebe, *Boston and the Boston Legend* (New York: D. Appleton-Century Company Inc., 1936), 262.

37   AL to OC, February 17, 1892, CFMC Box 83/Folder 1661 [HNE].

38   OC to AL, May 9, 1892, CFMC Box 87/Folder 1701 [HNE].

39   AL to OC, May 1, 1919, CFMC Box 83/Folder 1667 [HNE].

40   OC to AL, November 21–22, 1891, CFMC Box 87/Folder 1701 [HNE].

41   Seweryn Chomet, *Count de Mauny: Friend of Royalty* (New York: Begell House Inc., 2002), 69.

42   R. E. Lee Taylor to CHG, November 22, 1909 [GHM]; italics original.

43   OC to Sarah Bradlee Codman September 28, 1893, CFMC Box 49/Folder 1154 [HNE].

44   AL to OC, February 16, 1894, CFMC Box 86/Folder 1662 [HNE].

45   OC to AL, March 15 and 30, 1894, CFMC Box 87/Folder 1701 [HNE].

46   AL to OC, May 24, 1894, CFMC Box 83/Folder 1662 [HNE].

47   Cited in Ted Morgan, *Somerset Maugham* (New York: Random House, 1980), 263.

48   Augustus J. C. Hare to CHG, February 23, 1900, Manuscript Collection [GHM].

49   AL to OC, June 16, 1894, CFMC Box 83/Folder 1662 [HNE].

50   CHG [transl.], "Etching" (ca. 1894–1895), Manuscript Papers [GHM].

51   Maurice de Mauny, *The Gardens of Taprobane* (London: Williams and Norgate, Ltd., 1937), 218–19.

52   Holly Moran-Bates, "Love and Letters: An Edition of the Letters of Charles Hammond Gibson," unpublished manuscript, 2002 [GHM].

53   OC to Sarah Bradlee Codman, November 26, 1894, CFMC Box 49/Folder 1158; and February 8, 1895, Box 49/Folder 1159 [HNE].

54   OC to Sarah Bradlee Codman, March 5 and 25, 1895, CFMC Box 49/Folder 1159 [HNE].

55   OC to Sarah Bradlee Codman, April 24, 1895, CFMC Box 49/Folder 1160 [HNE].

56   Beverley Nichols, *Crazy Pavements* (London: Jonathan Cape, 1927), 72.

57   CHG, "A Prayer for Love," handwritten manuscript, June 9, 1895, Manuscript Papers [GHM].

58   Isabella Stewart Gardner Guest Books, Vol. II, 42, November 9–10, 1895, Isabella Stewart Gardner Museum Archives.

59   Count Carlo Emo to Isabella Stewart Gardner, June 26, 1896, Isabella Stewart Gardner Museum Archives.

60   Gibson later collected all of these poems, each with the date of its creation, in *The Spirit of Love and Other Poems* (Cambridge: Riverside Press, 1906).

61   CHG, "Rêve d'Amour" [author translation from original French], Manuscript Papers [GHM].

62   Letterhead printed above Gibson's letter to "Marque Costa de Beauregard" [?], June 20, 1897, Personal Papers [GHM].

63   OC to Sarah Bradlee Codman, November 5, 1896, CFMC Box 49/Folder 1166 [HNE].

64   OC to AL, February 23, 1898, CFMC Box 83/Folder 1664 [HNE].

65   Chomet, 46.

66   Chomet, 36.

67   CHG diary entry, July 28, 1899, Date Books [GHM]. While this entry bears no year, its recorded date ("July 28/Friday") places it in 1899.

68   CHG, "L'Envoi," June 1895, Manuscript Papers [GHM].

69   CHG, *Two Gentlemen in Touraine* (New York: Fox Duffield and Co., 1906), 4 and 16. This and the following citations derive from the 1899 book's identical "Automobile Edition" of 1906.

70   CHG, *Two Gentlemen in Touraine*, iv and 4.

71   CHG, *Two Gentlemen in Touraine*, 4 and 136.

72   CHG, *Two Gentlemen in Touraine*, 19.

73   CHG, "l'Envoie," handwritten fragment, dated June 17, 1895, Manuscript Papers [GHM].

74   *San Francisco Call*, April 22, 1900, and *Washington Times*, March 3, 1901, Manuscript Papers [GHM].

75   Francis Skinner to Rosamond Warren Gibson, undated; and Augustus Hare to CHG, April 13, 1900; Manuscript Papers [GHM].

76   Edith, Lady Playfair to CHG, February 20, 1900, Manuscript Papers [GHM].

77   CHG, January 13 and 17, 1900, Date Books [GHM].

78   Rodrigo de Saavedra y Vinent to CHG (the letter is dated only "Paris, the 20th 1901), Personal Papers [GHM].

79   Italics original.

80   As early as October 1900, Gibson recorded his family allowance was reduced to "£2 a week up to Xmas." Personal Papers [GHM].

81   CHG, *The Spirit of Love*, 53.

82   CHG to Edith, Lady Playfair, November 24, 1900, Personal Papers [GHM].

83   In the will that Gibson executed on October 7, 1952, he maintained that Gibson House would exemplify "the period from 1859 to 1900" [GHM].

84   In a 1953 profile Gibson told columnist Grace Davidson that his last trip abroad had occurred fifty years before. This would place the date at 1903, but as there is no evidence

of his travel in that year, he likely meant to round off the figure. Davidson, "About People," *Boston Post*, 1953 [GHM].

85 [No author indicated], "Great Luck for Mr. Gibson!" *Boston Daily Paper*, February 11, 1902, Manuscript Papers [GHM].

86 See, for example, Frank Chaffee's "Bachelor Bits," in *The Home-Maker*, February 1889, 356.

87 [No title or author indicated], *Boston Journal*, October 10, 1904, Manuscript Papers [GHM].

88 AL to OC, June 7, 1915, CFMC Box 83/Folder 1665 [HNE].

89 Marcel Proust (D. J. Enright, Scott Moncrief, Terence Kilmartin, and Andreas Mayor, translators), *In Search of Lost Time: Vol. III, The Guermantes Way* (New York: Modern Library, 2003; originally published in 1922), 386.

90 AL to OC, May 24, 1894, CFMC Box 83/Folder 1662 [HNE]; italics original.

91 CHG, *Little Pilgrimages Among French Inns* (New York: L. C. Pages and Co., 1905), vii.

92 CHG, *Little Pilgrimages*, 307.

93 CHG, *Little Pilgrimages*, 132.

94 *New York Herald*, December 17, 1905; *Chicago Record Herald*, December 2, 1905; *Chicago Post*, December 1, 1905; *Chicago Dial*, December 16, 1905; *Toledo Blade*, December 20, 1905; *New York Times*, December 1, 1905; and *Chicago Dial*, December 16, 1905; Manuscript Papers [GHM].

95 *Chicago Record Herald*, December 2, 1905; *Lewiston Weekly Journal*, December 27, 1905; *Boston Congregationalist*, December 9, 1905; and *Philadelphia Telegraph*, April 14, 1906; Manuscript Papers [GHM].

96 [No author indicted], "Writes of French Inns," *Boston Sunday Globe*, December 31, 1905, Manuscript Papers [GHM].

97 [No author indicted], "The Adventures of a Boston Don Quixote in an Automobile," *Boston Sunday Herald*, December 3, 1905, Manuscript Papers [GHM].

98 Jane Austen, *Emma* (London: Richard Bentley and Son, 1886; originally published 1815), 72.

99 As quoted in Todd S. Gernes, "Interior Designs: Charles Hammond Gibson and Literary Boston," delivered at Old South Meeting House, Boston, September 18, 1902), transcript, p. 12.

100 Beebe, 103.

101 Cited in Bunting, 17.

102 Anonymous, *Old Bachelors: Their Varieties, Characters, and Conditions* (London: John Macrone, 1835), 131.

103 CHG, *The Wounded Eros: Sonnets* (Riverside Press, 1908), xiii and xxxii.

104 *Chicago Evening Post*, July 23, 1909 [GHM].

105 Isabelle Harris Metcalf to CHG, "Easter 1909," Personal Papers [GHM].

106 Gibson's birthday poems appear in *The Spirit of Love and Other Poems*; his "Women's Page" clippings from the *Globe* are preserved in his Personal Papers [GHM].

107 Laura Anne Etnier Austin, cited in Eugene R. Gaddis, *Magician of the Modern: Chick Austin and the Transformation of the Arts in America* (New York: Alfred A. Knopf, 2000), 74.

108 CHG, *Two Gentlemen*, 219.

109 1906 business card, Manuscript Collection [GHM]; AL to OC, March 4, 1918, CFMA Box 83/Folder 1666 [HNE]; for shopping inventory, see Personal Papers [GHM].

110 *Boston Globe*, February 17, 1907, Manuscript Papers [GHM].

111 No author indicated, "Curley Goes to Washington," *Boston Daily Globe*, March 15, 1914, Personal Papers [GHM].

112 James Michael Curley, *I'd Do It Again! A Record of All My Uproarious Years* (Englewood Cliffs: Prentice-Hall, Inc., 1957), 97.

113 Gibson purchased the coat in 1912 from Edward F. Kakas Fine Furs in Boston for $30. In a handwritten note on the receipt, Gibson recorded: "Worn as Parks Commissioner of Boston 1914-16." Personal Papers [GHM]. The *Boston Globe* reported on December 5, 1915, that the new commissioner had exchanged the official Municipal Park and Recreation Commission car for a "newer open touring car." Personal Papers [GHM].

114 William Carpan, special representative of her Majesty Princess Eleonore of Bulgaria, to CHG, April 14, 1914, Personal Papers [GHM].

115 No author indicated, "Gibson Attacks Art Commission," *Boston Globe*, January 20, 1916, Personal Papers [GHM].

116 "Gibson Attacks Art Commission"; italics mine.

117 Russ Lopez, *The Hub of the Gay Universe: An LGBTQ History of Boston, Provincetown, and Beyond* (Boston: Shawmut Peninsula Press, 2019), 100–102.

118 Beginning in 1914 Gibson's insurer, Obrion, Russell, and Co., covered only his belongings at 121 Beacon Street ($2,500 for furniture, $1,500 for manuscripts). Personal Papers [GHM].

119 OC to AL, May 9, 1892, CFMC Box

71/Folder 1701 [HNE].

120 This curious document, titled "The Last Words of Charles Hammond Gibson," was first written March 24, 1929, when Gibson believed himself to be dying of influenza; he revised the document in 1934 [GHM].

121 OC to Thomas Newbold Codman, June 9 and July 11, 1925, CFMC Box 87/Bound Vol. (1923–1925) [HNE].

122 CHG to Jack Dempsey, October 20, 1928, Personal Papers [GHM]; all spelling original.

123 This card is tucked into Gibson's 1928 date book. Date Books [GHM].

124 Gibson's poem "England: A Pindaric Ode" (first drafted 1929) looked back nostalgically on his time in England decades before. Manuscript Papers [GHM]; italics mine.

125 AL to OC, June 7, 1915, CFMC Box 83/Folder 1165 [HNE].

126 AL to OC, June 10, 1918, CFMC Box 83/Folder 1666 [HNE]. The defendant, "Phil Beek," appears to have been someone familiar to them all.

127 OC to Thomas Newbold Codman, October 14 and November 30, 1925, CFMC Box 87/Bound Vol. (1923–1925) [HNE].

128 Little wrote to Codman 1919 to say, "the Widow Gibson and Charlie go walking around [illegible] in the P.M. Rossie in deepest crape [*sic*]" (May 1, 1919, CFMC Box 83/Folder 1667 [HNE]).

129 Rosamond Gibson, *Recollections*, 74.

130 CHG, date book entry, September 22, 1934, Date Books [GHM].

131 CHG date book entry, November 21, 1934, Date Books [GHM].

132 CHG, "The Library at Gibson House," 1 [GHM].

133 Davidson, 2.

134 Davidson, 1; CHG to Miss Nel K. McCraer, November 21, 1949, Manuscript Collection [GHM]; Eileen Sharpe, interview with Lester Beck, October 29, 1988, 4 [GHM].

135 Sharpe, 4.

136 Gibson notes on May 6, 1935, "two men came to put down pink carpeting in Pink Bedroom." Date Books [GHM]. For his unfinished Room Guide for this space, he made a draft title page titled "The Pink Bed Room," 1938 [GHM].

137 "Writes of French Inns," *Boston Sunday Globe*, December 31, 1905, Manuscript Papers [GHM].

138 Virginia Woolf, "Great Men's Houses," in Woolf, *The London Scene: Six Essays on*

London Life (New York: Ecco, 1975), 29.

139 Sharpe, 2.

140 CHG, May 22, 1935, Date Books [GHM]; italics and capitalization original.

141 CHG to Mrs. William Hooper, October 1, 1931, Manuscript Papers [GHM].

142 This browned, brittle slip of paper—no longer attached to any desk or pen—has been filed in Manuscripts Papers [GHM].

143 CHG, "The Music Room at Gibson House," 6; and "The Library at Gibson House," cover [GHM].

144 CHG, "The Music Room," 6.

145 CHG, "The Music Room," 6.

146 Elsie de Wolfe, *The House in Good Taste* (New York: The Century Company, 1913), 164.

147 Beverley Nichols, *Crazy Pavements* (London: Jonathan Cape, 1927), 69.

148 Transcribed remarks, March 31, 1983, by H. Shippen Goodhue to the Gibson House Board of Directors, Personal Papers [GHM].

149 Gibson, *Two Gentlemen in Touraine*, 281 and 228.

150 Beebe, 261.

151 Seiberling, Vol. II, 4.

152 John P. Marquand, *The Late George Apley* (New York: Modern Library, 1936), 344.

153 Marquand, 345 and 261.

154 Cited in Martha Spaulding, "Martini-Age Victorian," *The Atlantic*, May 2004.

155 "The Gibson Society, Inc.: Agreement of Association," January 18, 1936 [GHM].

156 William Sumner Appleton to Boyslton Beal, May 2, 1938, Microfiche Files [HNE].

157 CHG to William Sumner Appleton, May 3, 1938, Microfiche Files [HNE].

158 Thomas Frothingham to William Sumner Appleton, May 5, 1938, Microfiche Files [HNE].

159 Herbert Browne to Boylston Beal, May 10, 1938, and Frederick Whitwell to William Sumner Appleton, May 9, 1938, Microfiche Files [HNE].

160 William Sumner Appleton to Roger Hale Newton, March 15, 1942, Microfiche Files [HNE].

161 [No author indicated], "The Hammond Rose Gardens, Nahant," *The Breeze: A News Magazine of Society*, August 5, 1932, 10, Manuscript Papers [GHM].

162 Lawrence Dame, "A Minstrel and Horticulturalist Looks Back on an Independent Life," *Boston Herald*, October 8, 1950, 44 [GHM].

163 *The Breeze*, 10.

164 Dame, 44.

165 In a letter to Monsignor J. F. Minihan after Cardinal O'Connell's death in 1944, Gibson recalled "the pleasant hours in summer . . . when you came with his eminence to tea at the garden in Nahant." Manuscript Papers [GHM].

166 Dame, 44.

167 Gibson to Minihan.

168 CHG to Mrs. Carolyn Hillman, August 30, 1939, Personal Papers [GHM].

169 CHG, "To My Honorary Gardeners (Coralled from the Navy), April 12, 1945, at 'Forty Steps,'" Manuscript Papers [GHM].

170 The Count de Mauny, *The Gardens of Taprobane* (London: Williams and Norgate, 1937), 94.

171 CHG, "Ode to Taprobane," February 1938, Manuscript Papers [GHM].

172 Maurice de Mauny Talvande to CHG, January 22, 1940, Personal Papers [GHM].

173 De Mauny to CHG, October 6, 1941, Personal Papers [GHM].

174 De Mauny to CHG, January 22, 1940, Personal Papers [GHM].

175 De Mauny to CHG, October 1941, Personal Papers [GHM].

176 De Mauny, *The Gardens of Taprobane*, 315–16.

177 CHG to de Mauny, February 3, 1942.

178 CHG to de Mauny, November 28, 1941, Personal Papers [GHM]. De Mauny had died the day before Gibson wrote this letter.

179 CHG to de Mauny, November 21, 1939, Personal Paper [GHM].

180 CHG to de Mauny, February 3, 1942, Personal Papers [GHM]. Lester Beck related the story of Gibson's "soup" in his 1988 interview with Sharpe, 4 [GHM].

181 Gibson confessed to de Mauny as early as 1939 that "it is cheaper to live at the hotel" (November 21, 1939, Personal Papers [GHM]). Gibson wrote a series of poems devoted to the hotel in this period, "The Epic of Brunswick" (1944–1949), first drafted on the backs of menus from its Red Café. Manuscript Papers [GHM].

182 [No author indicated], "Marquand's Boston: A Trip with America's Foremost Satirist," *Life* 10, no. 12 (March 24, 1941): 64.

183 CHG to de Mauny, February 3, 1942, Personal Papers [GHM]. Margaret McDonald, a housemaid, testified to the "gross neglect" charge (April 18, 1940, Personal Papers [GHM]).

184 CHG to Curtis Brown, April 15, 1945, Manuscript Papers [GHM].

185 Dame, 44

186 CHG to Edward F. O'Brien, 1943, Personal Papers [GHM].

187 As quoted in Brenda Wineapple, *Sister Brother: Gertrude and Leo Stein* (New York: G. P. Putnam, 1996), 157.

188 CHG, January 3, 1900, Date Books [GHM].

189 Evelyn Waugh, *Put Out More Flags* (Boston: Little Brown and Co., 1942), 223.

190 [No author indicated], "Charles Hammond Gibson Dies, Poet, 79," *Boston Herald*, November 18, 1954, Personal Papers [GHM].

191 Marquand, 198.

192 Dame, 44.

193 The Packard Collection—an archive its creator called his "vocarium," or "library of voices"—includes approximately 2,500 discs assembled between 1933 and 1963. The collection is now housed in Harvard University's Woodbury Poetry Room. To access Gibson's recording, visit: https://library.harvard.edu/poetry/listeningbooth/poets/charles_gibson.html.

194 "Excerpts from the *Boston Herald* interview," Harvard University's Woodbury Poetry Room.

195 Davidson, 1.

196 Visitor Books [GHM]. The only guest books to survive from Gibson's lifetime cover 1950–1954. He received thirty-seven guests in 1950, thirty in 1951 (nineteen of whom came for Christmas Eve), and twenty-one in 1952.

197 "Mrs. Cole's Birthday Party," February 24, 1953, Visitor Books [GHM].

198 Joan Lancourt interview with Kenneth MacRae, May 2, 2005, Personal Papers [GHM].

199 Susan Farley Nichols Pulsifer to CHG, March 4, 1953, Personal Papers [GHM].

200 This entry is signed "Isabel Hickey of Hotel Brunswick," February 8, 1954, Visitors Book [GHM].

201 CHG, "Remembrance: A Sonnet" ("written at The Spur, N.Y., 1938"), Manuscript Papers [GHM].

202 [No author indicated], "Charles Hammond Gibson Dies/Poet, 79, Was 'Proper Bostonian," *Boston Herald*, November 18, 1954, Personal Papers [GHM].

203 "Inventory and Appraisal of House Furnishings and Personal Property/Estate of Charles Hammond Gibson, Jr./Date of Death November 17, 1954," compiled by Harold M. Hill, Boston, Black Binder [GHM].

204 CHG to Dr. and Mrs. MacKinlay Helen, January 28, 1946, Personal Papers

[GHM].

205 [No author indicated], "Boston's 'Victorian Center' Opens Doors June 11," *Boston Herald*, June 2, 1957 [GHM].

206 [No author indicated], "Era of Black Walnut and Clutter," *Panorama*, June 10, 1957, 10 [GHM].

207 Elizabeth Bernkopf, "Last Tuesday," June 10, 1957, otherwise unidentified newspaper clipping [GHM].

208 Gibson and Ladd's first meeting is noted in Albert Hughes's "New Stop for Tourists," *Christian Science Monitor*, June 1957 [GHM]. In 1933 Ladd won Second Prize for Best Costume at a "Gay Nineties" pop concert in Boston, wearing a "frock coat and trousers of Victorian grey" (*Boston Herald*, January 28, 1933 [GHM]).

209 Bernkopf, 10.

210 *Panorama*, 10.

211 [No author indicated], "Victorian Museum is Given to Boston in Charles Gibson's Will," *Boston Herald*, May 1957 [GHM].

212 As quoted in Seiberling, Vol. II, 43.

213 Ellen Rockefeller interview with Michael Robbins, February 28, 2007 [GHM].

214 During the museum's inaugural "Pride Tour" ("Charlie Gibson's Boston," June 7, 2019), attendee Gordon characterized the Gibson House Museum as "more of a closed society" through the 1980s.

215 Seiberling, Vol. II, 45.

216 Seiberling, Vol. II, 25. In a 1990 article, Seiberling confessed she was "frequently overwhelmed by the lingering scent of cherry tobacco in the [Red] study." Catherine Seiberling, "The Young Mistress of Gibson House," *Victoria* magazine, January 1991 [GHM].

217 For a subsequent reference to the same story, see *Leaves*, 1990, 104, an otherwise unidentified clipping at GHM. The "kimono" story was recounted by a guide during the author's first tour of Gibson House in 2013.

218 Steve Gross and Susan Daley with text by Henry Wienceck, *Old Houses* (New York: Stewart, Tabori & Chang, 1991), 10.

219 Lisa Birnbach, *The Official Preppy Handbook* (New York: Workman Publishing, 1980), see illustration p. 48.

220 CHG, *Two Gentlemen in Touraine*, 54; and Gibson, *Little Pilgrimages Among French Inns*, 104.

221 Cited in Will Fellows: *A Passion to Preserve: Gay Men as Keepers of Culture* (Madison: University of Wisconsin Press, 2004), 252.

222 Nell Porter Brown, "Preserving Heirs and Airs: Boston's History Glimpsed Through One Eccentric's Home," *Harvard Magazine* 117, no. 3 (January–February 2015): CI.

223 Cate McQuaid, "Family Portraits, With a Twist," *Boston Globe*, May 9, 2010.

224 Email communication with the author, December 20, 2022.

225 CHG to Mr. and Mrs. Gordon Hillman, July 4, 1944, Manuscript Papers [GHM].

FOUR
LOVE AND MAGIC ON EASTERN POINT

The following acronyms in these notes represent frequently cited collections or institutions:
[HNE] Historic New England Library and Archives
[ISGM] Isabella Stewart Gardner Museum Archives
[WM] Winterthur Museum Archives

Given the frequency of their appearance, the following names have been abbreviated following their first appearance:
[APA] A. Piatt Andrew
[HDS] Henry Davis Sleeper
[ISG] Isabella Stewart Gardner

1 Francis Coventry, *The World* 15 (April 12, 1753), cited in Lillian Dickins and Mary Stanton, eds., *An Eighteenth-Century Correspondence* (London: John Murray, 1910), 264.

2 Ralph Waldo Emerson, *Nature* (Boston: James Munroe and Co., 1836), 92.

3 Philip Hayden, *Beauport Binder Three* [HNE].

4 Frank E. Clark, August 27, 1912, Red Roof Guest Books, Volume 1 [HNE].

5 A. Piatt Andrew, April 19, 1906; E. Parker Hayden Jr. and Andrew L. Gray, eds., *Diary of Abram Piatt Andrew 1902–1914* (Princeton: Privately printed, November 1986), 171 [ISGM].

6 Henry Davis Sleeper to APA, April 19, 1906; Hayden Jr. and Gray, *Beauport Chronicle*, 1.

7 HDS to APA, January 28, 1907; Hayden and Gray, *Beauport Chronicle*, 3.

8 HDS to APA, May 27, 1906, and January 28, 1907; Hayden and Gray, *Beauport Chronicle*, 2–3.

9 HDS to APA, April 11, 1907; Hayden and Gray, *Beauport Chronicle*, 8.

10 APA, April 16, 1907; Hayden and Gray, *Diary*, 201 [ISGM].

11 HDS to APA, undated letter, likely April 16, 1907; Hayden and Gray, *Beauport Chronicle*, 9.

12 HDS to APA, April 11, 1907; Hayden and Gray, *Beauport Chronicle*, 7.

13 APA to Isabella Stewart Gardner, March 14, 1909 [ISGM].

14 APA, April 17, 1904; Hayden and Gray, *Diary*, 71 [ISGM].

15 APA, September 24, 1904; Hayden and Gray, *Diary*, 71 [ISGM].

16 APA, April 26, 1902; Hayden and Gray, *Diary*, 201 [ISGM].

17 APA, March 15, 1903; Hayden and Gray, *Diary*, 33 [ISGM]; italics original.

18 APA painted the roof on July 14, 1903, and first referred to the home (in print) as "Red Roof" on September 20, 1903. Hayden and Gray, *Diary*, 42 and 36 [ISGM].

19 APA, "shanty" (October 25, 1902) and "my wife" (November 30, 1902); Hayden and Gray, *Diary*, 18 and 21 [ISGM].

20 Isaac Patch, *Growing up in Gloucester* (Gloucester: The Curious Traveler Press, 2004), 1.

21 [No author indicated], "A Charming Gloucester Home," *The Gloucester Daily Times*, December 11, 1909 [HNE].

22 "Decorating History: Henry Davis Sleeper's Beauport House—A Dialogue with Mitchell Owens and Thomas Jayne," sponsored by the Sir John Soane's Museum Foundation, March 23, 2023.

23 Paul Hollister, *Beauport at Gloucester: The Most FASCINATING House in America* (New York: Hastings House, 1951), 2–4; Nancy Curtis and Richard Nylander, *Beauport* (Boston: Society for the Preservation of New England Antiquities, 1990), 11; and Kate Colby, *Beauport* (Brooklyn: Litmus Press, 2010), 104.

24 William Sumner Appleton to Mrs. Charles E. F. McCann, October 7, 1936, cited in Charles B. Hosmer Jr., *Preservation Comes of Age: From Williamsburg to the National Trust, 1926–1949, Volume I* (Charlottesville: University Press of Virginia, 1981), 147.

25 Antoinette Perrett, "A Notable Collection of Tole," *The House Beautiful*, February 1924, 137 [HNE]; Felicia Doughty Kingsbury, "First Impressions of Some Society Houses," *Old-Time New England* XL, no. 1 (July 1949): 109 [HNE]; and Nell Porter Brown, "Beauport's Lovely Creative Spirit," *Harvard Magazine*, May–June 2018, 12K; cited in Joseph Garland, *Eastern Point: A Nautical, Rustical and More or Less Sociable Chronicle of Gloucester's Outer Shield and Inner Sanctum, 1606–1990* (Beverly: Commonwealth Edi-

tions, 1999), 322.

26 Hollister, *Beauport at Gloucester*, 5; capitalization original.

27 Hollister, *Beauport at Gloucester*, 8.

28 Reginald T. Townsend, "An Adventure in Americana," *Country Life*, February 1929, 37 [HNE].

29 Douglass Shand-Tucci, *Boston Bohemia: 1881–1900* (Amherst: University of Massachusetts Press, 1995), 224.

30 Telephone interview with Sleeper's great-nephew, conducted by "G.E.B." for the Society for the Preservation of New England Antiquities (March 24, 1981, Beauport "Properties" File [HNE]).

31 Philip Hayden, *Beauport Binder Two*, "Biographies" [HNE].

32 The apocryphal story of Sleeper's Parisian training first appeared in Hollister, *Beauport at Gloucester*, 1; it is possible that Sleeper—who knew the teenage Hollister— might have first suggested it. As late as 1976, the writers of Beauport's nomination for National Register of Historic Places continued to repeat this fallacy [HNE].

33 Curtis and Nylander, 20.

34 Editor's note in Hayden and Gray, *Beauport Chronicle*, 13; Philip Hayden remarks upon Sleeper's western travels in *Beauport Binder Two*, "Biographies" [HNE].

35 Matthew Wills, "Go West, You Nervous Men," *JSTOR Daily*, May 1, 2019, 1.

36 HDS to Helen Andrew Patch, July 8, 1918; Philip Hayden, *Beauport Binder Two* [HNE].

37 Philip Hayden, *Beauport Binder One: 1609–Present* [HNE].

38 [No author indicated], "Carryl's Italian Protégé," *Boston Globe*, October 7, 1906, 1.

39 "Carryl's Italian Protégé," 1.

40 As related by Philip Hayden in "Private Lives, Public Faces: Sexuality and Beauport in the Early Twentieth Century," a lecture sponsored by HNE, August 22, 2014.

41 Unpublished typescript, Beauport Manuscript MS036/Folder 1.28 [HNE].

42 Guy Wetmore Carryl, *Far From the Maddening Girls* (New York: McClure, Phillips & Co., 1904), 2.

43 Carryl, 6.

44 Carryl, 33 and 58.

45 [No author indicated], "News of the Book World," *Minneapolis Journal*, January 9, 1905, 4 [HNE].

46 Editor's note, Hayden and Gray, *Beauport Chronicle*, 24. The editors suggest the later acronymic version of "Dabsville" may also date to this earlier period, a reference to the "D," "B," and "S" of Davidge, Beaux, and Sinkler.

47 HDS to APA, September 7, 1908; Hayden and Gray, *Beauport Chronicle*, 42.

48 Joseph E. Garland, *Boston's Gold Coast: The Northern Shore, 1890–1929* (Boston: Little, Brown and Co., 1981), 214.

49 Cited in Charlotte Gere and Marina Vaizey, *Great Women Collectors* (New York: Harry N. Abrams, 1999) 126.

50 APA, April 15, 1903; Hayden and Gay, *Diary*, 36 [ISGM].

51 Isabella Stewart Gardner to APA, September 7, 1907; *From Y to A: Letters from Isabella Stewart Gardner to A. Piatt Andrew*, 1 [ISGM].

52 ISG to APA, September 12, 1907; *From Y to A*, 2 [ISGM]; italics original.

53 ISG to APA, August 9, 1908; *From Y to A*, 5 [ISGM].

54 ISG to APA, August 9, 1908; *From Y to A*, 5 [ISGM]; and ISG to APA, 1917, Andrew Gray manuscript fragment, 6a [ISGM].

55 Alice A. Carter, *Cecilia Beaux: A Modern Painter in the Gilded Age* (New York: Rizzoli, 2005), 134.

56 HDS to APA, September 1 and 15, 1908; Hayden and Gray, *Beauport Chronicle*, 39 and 46; Cecilia Beaux, diary entry, March 15, 1912, Cecilia Beaux Papers, Archives of American Art.

57 Jane C. Nylander and Diane L. Viera, *Windows on the Past: Four Centuries of New England Homes* (Boston: Little, Brown and Co., 2000), 186.

58 Richard Guy Wilson, *The Colonial Revival House* (New York: Harry N. Abrams, 2004), 79.

59 Wilson, 80.

60 Philip Hayden, *Beauport Binder Eight* [HNE].

61 HDS to APA, August 28 and September 12, 1908; Hayden and Gray, *Beauport Chronicle*, 38 and 44.

62 Philip A. Hayden was the first to identify this source. See Hayden Jr., "Inspiring Beauport: The Design Source for Henry Davis Sleeper's Summer Cottage," *Historic New England* 15, no. 2 (Fall 2014): 5.

63 Charles Holme, ed., "Old English Country Cottages," *The Studio*, Special Winter Number (1906–1907): iii.

64 Oliver Bell Bunce, *Bachelor Bluff: His Opinions, Sentiments, and Disputations* (New York: D. Appleton and Co., 1881), 62.

65 Emily Post, *The Personality of a House* (New York: Funk and Wagnalls, 1930), 405.

66 Bunce, 60.

67 "A Charming Gloucester Home" [HNE].

68 "Carryl's Italian Protégé," October 7, 1906.

69 Linda L. Brayton and Jannifer A. Holmgren, "Halfdan M. Hanson: The Making of an Architect," *Historic New England* 15, no. 2 (Fall 2014): 3.

70 "Famous Architect in Denver Builds Daughter's Doll House" [no author indicated], *The Denver Post*, June 1, 1924 [HNE].

71 Paul Hollister Jr., "The Building of Beauport, 1907–1924," *The American Art Journal* 13, no. 1 (Winter 1981): 79.

72 HDS to APA, December 23, 1908 [HNE]; Hayden and Gray, *Beauport Chronicle*, 11.

73 ISG to APA, September 5, 1908; *From Y to A*, 7 [ISGM].

74 "A Charming Gloucester Home" [HNE].

75 ISG to APA, September 26, 1908; *From Y to A*, 8 [ISGM].

76 APA, September 6–8, 1902; Hayden and Gray, *Diary*, 15 [ISGM].

77 APA, May 12, 1908; Hayden and Gray, *Diary*, 232 [ISGM].

78 APA, November 10, 1907; Hayden and Gray, *Diary*, 208 [ISGM].

79 APA, February 25, and March 2, 1908; Hayden and Gray, *Diary*, 222–23 [ISGM].

80 James Fiske ("Jack") Mabbett to ISG, December 23, 1907 [ISGM].

81 APA, December 9–10, 1907; Hayden and Gray, *Diary*, 212 [ISGM].

82 HDS to APA, December 23, 1907; Hayden and Gray, *Beauport Chronicle*, 11–12.

83 HDS to APA, December 31, 1907; Hayden and Gray, *Beauport Chronicle*, 15.

84 HDS to APA, January 1, 1908; Hayden and Gray, *Beauport Chronicle*, 24.

85 APA, May 24, 1908; Hayden and Gray, *Diary*, 233 [ISGM].

86 APA, June 4, 1908; Hayden and Gray, *Diary*, 235 [ISGM].

87 APA, June 25, 1908; Hayden and Gray, *Diary*, 236 [ISGM].

88 APA, July 6 and 14, 1908; Hayden and Gray, *Diary*, 238–39 [ISGM].

89 ISG to APA, September 26, 1908; *From Y to A*, 8 [ISGM].

90 Cited by editors; Hayden and Gray, *Beauport Chronicle*, 26.

91 Editors' note; Hayden and Gray, *Beauport Chronicle*, 19.

92 HDS to APA, August 2, 1908; Hayden and Gray, *Beauport Chronicle*, 17.

93 HDS to APA, August 28, 1908; Hayden and Gray, *Beauport Chronicle*, 36.

94   HDS to APA, August 6 and September 30, 1908; Hayden and Gray, *Beauport Chronicle*, 20 and 57.

95   HDS to APA, August 4 and 6, 1908; Hayden and Gray, *Beauport Chronicle*, 18 and 2.

96   HDS to APA, April 29, 1915; Hayden and Gray, *Beauport Chronicle*, 92.

97   HDS to APA, April 21, 1915; Hayden and Gray, *Beauport Chronicle*, 90.

98   HDS to APA, July 18, 1915; Hayden and Gray, *Beauport Chronicle*, 100.

99   HDS to APA, September 12, 1908; Hayden and Gray, *Beauport Chronicle*, 44.

100   HDS to APA, March 23, 1915; Hayden and Gray, *Beauport Chronicle*, 79.

101   HDS to APA, September 19 and March 1, 1909; Hayden and Gray, *Beauport Chronicle*, 49 and 59.

102   HDS to APA, September 3, 1908; Hayden and Gray, *Beauport Chronicle*, 41.

103   Italics mine.

104   Italics original.

105   Author interview with Corinna Fisk, August 27, 2018.

106   Cited in Gray, "An American Bloomsbury," 3 [ISGM].

107   Author interview with Fisk, August 27, 2018.

108   Andrew L. Gray, "Mrs. Gardner as Matchmaker," *Fenway*, 52, n.d. [ISGM].

109   APA, June 5, 1909; Hayden and Gray, *Diary*, 279 [ISGM].

110   APA to ISG, March 14, 1909 [ISGM]. For entries related to Mabbett and Andrew's time together that winter, see APA, December 21, 1908–January 3, 1909; Hayden and Gray, *Diary*, 260–62 [ISGM].

111   Garland, 31.

112   Hayden, *Beauport Binder Two* [HNE].

113   HDS entry, July 11, 1911; Isabella Stewart Gardner Guest Books, Vol. XI, 18 [ISGM].

114   Townsend, 37.

115   Mitchell Owens, "An Afternoon with Henry Davis Sleeper," sponsored by the Institute of Classical Architecture and Art (Stillington Hall, Gloucester; June 10, 2023).

116   "Decorating History: Henry Davis Sleeper's Beauport House—A Dialogue with Mitchell Owens and Thomas Jayne," March 23, 2023.

117   HDS to APA, December 26, 1911; Hayden and Gray, *Beauport Chronicle*, 63.

118   HDS to Helen Andrew Patch, December 26, 1911; Hayden, *Beauport Binder Eight* [HNE].

119   The erroneous story of the Strawberry Hill wallpaper was first told in Beauport's August 1916 *House Beautiful* profile, written by "A.M.B." and was repeated in the house's 1929 *Country Life* profile [HNE]. The wallpaper's actual origin is noted in Curtis and Nylander, 85.

120   Matthew Reeve, "Gothic Architecture, Sexuality, and License at Horace Walpole's Strawberry Hill," *The Art Bulletin* XCV, no. 3 (September 2013): 411.

121   Matthew Reeve, "Dickie Bateman and the Gothicization of Old-Windsor: Gothic Architecture and Sexuality in the Circle of Horace Walpole," *Architectural History* 56 (2013): 112.

122   Reeve, "Dickie Bateman," 120–21.

123   Cited in Reeve, "Gothic Architecture," 426.

124   Cited in Stephen Clarke, "The Strawberry Hill Sale of 1842: 'The Most Distinguished Gem that Has Ever Dorned the Annals of Auctions,'" in *Horace Walpole's Strawberry Hill*, ed. Michael Snodin (New Haven: Yale University Press, 2009), 265.

125   Grace and Philip Wharton, *The Wits and Beaux of Society in Two Volumes* (Philadelphia: Porter and Coates, 1890), Vol. II, 64–65.

126   APA, July 6, 1912; Hayden and Gray, *Diary*, 368 [ISGM].

127   Elizabeth Stillinger, *The Antiquers* (New York: Alfred A. Knopf, 1980), 27 and 29.

128   William Sumner Appleton to J. G. Gremse, February 20, 1940, cited in Hayden, *Beauport Binder Three* [HNE].

129   Edith Wharton and Ogden Codman, *The Decoration of Houses* (New York: Charles Scribner's Sons, 1897), 22.

130   HDS to Henry Francis du Pont, July 29, 1925; "Antique Dealers Correspondence," Box 54 [WM].

131   Cited in Hollister, 2.

132   Thomas Jayne, "Decorating History," March 23, 2023.

133   Cited in Aaron Betsky, *Queer Space: Architecture and Same-Sex Desire* (New York: William Morrow and Co., 1997), 81.

134   APA to Caroline Sinkler, September 5, 1908, cited in Hayden and Gray, *Beauport Chronicle*, 31.

135   William B. and Elizabeth Clay Blanford, *Beauport Impressions: An Introduction to Its Collections* (Boston: Society for the Preservation of New England Antiquities, 1965), 9; Hollister, *Beauport at Gloucester*, 5.

136   HDS to Henry Francis du Pont, July 27, 1925; "Antique Dealers Correspondence," Box 54 [WM].

137   Hollister, *Beauport at Gloucester*, 4.

138   Nancy McClelland, *The Practical Book of Decorative Wall-Treatments* (Philadelphia: J. B. Lippincott Company, 1926), 187.

139   Cited in Doreen Bolger Burke et al., *In Pursuit of Beauty: Americans and the Aesthetic Movement* (New York: Rizzoli, 1986), 177.

140   Hollister, *Beauport at Gloucester*, 5.

141   Curtis and Nylander, 7.

142   Ora Dodd, "Beauport," unpublished typescript, 1957 [HNE]; and John Cornforth, "Beauport, Gloucester, Massachusetts," *Country Life*, October 28, 1982, 1318.

143   Charles Dickens, *Bleak House* (Boston: Houghton Mifflin, 1956; originally published in 1853), 50.

144   Garland, *Boston's Gold Coast*, 214.

145   HDS to Henry Francis du Pont, October 26, 1928; "Antique Dealers Correspondence," Box 54 [WM].

146   Stillinger, 222.

147   HDS to Henry Francis du Pont, October 22, 1928; "Antique Dealers Correspondence," Box 54 [WM].

148   HDS to Henry Francis du Pont, September 2, 1924, and October 26, 1928; "Antique Dealers Correspondence," Box 54 [WM].

149   HDS to Henry Francis du Pont, June 11 and July 7, 1925; "Antique Dealers Correspondence," Box 54 [WM].

150   HDS to Henry Francis du Pont, August 9, 1929; "Antique Dealers Correspondence," Box 54 [WM].

151   HDS to Henry Francis du Pont, November 12, 1930; "Antique Dealers Correspondence," Box 54 [WM].

152   Stillinger, 282.

153   HDS to APA, May 5, 1912; Hayden and Gray, *Beauport Chronicle*, 65.

154   APA's letter to his parents, February 9, 1909, is cited in Hayden and Gray, *Beauport Chronicle*, 58.

155   APA notes Butt's service on May 5, 1912; Hayden and Gray, *Diary*, 361 [ISGM].

156   Sleeper's appearances at APA and Mabbett's dinners crop up several entries in late May and early June. Hayden and Gray, *Diary*, 361–62 [ISGM].

157   [No author indicated], "Society: One of Cleopatra's Nights," *Vogue* 41, no. 6 (March 15, 1913), 56.

158   Leslie Buswell to HDS, September 29, 2015, cited "A Celebration of Pride and History Tour" at Beauport, June 10, 2018.

159   APA's letter of December 3, 1914, is cited in Isaac Patch IV, *Closing the Circle (A Buckalino Journey Around Our Time)* (Wellesley: Wellesley College Printing Series, 1996), 16.

160 HDS to APA, December 21, 1914; Hayden and Gray, *Beauport Chronicle*, 71.

161 HDS to APA, March 7, 1915; Hayden and Gray, *Beauport Chronicle*, 77.

162 HDS to APA, April 14, 1915; Hayden and Gray, *Beauport Chronicle*, 88.

163 HDS to APA, March 7, 1915; Hayden and Gray, *Beauport Chronicle*, 78.

164 HDS to APA, July 18, 1915; Hayden and Gray, *Beauport Chronicle*, 100.

165 HDS to APA, July 18, 1915; Hayden and Gray, *Beauport Chronicle*, 101.

166 HDS to APA, June 11, 1915; Hayden and Gray, *Beauport Chronicle*, 98.

167 ISG to APA, July 1917, cited in unpublished Andrew Gray manuscript, 6a [ISGM].

168 HDS to Helen Andrew Patch, July 8, 1918, cited in Hayden, *Beauport Binder Seven* [HNE].

169 Blanford and Blanford, 5.

170 Cited in Nylander and Viera, 135.

171 Kevin D. Murphy, "Secure from all Intrusion: Heterotopia, Queer Space, and the Turn-of-the-Century Resort," *Winterthur Portfolio* 43, no. 2/3 (Summer/Autumn 2009): 37.

172 HDS to Halfdan Hanson, September 13, 1921; Halfdan Hanson Papers, Box 1/Folder 1.14 [HNE].

173 Hayden, *Beauport Binder Two* [HNE].

174 HDS to ISG, March 10–13 1920, cited Hayden, *Beauport Binder Two* [HNE].

175 Townsend, 41; Cornforth, 1402.

176 Hollister, 6; Blanford and Blanford, 22.

177 APA, August 5, 1903; Hayden and Gray, *Diary*, 44 [ISGM].

178 Editor's note, Hayden and Gray, *Beauport Chronicle*, 57; ISG to APA, September 26, 1908; *From Y to A*, 8 [ISGM].

179 HDS to APA, March 7, 1915; Hayden and Gray, *Beauport Chronicle*, 78.

180 Blanford and Blanford, 46.

181 Halfdan Hanson to Helena McCann, November 12, 1935; cited in Hayden, *Beauport Binder Two* [HNE].

182 Richard C. Nylander, Elizabeth Redmond, and Penny J. Sandler, *Wallpaper in New England* (Boston: Society for the Preservation of New England Antiquities, 1986), 93.

183 Hollister, *Beauport at Gloucester*, 11.

184 Gaston Bachelard, *The Poetics of Space* (Boston: Beacon Press, 1969), 6.

185 Hayden, *Beauport Binder Two* [HNE].

186 Total costs for Beauport's construction are believed to be approximately $60,700. Sleeper spent $19,000 to build these three rooms. Hayden, *Beauport Binder Two* [HNE].

187 Halfdan Hanson to HDS, March 8, 1921; Halfdan Hanson Papers Box 1/Folder 1.14 [HNE].

188 Andrew Gray to Mrs. Nugent, January 14, 1984; Beauport Manuscript File MS036/File 1.24 [HNE].

189 Author interview with Fisk, August 27, 2018.

190 "Barbara Hutton May Bring Son to North Shore," [no author indicated], *Boston Evening Transcript*, August 13, 1936 [HNE].

191 HDS to APA, July 1, 1915; Hayden and Gray, *Beauport Chronicle*, 99; Townsend, 42.

192 [No author indicated], "A Five and Ten Heiress at Gloucester this Summer," *Boston Sunday Globe*, August 23, 1936 [HNE].

193 Cited in Hayden, *Beauport Binder Two and Beauport Binder Eleven* [HNE Archives].

194 Hayden, *Beauport Binder Two* [HNE].

195 Paul Hollister to Linda Wesselman, April 20, 1981; Beauport Manuscript File MS036 Box 1/Folder 1.13 [HNE].

196 HDS to APA, August 19, 1934; Beauport Manuscript File, MS036/Folder 1.12 [HNE].

CODA

1 Lisa Cohen, *All We Know: Three Lives* (New York: Farrar, Straus, and Giroux, 2012), 356.

INDEX

Ay me, what act, / That roars so loud, and thunders in the index?
—William Shakespeare, *Hamlet* (Act III, Scene 4)

Page references for figures are *italicized*.

ABOUT THE AUTHOR

R. Tripp Evans is a professor of the history of art at Wheaton College in Norton, Massachusetts, where he specializes in American material culture of the late nineteenth and early twentieth centuries. He earned his BA in architectural history from the University of Virginia and his MA and PhD in the history of art from Yale University, where he was named the Henry S. McNeil Fellow in American Decorative Arts. He is the author of two previous books, *Romancing the Maya: Mexican Antiquity in the American Imagination, 1820–1915* (University of Texas Press, 2004) and *Grant Wood: A Life* (Alfred A. Knopf, 2010), the latter of which received the National Award for Arts Writing. A frequent public lecturer on topics ranging from historic preservation to house museums to LGBTQ history, he has served on the boards of the Providence Preservation Society, the Providence Athenaeum, the Grant Wood Art Colony, and in 2017 he was appointed State Commissioner on the Rhode Island Historical Preservation and Heritage Commission. He and his husband live in the former New England Butt Company in Providence, Rhode Island.